FURNITURE
DESIGN &
CONSTRUCTION

also by
Graham Blackburn

for BK

Dziękuję

Pl. 276.

Plans Coupes et Elévations d'un Secretaire en forme d'Armoire.

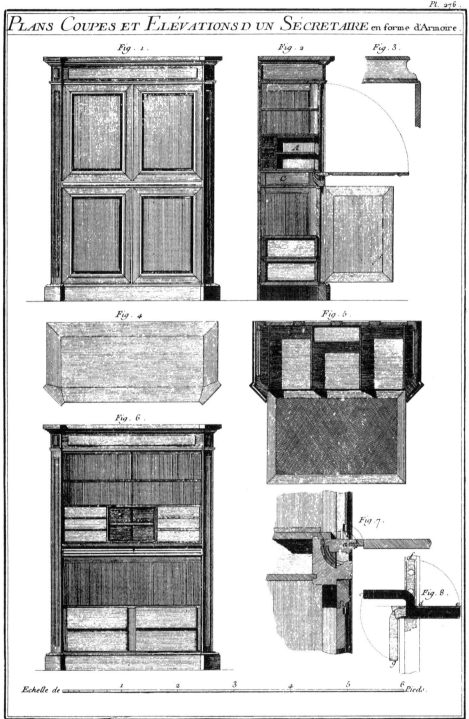

Fig. 1.

Fig. 2.

Fig. 3.

Fig. 4.

Fig. 5.

Fig. 6.

Fig. 7.

Fig. 8.

Echelle de | 1 | 2 | 3 | 4 | 5 | 6 Pieds.

A. J. Roubo. Inv. Del. et Sculp.

FURNITURE DESIGN & CONSTRUCTION

CLASSIC PROJECTS & LESSONS *of the* CRAFT

written & illustrated
by

GRAHAM BLACKBURN

SPRING HOUSE PRESS

NASHVILLE : TENNESSEE

M M X I V

Published by
SPRING HOUSE PRESS
3613 BRUSH HILL CT, NASHVILLE,
TENNESSEE 37216
WWW.SPRINGHOUSEPRESS.COM

Library of Congress Control Number: 2009900700
International Standard Book Number: 1-940611-05-9

Designed by Graham Blackburn
Set in 11 point Caslon

First Edition
0 9 8 7 6 5 4 3 2 1

Printed in China

ACKNOWLEDGEMENTS

Grateful acknowledgement is made to the magazine *Fine Woodworking*, in which articles substantially similar, but now much enlarged, to chapters 1, 2, 3, 4, 12, and 16 first appeared; to the magazine *Popular Woodworking*, in which much of chapters 8 and 10 first appeared; and to the magazine *Woodwork*, for much of the material in chapters 5, 6, 7, 9, 11, 13, 14, and 15.

CONTENTS

PART TWO

THE PROJECTS

PLATES

CONTENTS

PREFACE

Of all the books that I have written over the years, this volume and the other three in this *Illustrated Workshop* series represent the most complete distillation of everything that I have learned about woodworking. It has been a long process, beginning as a young man in my father's shop and continuing to the present day. It is, indeed, the fact that woodworking is a never-ending process of learning and discovery that makes it one of the more fascinating pursuits, especially in this day and age of increasing technological estrangement for many people who know less and less about the wonders that surround them. Few of us could construct a smartphone, or even in an era of greater computer dependency even fix their automobile, but we remain by definition 'the tool-using animal', so something like woodworking assumes an ever more important role in a fuller self-realization.

There is an enormous satisfaction to be obtained by making something, and by making it well. Little that I have written is fundamentally difficult, but much is the result of many generations of discovery and practice. It would be a lasting shame if any of this were to be lost or forgotten, and it is my fondest hope that these books may do something to preserve what has been one of the building blocks of everything that we consider current civilization.

•

The Illustrated Encyclopedia of Woodworking Handtools

••

Traditional Woodworking Handtools

•••

Traditional Woodworking Techniques

••••

Furniture Design & Construction

INTRODUCTION

The Art & Mysteries of the Craft

*"Every decision should be justifiable not only
in terms of function, structure, and strength, but also
in terms of optimum proportions."*

THIS BOOK IS INTENDED TO SERVE MAINLY AS A PRACTICAL INTRODUCTION TO BOTH THE CRAFT AND THE ART OF FURNITUREMAKING. ALTHOUGH it may be read purely as a construction guide for various pieces of furniture, it also aims to make the woodworker aware of other aspects necessary for successful furnituremaking that are often poorly appreciated or even ignored, such as style and proportion. The first four chapters are therefore concerned purely with the theoretical underpinnings of design. The projects that follow also address these concerns, sometimes focusing on one element, sometimes focusing on another, but always with the intention of showing how the art must be considered as much as the craft. The subtitles of each chapter indicate which aspects of the design process are particularly exemplified by the subject piece.

Woodworking as a hobby is admirably served by a wealth of books on tools, joints, joinery, construction, as well as many published plans and projects. In so far as many people are drawn to woodworking primarily by the desire to make some sawdust, use some tools, or simply enjoy the smell and feel of one of nature's most beautiful and versatile materials, this is fine. What is all too often overlooked, however, is one of the more important reasons for the craft in the first place: the designing of potentially utilitarian objects *with as much beauty as possible*. Furniture does not exist to make woodworking possible; woodworking is the result of the need to make furniture. Unfortunately, not only style and proportion but also the rationale behind various construction techniques and the niceties of joinery frequently remain a mystery to many woodworkers, who are then forced to rely on other people's designs.

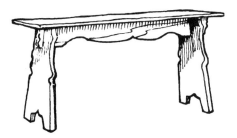

If you want freedom from other people's plans and the ability to produce furniture that has no exact counterpart in published projects and cutting lists, then you need to understand how designs are arrived at.

Furniture design consists of fulfilling specific needs in the most pleasing manner possible. Furniture that is to be primarily utilitarian is largely designed according to the dictum 'form follows function'. If the bookcase must hold a hundred books it needs to be a certain minimum size. If the table must seat sixteen you cannot get by with something that measures only 4 ft by 4 ft. Function demands that you must always start with these givens. But arriving at the most pleasing manner is equally important and can no more be left to chance than the choice of the right material and the right construction technique. Fortunately, this can be learned and does not have to depend on what is often referred to as a 'good eye' — something few professional designers are born with.

As a woodworker there is another element in the design problem: you have to be able to figure out how to build the piece. This is not just a question of knowing how to operate whatever machinery you own or use whatever tools you have to construct the design, but also of how to apply this knowledge to the design in question.

How you make things will also affect the design. Although you should try not to fall into the trap of only designing things for the construction of which you already have the technical ability — since you will never learn anything more unless you challenge yourself occasionally — it is, at the same time, pointless to attempt a project which possesses problems for which there is no imaginable solution.

The French Art-Nouveau designer Jacques-Émile Ruhlmann was noted for designing pieces that included elements no one had attempted before.

He was fortunate in having his own master cabinetmaker to figure out how these designs might be realized. Together these two masters produced wonderful new designs. You must be both people.

In the final analysis, each project must be considered in various ways: what do I want it to do, how can it be made, and how do I want it to look? These three elements — function, construction, and proportion — constitute the Three Pillars of Design, upon which every truly successful piece of furniture must rest equally.

Note that the *Parts Lists* included at the end of chapters in PART TWO represent dimensions of the pieces as illustrated, and as such are intended only as a guide from which overall proportions may be ascertained. One of the aims of this book is to enable you to be able to make any needed adjustments intelligently, without compromising function or form. You should therefore regard them only as a jumping-off point for similar pieces of different sizes that may better suit your purposes.

Lastly, the sequence of the lessons that may be learned by attempting the projects either as described, or by making your own adaptations thereof, proceeds from the general to the specific and, in general, from the simple to the complicated. The first project, a media cabinet, provides an introduction to the awareness needed to design intelligently, and illustrates the different needs that may have to be considered when trying to decide on stylistic concerns. Succeeding chapters may be read in whatever order you prefer. While there is a certain amount of referring back to points made in previous chapters, each chapter nevertheless constitutes a stand-alone project exemplifying one or more aspects of the design process.

Graham Blackburn
Bearsville, New York, 2012

PART ONE

THE LESSONS

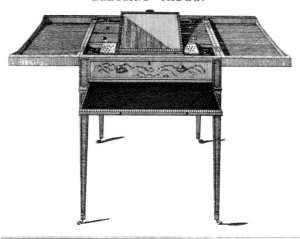

DRESSING TABLE.

Publiſhed as the Act directs, by T. Sheraton. July 24.ᵗʰ 1793.

REGINA VIRTUS

THE FOUR BOOKS
OF
ANDREA PALLADIO's
ARCHITECTURE:
WHEREIN,
After a short Treatise of the Five ORDERS,
Those Observations that are most necessary in
BUILDING,
PrivateHouses, Streets, Bridges, Piazzas,
Xisti, and Temples are treated of.

LONDON,
Published by
ISAAC WARE,
Anno MDCCXXXVIII.

Frontispiece from Isaac Ware's 1738 edition of *The Four Books of Architecture* by Andrea Palladio
(see page 14)

1

THREE PILLARS *of* DESIGN

Function, Construction, & Form

FOR THE GENERAL WOODWORKER OR BEGINNING FURNITUREMAKER ANY THEORY OR EXPLICATION OF DESIGN IS PERHAPS BETTER UNDERSTOOD AND more readily accepted as necessary when applied directly to concrete examples. As such, I have chosen to use tables as a vehicle for the initial discussion of the design process since they constitute a class of furniture that is both extremely common and almost infinitely varied. Much of what can be said about tables applies to other furniture forms, such as chairs, chests, and cabinets, and this chapter may be taken as a method of approach for whatever you may be considering designing.

Tables designed and built primarily as art objects — expressions of emotion, inspiration, or pure whimsy — may be perfectly legitimate examples of woodwork, but depend chiefly for their success on how well they manifest their maker's intent in these regards. How well they work as tables — how appropriate is the choice of species, how strongly they are put together, how finely the joinery details work, and how well they are finished — may be of lesser importance than their esthetic impact on the senses.

Tables designed for more prosaic and utilitarian reasons than those of making an esthetic statement, on the other hand, must above all function on a practical level. So far as function goes, the choice of material, construction method, joinery details, and ergonomic success are all of prime importance. But — and this is a very big 'but' — for these tables to be completely successful as satisfying examples of furniture, esthetic considerations remain equally important.

Woodworkers often shy away from such esthetic considerations, believing, incorrectly, that such considerations are largely subjective, and as such dependent on the extent of the woodworker's exposure to fine art and other sophisticated cerebral machinations, such as are usually only gained at art school. But as every successful professional designer knows, reliance on one's own eye or intuition can be a risky proposition. Instead, he or she typically makes use of many often surpisingly simple tools that guarantee that whatever is being designed will both function and look well.

Regardless of your experience as a woodworker, if you adhere to the following three-part plan you are more likely to achieve a satisfying result than if you approach your next table, or any other project, in a more random manner. Most simply stated, the plan consists of identifying the precise function of your particular table, giving careful consideration to the material and the construction, and following some form of esthetic rationale throughout the entire design process. These three elements — function, construction, and form — constitute what may be referred to as *The Three Pillars of Design*, upon which, equally, every truly successful piece of furniture must rest.

FUNCTION

CLOSE ATTENTION TO FUNCTION IS THE DESIGNER'S FIRST responsibility. You may, of course, regard the function of a table as being any one of a variety of things: the art object mentioned above, an excuse to make shavings or sawdust, an opportunity to spend time alone in the workshop, or a vehicle for practising your woodworking skills. In all of which cases its functionality as a usable piece of furniture is largely irrelevant. But whatever your motivation, be absolutely clear about it from the outset.

Considered solely as a utilitarian piece of furniture, the quintessential function of a table is to provide a flat surface that may be used for writing on (hence the secondary meaning of 'table': something that has been written, such as a 'table of contents'). Further employed as a surface on which to play games or at which to eat or work, a table in the furniture sense suggests a flat surface supported on legs or pillars. The form of any given table may therefore be as varied as are these several uses.

A partial list of tables drawn from *The Dictionary of English Furniture* by Percy Macquoid and Ralph Edwards (see the Select Bibliography) illustrates how many and varied these uses may be, for example: artist's table, reading and writing table, billiard table, breakfast table, coffee table, dining table, card and gaming table, massage table, end table, library table, dressing table, occasional table, shaving table, hall table, night table, sofa table, communion table, and tea table.

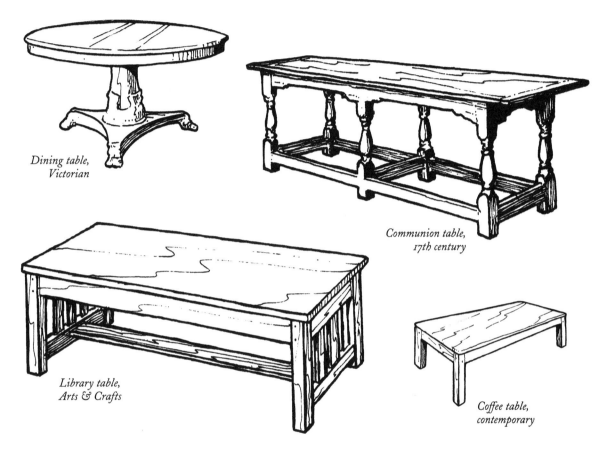

Dining table,
Victorian

Communion table,
17th century

Library table,
Arts & Crafts

Coffee table,
contemporary

FIG. I TABLES FOR DIFFERENT USES

Faced with such a multiplicity of uses, it is of the utmost importance to be perfectly clear at the outset about the particular requirements of the table you intend to design. These include not only structural requirements, so that the table can do the job intended for it, but also the ergonomic requirements. The best-made library table in the world, for example, will be a failure if made with legs too weak to support a heavy load of books. The most exquisite dining table will similarly be a complete failure if it proves too small to sit at. And the most commodious drafting table will be useless if the top does not slope.

Over the centuries, with the development of newer techniques and advances in joinery, structural requirements have gradually become less intrusive. Massive 16th and 17th century tables needed heavy stretchers close to the floor to provide stability for the legs. Excessive wear on these members is evidence of their inconvenience. Few people would today design a dining table with such an obstruction. Similarly, the large feet necessary to withstand wear on stone floors are usually no longer needed.

Having ascertained your proposed table's functions, familiarize yourself with other examples of tables designed for identical functions, and note features designed for specific purposes, such as sturdy legs for heavy loads, drop- or draw-leaves for variable-size tables (occasionally called upon to accommodate greater numbers), lipped tables designed to prevent objects placed upon them from falling off, and added drawers or shelves for tables designed to include storage. A reference such as *Architectural Graphic Standards* by Charles G. Ramsey and Harold R. Sleeper (see the Select Bibliography) is a useful place to explore table types by function, and a good basic reference for the relevant standard or average dimensions.

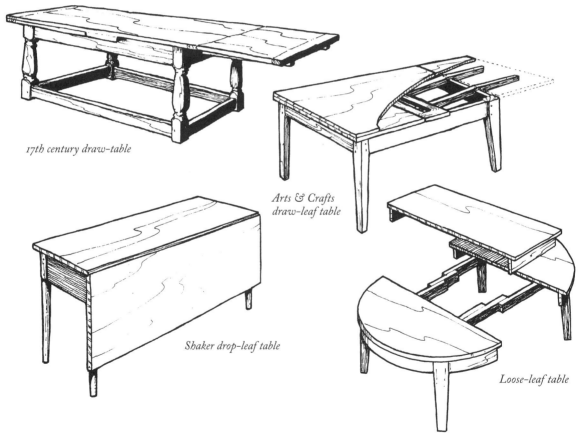

17th century draw-table

Arts & Crafts draw-leaf table

Shaker drop-leaf table

Loose-leaf table

FIG. 2 VARIABLE-SIZE TABLES

Even though they can be a useful place to start, beware of slavishly following so-called standard dimensions. While most people might find a table designed for writing, for example, to be more convenient if made somewhat higher than a table designed for eating, few people are exactly standard. Unless you are involved in the production of many examples of a particular table, your client will be better served if the dimensions are uniquely suited to him or her. Nevertheless, certain aspects of many tables are relatively unalterable, such as the amount of leg room required beneath an apron or the size of the area required before a diner for greatest convenience. Furthermore, a table rarely exists *in vacuo;* other factors, such as pre-existing furniture or the seating to be used with the table, can influence the choice of dimensions.

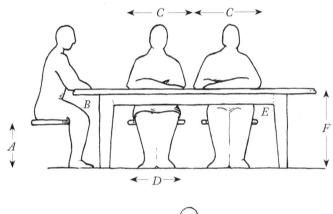

AVERAGE ERGONOMIC REQUIREMENTS

A = average seat height: 16 in.
B = average distance between seat
*   and tabletop: 11 in.*
C = average space per person: 2 ft.
D = average chair width: 1 ft. 2 in.
E = average space between seat and
*   apron (thigh space): 7 in.*
F = average table height: 2 ft. 5 in.

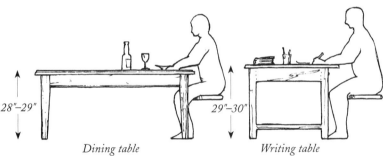

Dining table

Writing table

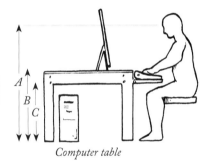

Computer table

COMPUTER TABLE ERGONOMICS

A = optimum direct line of sight
B = average height of table: 26 in.– 27 in.
C = optimum height of keyboard:
*   3 in.– 4 in. below table height*

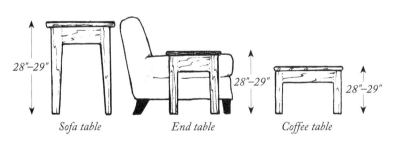

Sofa table

End table

Coffee table

FIG. 3 STANDARD DIMENSIONS

CONSTRUCTION

A TABLE MAY ALSO BE DEFINED BY VARIOUS STRUCTURAL features and construction methods, such as clap table, console table, demi-lune table, draw table, gate-leg table, trestle table, nesting (or quartetto) table, pier table, Pembroke table, or refectory table.

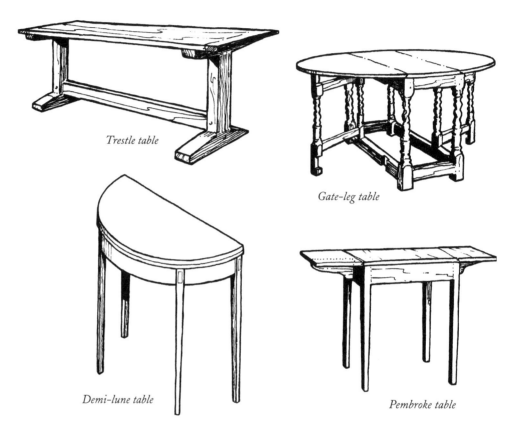

Trestle table

Gate-leg table

Demi-lune table

Pembroke table

FIG. 4 CLASSIFICATION OF TABLES BY CONSTRUCTION

The construction should, of course, be consistent with the intended use: a knock-down trestle table for portability, a drawer-leaf table for occasional enlargement, or a sectional table for alternative disposition of its various parts.

While your own experience and available tools will dictate to a large extent how any given table is constructed, it is a good design principle to resist the impulse to build only what you know. No one person can be expert in everything, but be assured that many things are possible; it is worth the effort to research a new technique or a new joint for the sake of better function or more pleasing shape. One of the most innovative early 20th century designers, Jacques-Émile Ruhlman, achieved greatness by pushing the construction envelope. He was fortunate, however, in having gifted cabinetmakers in his employ, and so was able to increase the structural vocabulary of the craft by refusing to be limited by what had been done before.

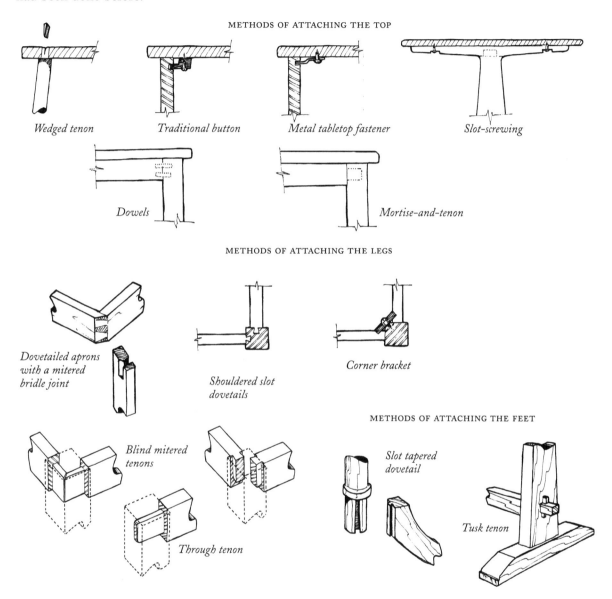

METHODS OF ATTACHING THE TOP

Wedged tenon

Traditional button

Metal tabletop fastener

Slot-screwing

Dowels

Mortise-and-tenon

METHODS OF ATTACHING THE LEGS

Dovetailed aprons with a mitered bridle joint

Shouldered slot dovetails

Corner bracket

METHODS OF ATTACHING THE FEET

Blind mitered tenons

Through tenon

Slot tapered dovetail

Tusk tenon

FIG. 5 JOINERY DETAILS

At the same time, do not get carried away by the urge for novelty. Successful construction entails the use of appropriate species, such as scrubbable pine for kitchen tables, hard-wearing maple for butcher-block chopping tables, expensive but figured veneer for elegant dining tables, or a stable species for use in climatically extreme locations. Successful construction also entails relevant construction methods, such as stack lamination for sculptural shapes, veneered surfaces for large conference tables, or gatelegs for storable tables, as well as the right joint for the job: dovetail, mortise-and-tenon, dowels, biscuits, or splines, for example, and, last but not least, a finish consistent with the intended use.

Chapters 5 through 16, while each exemplifying a particular aspect of the overall design process, may at the same time be read as in-depth practical illustrations of various construction methods. Increasing your construction expertise is a never-ending part of the craft.

FORM

THE THIRD INGREDIENT FOR SUCCESSFUL TABLE DESIGN requires that every detail be considered from the point of view of how well the table will look. Such details include color, figure, ornament, decoration, carving, stylistic consistency, and proportion.

Given that the functional requirements have been satisfied, and that the construction is sufficiently workmanlike, the most striking feature of any table is how well it fits in with its surroundings. For any given piece to work well in a particular environment may require that you design in an established style, Queen Anne or Arts & Crafts, for example, or — perhaps more simply — design so that the general proportions, shapes, and even colors that you choose are compatible with those of the neighboring pieces. Compatibility, of course, can result both from similarity or contrast. A severely modern design might fit very well with the relatively simple lines of a room full of Shaker furniture, whereas it might look uncomfortably out-of-place in a room furnished in a ponderously Gothic, or an ornate 18th century style.

Designing in the style of a particular period can be difficult if the underlying design sensibility of the particular period is not completely understood. It is not enough to employ superficial features of a particular period to achieve the right feeling. Slapping some mis-proportioned cabriole legs onto a table does not guarantee that it will look Chippendale. Incorrect details can produce ludicrous and unhappy results similar to applying a distinctive Rolls-Royce hood to a Volkswagen Beetle. Arts & Crafts furniture is nowhere as square and rectilinear as it may initially appear. And Shaker furniture, for all its apparent simplicity and lack of ornament, is often surprisingly sophisticated in its proportions. Before attempting to design a table in a period style, therefore, ensure that you are familiar not only with the typical construction techniques and the usual materials of the period, but also that you understand the forms that governed the proportions.

This last point is, in fact, more important than almost anything else, more important than any amount of carving, inlay, or applied moulding, and more important than the tightness of the joints or the perfection of the finish.

DESIGN PARADIGMS

A MOST UNFORTUNATE FACT IS THAT, FUNCTIONAL AND structural requirements aside, unless a piece has been designed using some kind of plan to decide on the relative proportions of all the parts, it is unlikely to be a complete success Making decisions about the exact width of a leg or the depth of an apron based on structural requirements alone may guarantee solid joinery, but unless you are that rare designer possessed of an inherently perfect eye, it is unlikely that your table will look as balanced, graceful, felicitous (or any other term used to mean that it looks well) as it could if designed according to some plan.

The plan, more usually spoken of as the 'design paradigm', is the 'Mysterie' of 'The Art and Mysterie of the Craft', the expression used by trade guilds in the days when furnituremaking required a long indentured apprenticeship and when design paradigms were closely guarded secrets that apprentices were sworn not to reveal. There are, in fact, numerous design paradigms commonly used by designers, some exceedingly simple, others more sophisticated. You may, indeed, invent your own paradigm; the point being that using virtually any plan will produce better results than making decisions about exact dimensions based on nothing more than what material is conveniently to hand, or what size router bits are available. All paradigms work towards establishing balance and grace, lacking which a table — any table, from the smallest to the largest — will look clumsy and uncomfortable, no matter how well made.

The following five paradigms are among the most commonly used. They may be taken as suggestions — to be mixed and matched if needed, and followed only as closely as function, ergonomics, and structure will allow. Do not fall into the trap of designing a table that adheres so perfectly to any particular paradigm that other requirements are compromised:

1. Basic Geometric Shapes
Basic geometric shapes, such as squares, cubes, circles, ovals, or ellipses based on regular conic sections such as parabolas and hyperbolas can be used to define both the overall shape and the details of a table, especially when repeated, either in similar sizes or by regular increments or multiples thereof. Such an underlying repeated pattern will unify the whole structure and produce a design that not only possesses an overall logic, but whose parts belong together.

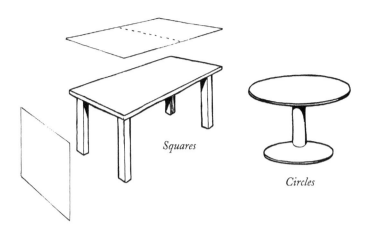

Squares

Circles

FIG. 6 BASIC GEOMETRIC SHAPES

2. Common Integer

Using a basic unit of measurement to determine the sizes of constituent parts is another method of producing a cohesive whole. Starting with a tabletop with a given thickness of 1 in., for example, you might construct legs that measured 2 in. square and an apron that was 4 in. deep. These measurements are likely to work better together than legs measuring an arbitrary 1¾ in. square, and an apron measuring 4⅝ ins. The more that you can relate all dimensions, both overall and internal, to some common unit, either in multiples or regular increments, the more you will have provided the table with an implied pattern that may not be immediately apparent but which will assuredly lend it a fundamental unity.

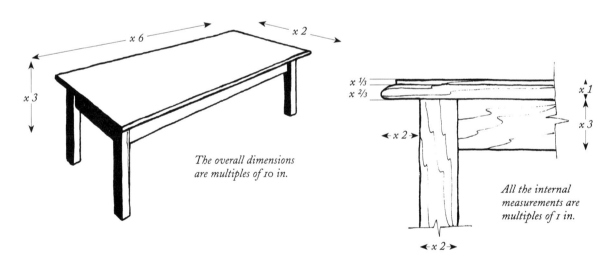

The overall dimensions are multiples of 10 in.

All the internal measurements are multiples of 1 in.

FIG. 7 COMMON INTEGER

3. The Golden Mean

The Golden Mean, more fully covered in chapter 2, and which is often referred to as Φ (phi), in honor of Phidias (φιδιασ), the architect who designed the Parthenon, is a well-known ratio that is frequently used to define the proportions of both areas and solids. It is typically expressed as the ratio of 1 to approximately 1.618. A tabletop might, for example, be designed so that its long side was 1.618 times longer than its short side, resulting in a so-called Golden Rectangle. Similarly, the volumetric space in which the table would fit might be designed as a Golden Solid — a solid whose various sides were in Φ ratio to each other.

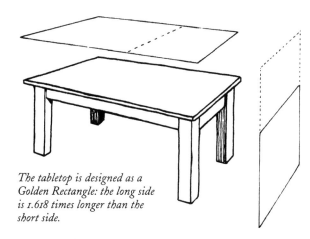

The tabletop is designed as a Golden Rectangle: the long side is 1.618 times longer than the short side.

The end of the table is the same as the squared part of the Golden Rectangle that forms the top; both parts are thus related, forming a Golden Solid.

FIG. 8 OVERALL DIMENSIONS BASED ON THE GOLDEN MEAN

The Φ ratio might additionally be used to determine all the relative dimensions of the various parts of a table. The apron might be Φ times the width of a leg, the leg Φ times the thickness of the table top, and even the different parts of a complex moulding profile might be in Φ ratio to one another.

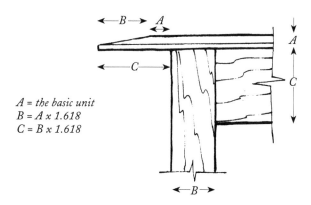

A = the basic unit
B = A x 1.618
C = B x 1.618

FIG. 9 INTERNAL GOLDEN MEAN RATIOS

4. The Five Orders of Architecture

An extremely common design paradigm, one that was much used by cabinetmakers in the 18th century, and that is still taught to every student of architecture today, is that based on *The Five* (sometimes *Seven*) *Orders of Architecture*. This term derives from books by the Roman architect and theorist Vitruvius, and various Renaissance authors, most notably Palladio (see the Select Bibliography), which systematically sought to analyze the proportions used to design many classical buildings.

The essence of each Order is characterized by a specific ratio, shown by the height of a column in relation to its basic width. The Tuscan Order, for example, may be illustrated by a column whose height is seven times its width, thereby establishing not only a basic ratio of 1 : 7, which may be used to determine the relative proportion of other parts of whatever is being designed, but also creating a fundamental module (one seventh of the column's height) that may be used to determine other constituent parts.

The actual determination of the various proportions of any given Order is a little more complicated, but an idea of the resulting relationships between the various parts may be understood from the construction of a column standing on a pedestal and surmounted by an entablature (shown below in FIG. 10) as follows:

Take any required height and divide it into five parts, as at *A*. One of these parts will be the height of the pedestal. The other four parts are now divided into five parts, the topmost of which becomes the entablature, while the lower four constitute the column, as at *B*, which, in the case of the Tuscan Order, being in turn divided into seven equal parts, as at *C*, provides the width of the column — hence the basic ratio of the Tuscan Order of 1 : 7. Further divisions are usual, such as the division of the column between the pedestal and the base into three

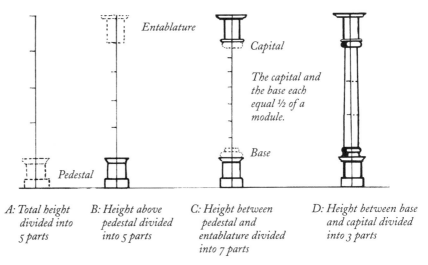

A: Total height divided into 5 parts

B: Height above pedestal divided into 5 parts

C: Height between pedestal and entablature divided into 7 parts

D: Height between base and capital divided into 3 parts

Entablature

Capital

The capital and the base each equal ½ of a module.

Base

Pedestal

FIG. 10 CONSTRUCTION OF THE TUSCAN ORDER

into three parts, the bottom third remaining cylindrical while the upper two taper (to form what is known as 'entasis', a procedure intended to reduce the optical illusion whereby a perfectly cylindrical column appears convex), and the further division of one of the seven parts shown in *C* into sixty smaller parts, used to determine the relative proportions of the various mouldings associated with the Order.

The other four Orders and their associated ratios are: Doric, 1 : 8; Ionic, 1 : 9; Corinthian, 1 : 10; and Composite, 1 : 11. These are sometimes further divided into Greek and Roman. The use of any particular Order as the basis for determining the relative proportions of the parts of any design not only assures a balanced whole, but also can add an emotional aspect, since each Order is considered to possess a particular character, in very much the same way as various musical keys (which are also defined by the internal proportional relationships of the notes) are representative of particular emotions.

Cabinetmakers trained in this tradition, such as Thomas Chippendale, who actually published an abbreviated methodology of *The Five Orders of Architecture* in what was essentially a trade catalog of the furniture that he was prepared to supply (see the Select Bibliography), typically used this system to determine not only overall dimensions but also the least detail, such as the relative proportions of mouldings that might form a table edge.

Length divided into 7 parts conforming to the ratio of the Tuscan Order (1 : 7)

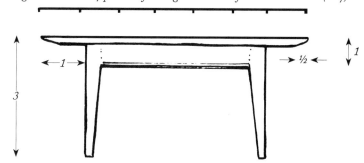

The length of the table having been divided into seven equal parts, all major dimensions are based on these modules, such as the height, the overhang of the top, the width of the beveled edge of the top, and the apron.

FIG. 11 CONSTRUCTION OF A TABLE BASED ON THE TUSCAN ORDER

5. Rhythmic Axes

A final example of a design paradigm that can be used to unify a table and provide balance and even movement is related to geometry, but in a more sophisticated manner than that described under *Basic Geometric Shapes* above. By using what are sometimes referred to as regulating lines, which connect salient features of the design — the corners of the table, the intersections of legs and aprons, the position of stretchers, even the placement of small details like edge mouldings, inlays, or apron carving — a geometric rhythm and a logic can be imposed that will make the table seem just right.

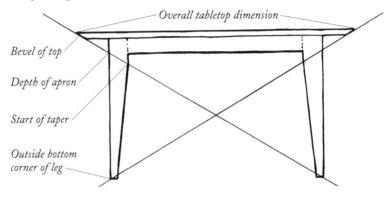

Overall tabletop dimension

Bevel of top

Depth of apron

Start of taper

*Outside bottom
corner of leg*

FIG. 12 REGULATING LINES DEFINING VARIOUS DETAILS OF A TABLE'S DESIGN

Regulating lines can be as simple as consistently angled vertices that connect certain points, or they can be more involved and consist of overlapping and intersecting arcs of circles. A well-known example is the area (known as a *vesica piscis*, Latin for a 'fish's bladder') formed by the overlap of two circles of the same diameter whose circumferences pass through each other's center. This flame or leaf-like shape occurs everywhere in nature and has been used for centuries as a paradigm for structural, philosophical, and esthetic design.

*Vesica piscis defines the
height of the table, the
width of the legs, and, by
extension of the circle
forming the upper part of
the vesica piscis, the overall
width of the tabletop and
the amount of overhang.*

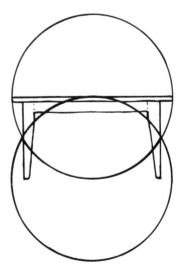

FIG. 13 TABLE BASED ON THE VESICA PISCIS

Using either a series of straight lines or enclosing arcs as the descriptive geometry of a table is another way to guarantee the formal logic which is the hallmark of a well-designed table. But never forget that function comes first, and that structural demands are equally important. In real life, tablemaking often proves to be a compromise between conflicting ideals. But almost any compromise will produce better results than if everything had been left to chance. So if one paradigm does not work exactly, feel free to adjust, and to mix and match.

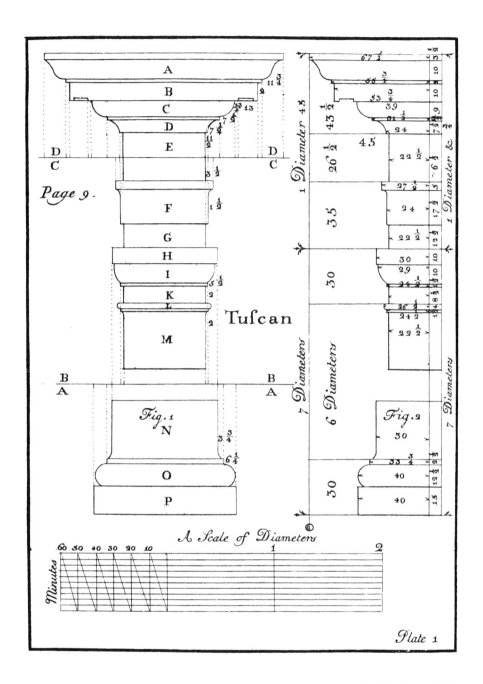

The Tuscan Order from *Magnum in Parvo; or, The Marrow of Architecture* by William Halfpenny, 1728
(see page 14)

2

THE GOLDEN MEAN

Pleasing Proportions

AS ALREADY MENTIONED IN CHAPTER ONE, THE THIRD PILLAR OF DESIGN IS FORM, THE PRACTICAL APPLICATION OF WHICH TYPICALLY DEPENDS ON the use of some plan, pattern, or design paradigm to ensure that whatever is made, in addition to functioning well and being soundly constructed, looks well.

Each of the paradigms described in that chapter might be described at much greater length — design theory in this regard is virtually infinite — but for the practicing furnituremaker much can be learned simply by bearing the need in mind and intelligent experimentation. Nevertheless, a much closer look at one of the more sophisticated paradigms, that commonly referred to as the Golden Mean, will provide some idea of the possible intriguing complexities involved.

Much has been written about this most interesting of paradigms, but do not fall into the trap of thinking that it is necessarily the best paradigm for every project. Furthermore, perfect adherence to it is often impossible and indeed seldom necessary. Lastly, remember also that it need not be used exclusively; feel free to mix and match paradigms.

DEFINITION

THE GOLDEN MEAN IS KNOWN TO MATHEMATICIANS AS
Φ (phi), in honor of Phidias (φιδιασ), the architect who designed the
Parthenon, which is largely based upon the Golden Mean. The ratio can
be expressed as the following equation:

$$\Phi = \frac{\sqrt{5}+1}{2}$$

which, when resolved, produces an infinite value:

$$1.61803398825751......$$

For most practical purposes, however, at least in so far as designing
furniture is concerned, we can think of Φ as 1.618, and we can most easily
visualize it by dividing any given line so that the longer part is 1.618 times
greater than the shorter part. Thus, in the following diagram, however
long AB may be, BC will be 1.618 times longer.

FIG. 14 THE RATIO Φ

One of the interesting and most useful things about this ratio is that the
shorter part (AB) is in the same proportion to the longer part (BC) as the
longer part is to the whole. Expressed mathematically the ratio is thus:

$$AB : BC :: BC : AC$$

WHY THE GOLDEN MEAN WORKS

THE RATIO Φ UNDERLIES MUCH OF NATURE AND THE WAY
the universe is constructed. Examples abound on every level, from
astro-physics to quantum mechanics. The planetary orbits of our own
solar system, despite being somewhat elliptical and not all exactly on the
same plane, are essentially arranged according to Φ, meaning that the
distance between successive planets' orbits is always approximately 1.618
times greater than the distance between the orbits of the previous two
planets. Indeed, the same holds true for the relationship between Venus
and Mercury, and Mercury and the Sun. Considering the prevalence
of this ratio in nature, as exemplified in countless examples from the

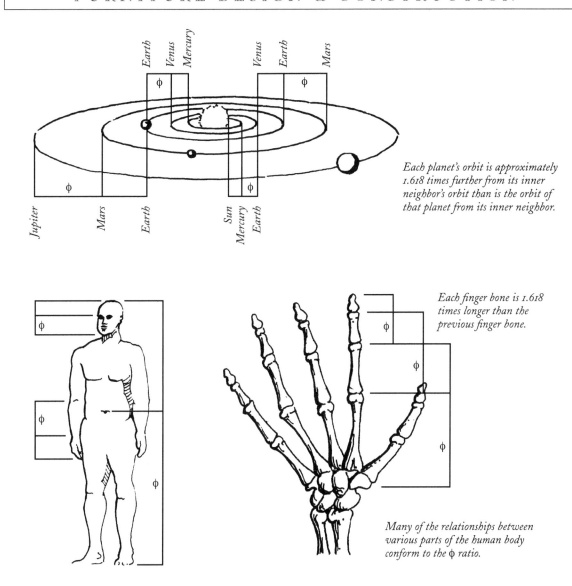

Each planet's orbit is approximately 1.618 times further from its inner neighbor's orbit than is the orbit of that planet from its inner neighbor.

Each finger bone is 1.618 times longer than the previous finger bone.

Many of the relationships between various parts of the human body conform to the φ ratio.

FIG. 15 THE RATIO Φ IN NATURE

body proportions of beetles to the arrangement of seeds in sunflowers it is hardly surprising that even the very structure of the human figure — from the large relationships shown in FIG. 15 to the ratio, measured in angstroms (one ten-billionth of a meter!) of one revolution of the double helix form of deoxyribonucleic acid (DNA) to its diameter — uses this ratio. It is no wonder that such a fundamental and all-pervasive ratio should appeal to us on a subconscious level as being essentially 'right', and that as such has been recognized and used for centuries by designers of everything from the pyramids to countless furniture masterpieces.

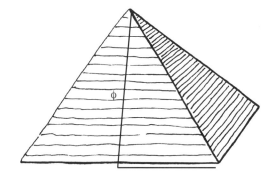

The height of the Great Pyramid of Ghiza is 1.618 times the length of half the base.

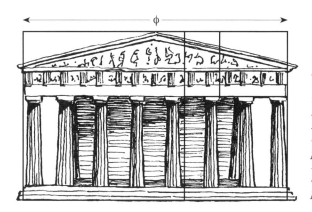

The Parthenon is designed to fit within a Golden Rectangle — a rectangle whose long side is 1.618 times its short side, the squaring of which (see FIG. 26) produces further Golden Rectangles, used to determine other major proportions.

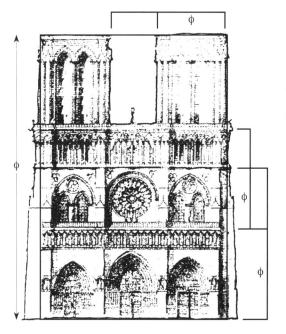

Not only does the west front of the cathedral of Notre Dame in Paris form a vertical Golden Rectangle, but many of the inner proportions are also based on φ.

FIG. 16 THE RATIO Φ IN ARCHITECTURE

Much professionally designed furniture uses the φ ratio, as does this high chest of drawers (known as 'the Pompadour'), made in Philadelphia between 1762 and 1790.
• The carcase is designed as a vertical Golden Rectangle.
• The waist (where the upper case sits on the lower case) is determined by dividing the overall height in φ proportion.
• The two lower drawers are Golden Rectangles, and in addition are 1.618 times deeper than the drawer above.

FIG. 17 THE RATIO Φ IN FURNITURE

Apart from various philosophical and metaphysical explanations concerning the qualities and attributes of this particular ratio, one of its most useful functions is that if used in regular increments it increases the size of any given object without altering its shape. Another expression of this ratio is known as a Golden Spiral (see FIG. 26), which keeps the same center as it increases. There are countless examples of this in nature, from the way in which the seeds of a sunflower are arranged to the form of the horns on a ram. Perhaps the best known example of a

The nautilus also grows in the form of a so-called Golden Spiral (see FIG. 26).

FIG. 18 NAUTILUS SHELL

Golden Spiral is the nautilus shell, each of whose chambers increases in Φ proportion to the previous chamber, and so, although larger, retains the same shape, which furthermore results in a shell that also stays the same overall shape, no matter how many chambers it may acquire.

Similarly, using regular Φ increments when designing a piece of furniture will not only enable you to produce a pleasing whole, but will also ensure that all the constituent parts, being fundamentally related, add up to a harmoniously balanced structure.

Door A has been randomly constructed with no considered relationship between any of its parts, and so is unbalanced and awkward compared to doors B and C.

Door B has been designed as a Golden Rectangle, as are its various panels.

Door C achieves an internal balance as a result of the various framing members having been designed according to the φ ratio: the top rail and stiles are 1.618 times wider than the muntin, and the bottom rail is 1.618 times wider than the top rail.

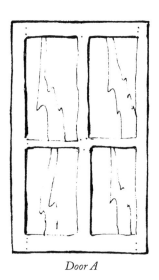

Door A

Door B

Door C

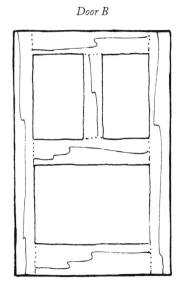

FIG. 19 DOORS BASED ON THE RATIO Φ

HOW TO PRODUCE A Φ RATIO

BEFORE YOU CAN CONVENIENTLY USE Φ AS A RATIO OR AS
a paradigm to design a piece of furniture, you must know how to produce
it. You could, of course, simply multiply or divide any given measurement
by 1.618, but this typically results in very clumsy numbers, especially when
using the Imperial system of feet and inches. It is much easier to construct
an arbitrarily sized Golden Rectangle and then adjust the size as required.
Two simple methods are shown below:

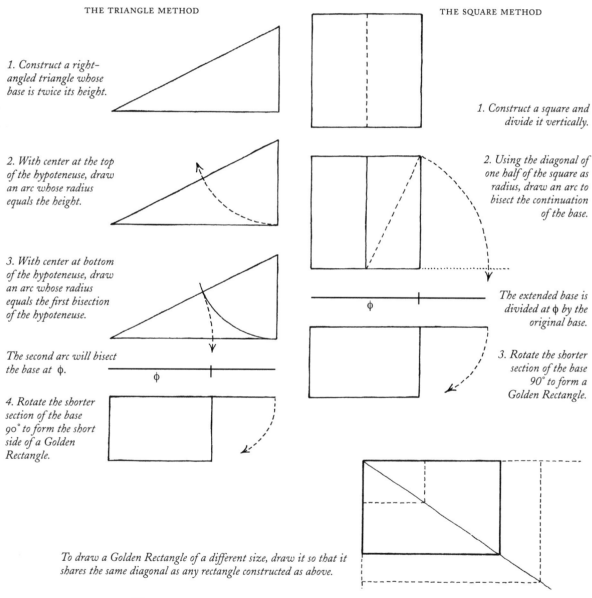

THE TRIANGLE METHOD

1. Construct a right-angled triangle whose base is twice its height.

2. With center at the top of the hypoteneuse, draw an arc whose radius equals the height.

3. With center at bottom of the hypoteneuse, draw an arc whose radius equals the first bisection of the hypoteneuse.

The second arc will bisect the base at φ.

4. Rotate the shorter section of the base 90° to form the short side of a Golden Rectangle.

THE SQUARE METHOD

1. Construct a square and divide it vertically.

2. Using the diagonal of one half of the square as radius, draw an arc to bisect the continuation of the base.

The extended base is divided at φ by the original base.

3. Rotate the shorter section of the base 90° to form a Golden Rectangle.

To draw a Golden Rectangle of a different size, draw it so that it shares the same diagonal as any rectangle constructed as above.

FIG. 20 CONSTRUCTION & ADJUSTMENT OF A GOLDEN RECTANGLE

25   **THE GOLDEN MEAN**

Note that once you have constructed a Golden Rectangle, if you square off one end you will be left with another Golden Rectangle (see FIG. 16 and FIG. 26) — which process can be repeated indefinitely to produce a whole series of Golden Rectangles all inherently related to one another. This is a handy way to discover a series of Φ ratios without having to resort to complicated calculations — with or without a calculator.

Yet another way to derive measurements that reflect the Golden Mean ratio is to use a Fibonacci series. This is simply a sequence of numbers each of whose values is the sum of the two preceding values. A very simple series starting with 1 and 2 produces the following:

1, 2, 3, 5, 8, 13, 21, 34, 55, 89, 144, 233, 377, 610, 987, 1597, etc.

A Fibonacci series is useful because after the first few values, any value divided by the previous value results in a value increasingly closer to Φ, or 1.618. This explains why items proportioned using ratios such as 3 : 5, or 5 : 8 are so common — they are based on Φ !

Perhaps more useful to the furniture designer looking for Φ ratios is the realization that a Fibonacci series can be generated using any two values that might represent certain given or required dimensions and adding them together to produce the third value and so on, thus resulting in a series of other potential dimensions all with a Φ relationship. For example the dimensions of a box measuring 4 in. by 9 in. could be used to produce the following series:

4, 9, 13, 22, 35, 57, 92, 149, 241, 390, 631, etc.

Once again, disregarding the first few values, you now have a series of pairs of numbers with a Φ ratio, which might be used as a basis for other required dimensions.

APPLYING THE GOLDEN RECTANGLE TO OVERALL DIMENSIONS

A WORD OF CAUTION BEFORE STARTING TO APPLY THE Golden Mean as a design paradigm: remember that form must follow function. This means that even the most sublimely proportioned piece of furniture, if it does not function — because it is too small or too large or otherwise unable to be used comfortably — will be a failure. Practical considerations must therefore come first. And, in fact, most of the time you will start out with a number of so-called givens when designing anything: a table must be a certain height, a cabinet may have to fit a particular space, or a bookcase may require a fixed number of shelves. But almost certainly you will be left with many other decisions regarding exact dimensions, both overall and internal. Deciding on these by eye alone — or, even worse, on the basis of whatever lumber is conveniently to hand — is a less certain way of achieving a well-balanced, nicely proportioned piece than is using a system or paradigm such as the Golden Mean. So start with function and then see how close you can come to the ideal.

You might, for example, want to build a table to a certain length, but be undecided about the exact width. It will be worth the effort to see if the proportions of a Golden Rectangle might work. In FIG. 21 below, note that not only is the top a Golden Rectangle, but also that the legs have been positioned within a small Golden Rectangle.

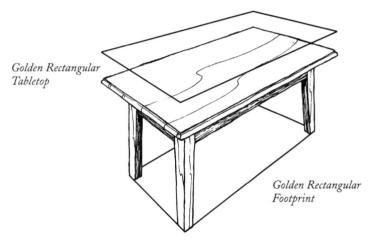

Golden Rectangular Tabletop

Golden Rectangular Footprint

FIG. 21 TABLETOP DESIGNED USING THE GOLDEN RECTANGLE

Similarly, if designing a cabinet that requires a fixed width but whose height is potentially flexible, try imposing a Golden Rectangle on the design.

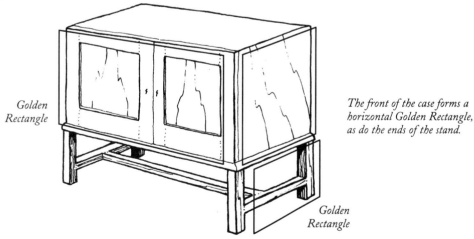

Golden Rectangle

The front of the case forms a horizontal Golden Rectangle, as do the ends of the stand.

Golden Rectangle

FIG. 22 CABINET DESIGNED USING THE GOLDEN RECTANGLE

Faced with the job of designing a built-in wall unit consisting of various modules — such as an entertainment center flanked by shelving — in a space that has no immediately apparent convenient relationships, consider starting with two Golden Rectangles for shelving at the sides, and allowing the central part to be what it may — perhaps dividing its height by the Golden Mean; or, alternatively, designing the central part as a Golden Rectangle and then dividing the remaining space equally between the two shelving units..

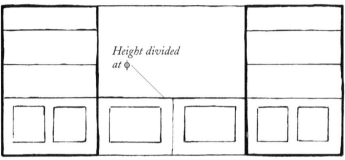

Height divided at φ

Two side Golden Rectangles;
the central part divided vertically at φ

A central Golden Rectangle;
the side units filling the remaining space equally

FIG. 23 WALL UNIT

THE GOLDEN SOLID & THE GOLDEN SPIRAL

MOST FURNITURE IS, OF COURSE, THREE-DIMENSIONAL, and the Golden Mean ratio can be applied between all three dimensions simply by turning a Golden Rectangle into a Golden Solid. Note that any side of a Golden Rectangle can be thought of as either the long side or the short side of an adjacent Golden Rectangle; consequently there is more than one choice when deciding on width relative to height or depth.

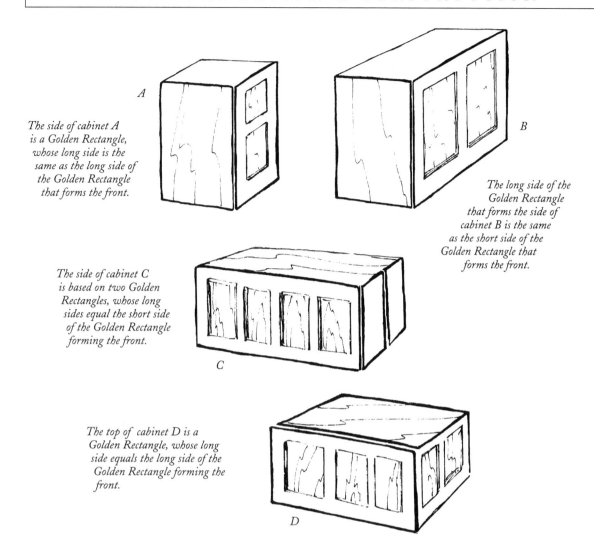

The side of cabinet A is a Golden Rectangle, whose long side is the same as the long side of the Golden Rectangle that forms the front.

The long side of the Golden Rectangle that forms the side of cabinet B is the same as the short side of the Golden Rectangle that forms the front.

The side of cabinet C is based on two Golden Rectangles, whose long sides equal the short side of the Golden Rectangle forming the front.

The top of cabinet D is a Golden Rectangle, whose long side equals the long side of the Golden Rectangle forming the front.

FIG. 24 GOLDEN SOLIDS

A design may be developed to approximate a single Golden Rectangle, or be based on multiples of a Golden Rectangle and thereby retaining an inherent Golden Relationship in its overall dimensions. As with other design paradigms, the effectiveness is often increased with repetition, since it provides a kind of underlying pattern, and pattern is one of the best ways of unifying any construction.

The concept of using the Φ ratio as the basis for an entire modular system is an idea made famous by the Swiss architect Charles Edouard Jeanneret (known as Le Corbusier), who designed the United Nations building in New York — the front of which is a perfect Golden Rectangle. Le Corbusier proposed a dimensioning system known as the *Modulor*, based on human measurements and Φ (see the Select Bibliography). The *Modulor* is developed into a grid that is used to determine the size of construction modules based on two series of Φ relationships. The first series is based on the conventional height of a man (72 in.) as divided by Φ at the navel; the second is based on the height of a man's upraised hand (which equals twice the height of his navel) and which is divided at Φ by his lowered hand.

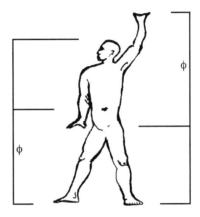

FIG. 25 LE CORBUSIER'S MODULOR MAN

The process mentioned in the illustration of the Parthenon (FIG. 16) of squaring a Golden Rectangle to produce a second, smaller Golden Rectangle, which may in turn be squared, is one way of arriving at a series of related shapes that can be useful when designing such multiples. But perhaps more importantly, it is also a simple method for producing a Golden Spiral. Simply continue the squaring process within the original Golden Rectangle four or five times, and then draw a curved line that connects the diagonals of all the square sections.

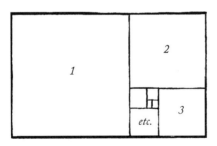

Note that every line in the Golden Rectangle, starting from the smallest square, is 1.618 times longer than the previous line.

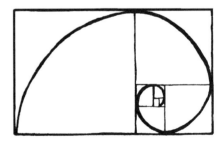

FIG. 26 CONSTRUCTION OF A GOLDEN SPIRAL

It is pattern and proportional relationships that provide a piece with the balance and harmony that is so pleasing to the senses, and this applies as much to curved, non-rectilinear shapes as it does to basic straight-sided pieces. It is not too difficult to fair a curve for an apron or a bonnet or some other part of a piece of furniture, but if in addition to being smoothly cut the curve possesses an inherent relationship to the rest of the piece — such as being part of a Golden Spiral derived from a Golden Rectangular section of the piece — the effect will be much better. Make sure your curves relate to the other dimensions of your piece, and are not simply arbitrary, albeit smooth, curves.

THE GOLDEN RATIO & INTERIOR PROPORTIONS

WHETHER OR NOT THE OVERALL DIMENSIONS OF A PIECE reflect proportions based on Φ, there will invariably be many internal proportions to be decided on, such as the proportions of aprons to table tops or thickness of legs, or the spacing of shelves, or the widths of drawers, or even the relative sizes of framing members such as stiles, rails, and muntins. All of these may be originally determined by functional and structural requirements, but many nice adjustments can often be made that without detracting from function or structure can add substantially to an inner harmony if viewed in light of how well they match or merely approach the Golden Mean.

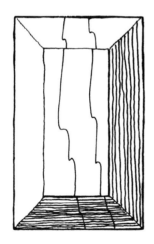

The width of the bevel defining the raised field of this panel is determined by progressively squaring the original Golden Rectangle.

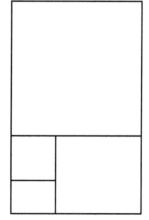

FIG. 27 PANEL PROPORTIONED BY RATIO Φ

The method of graduating drawers so that each drawer's height equals the height of the drawer above it plus the thickness of the rail it rests upon is well-known, but is not always convenient. The Golden Ratio offers another way to solve the problem of designing nicely graduated drawers, and the method can be applied equally effectively to other elements such as shelving, doors, or partitions.

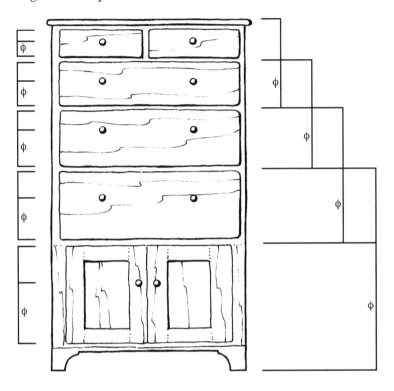

FIG. 28 PROPORTIONING DRAWERS & PULLS USING Φ

Similarly, consider using the ratio whenever you have to make decisions about the relative thicknesses or widths of the constituent parts of a piece, such as the table shown below.

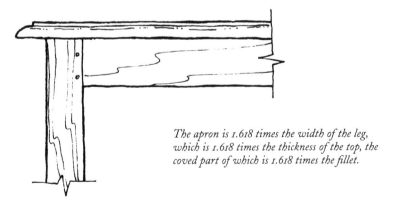

The apron is 1.618 times the width of the leg, which is 1.618 times the thickness of the top, the coved part of which is 1.618 times the fillet.

FIG. 29 INTERNAL Φ PROPORTIONS

PRACTICAL ADJUSTMENTS

DESIGNING SOMETHING WITH PERFECT PROPORTIONS IN all its details is rarely possible in the real world. Almost every piece of furniture or woodwork will need to accommodate unavoidable constraints imposed by details of function, joinery, or even economics. But even just the attempt to approach perfection (which might, for example, be defined as measurements that correspond precisely to a system such as the Golden Mean), is guaranteed to produce a better result than designing with no regard for any such paradigm, since the eye is inclined to accommodate slight imperfections and fill in the gaps, so do not think that everything has to fit the formula exactly.

Lastly, remember that we often adjust things by eye in an attempt to make a piece look lighter or better balanced, and we do so by using a variety of tricks and techniques that are part of the normal day-to-day woodworking vocabulary. Using these tricks and techniques to approach more closely to the ideal Golden Mean is a surer way of achieving balance than trying to do so by eye alone.

Such tricks include the calculated use of any pronounced figure to help the eye see curves where none exists, grain direction to imply movement, various ways to finish edges and corners to give the impression of greater thickness or thinness, the use of moulding (whose proportions might also be considered in the light of how closely they fit Φ) to adjust an apparent Golden Rectangle or Golden Solid, the use of tapered legs to give the appearance of more closely approximating an ideal proportion, and most certainly the mixing and matching of many other design paradigms in combination with the use of the Golden Mean.

Designing is fun. You must consider function, and the more technical ability you develop the better made your furniture will be, but making sure that the piece looks good is no more complicated than working to some paradigm such as the Golden Mean. It should certainly not depend exclusively on a 'good eye'.

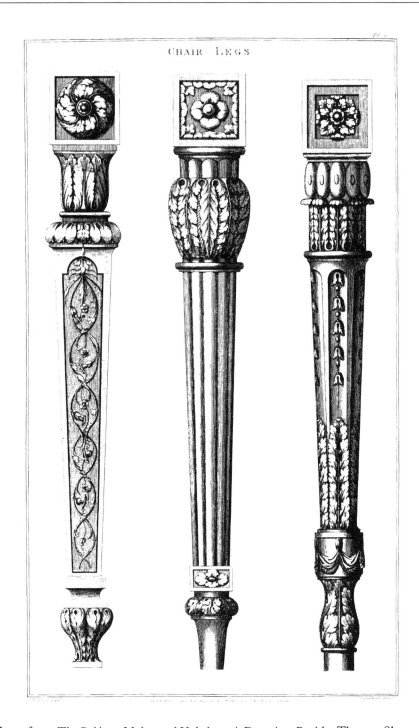

CHAIR LEGS

Chair Legs from *The Cabinet-Maker and Upholsterer's Drawing-Book* by Thomas Sheraton, 1793

3

FUNCTIONAL & STYLISTIC APTNESS

Including a Short History of Styles

A N IMPORTANT ELEMENT OF THE THIRD PILLAR, PROPORTION, IS ENVIRONMENTAL PROPORTION, OR HOW WELL ANY GIVEN PIECE FITS WITH ITS neighbors and its surroundings in general. Continuing our use of a table as a vehicle to illustrate the design process as it might be applied to any piece of furniture, this chapter discusses how to design the legs of a table in the light of both functional and stylistic aptness or appropriateness.

THE BEWILDERING ARRAY

ONCE YOU DECIDE ON THE SHAPE AND COLOR OF A tabletop, its fabrication is largely a question of providing the required surface area with the chosen material. Flatness, stability, and finish are the chief concerns. But the support for the tabletop is a different matter. Legs, whether in the form of monolithic blocks, single pedestals, trestles, or in groups of three, four, or more, may be provided in a bewildering array of forms.

Providing reliable support may be the most fundamental requirement demanded of any leg, but deciding on an appropriate form and shape requires a reasoned understanding not only of the table's function but also, and most importantly, of the table's style.

FUNCTION

VERY OFTEN THE TABLE'S USE WILL LARGELY DETERMINE how its legs are designed. If, for example, it is a dining table the legs must not make sitting at it difficult: no matter how handsome any given leg may be, if it prevents a comfortable seating arrangement it will be a functional failure. Similarly, if it is to be a load-bearing library table it should not have delicate, spindly legs; if it is to be movable or adjustable or expandable it should not rest on massive, stretcher-bound legs.

FORM

EVEN AFTER THE TABLE'S FUNCTION HAS BEEN TAKEN INTO account the question of stylistic appropriateness remains. Sometimes this is merely a question of designing legs that are simply coherent with the table's essential character — stout, sturdy legs for a chunky, heavy-duty piece, or more delicate legs for a more refined piece — but more often the table will contain references to a particular period or style, and adding inappropriately designed legs can result in an awkward combination that will spoil an otherwise soundly constructed piece.

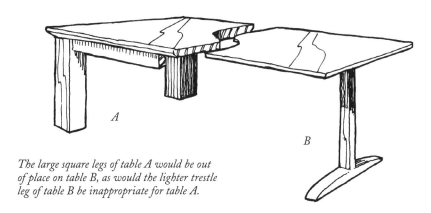

The large square legs of table A would be out of place on table B, as would the lighter trestle leg of table B be inappropriate for table A.

FIG. 30 CHARACTER-COHERENT TABLE LEGS

Words like 'inappropriately' and 'awkward' may sound ambiguously subjective, but, in fact, stylistic design appropriateness can be analyzed and understood quite objectively using the following guidelines:

1. The Use of Congruent Material

If, for example, the table is an Arts & Crafts-style piece made of solid oak — a material that accounts for much of the character of this style — then the material of the legs, if not also oak should be made of something close, both in color and grain pattern, such as ash or elm, as well as in size and style, to match or complement the rest of the table.

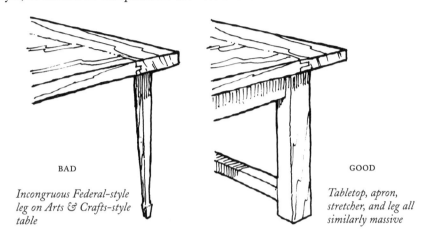

BAD

Incongruous Federal-style leg on Arts & Crafts-style table

GOOD

Tabletop, apron, stretcher, and leg all similarly massive

FIG. 31 STYLISTICALLY CONGRUENT TABLE LEGS

2. Desired Effect

Some of the styles described below in the *Brief History* are characterized by features producing particular effects. These effects may be duplicated in original designs not intended to reproduce any particular style if their essence is understood. Such effects and the ways to reproduce them include:

i. Solid Grounding:

Designing a leg that rests on a solid base and that is perhaps joined to other legs by low rails or stretchers, and that perhaps also finishes in a substantial foot will create the effect of sturdy, well-balanced solidarity.

ii. Lightness:

A tapered leg, whether plain, square, or turned, will give the effect of delicacy, even of floating. This idea can be further developed by altering the form of the tapering, for example tapering a square leg on one, two, three, or four sides, as in FIG.32, below.

iii. Sobriety:

A classicly designed leg after the manner of Adam- or Federal-style pieces can be more appropriate for tables requiring dignity, such as conference tables, library tables, or formal dining tables.

iv. Playfulness:

Flights of fancy embodied in curvilinear pieces, both regular and freeform, will transform a table to a contemorary expression of individuality.

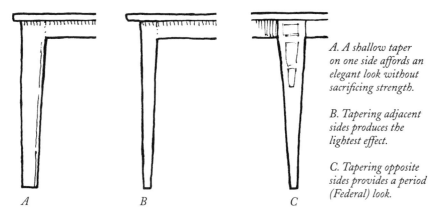

A. A shallow taper on one side affords an elegant look without sacrificing strength.

B. Tapering adjacent sides produces the lightest effect.

C. Tapering opposite sides provides a period (Federal) look.

FIG. 32 TAPER EFFECTS

3. Environmental Compatibility

This simply means taking the surroundings into account — either locally in terms of adjacent pieces, or globally in terms of the larger surroundings in which the piece will live. Sometimes, of course, none of this is known and you can do no more than aim to be as true as possible to the piece's own character — square legs on square tables, for example.

4. Stylistic Authenticity

Designing legs that are, in fact, appropriate to, and therefore in harmony with a particular style requires that you can recognize the underlying design parameters of the style in question. Knowing how particular styles developed, and the features and techniques that were used to achieve their various characteristics, will help you design legs for any given table that look comfortable and right, and protect you from making unfelicitous mistakes such as trying to graft Jacobean legs on a Chippendale piece.

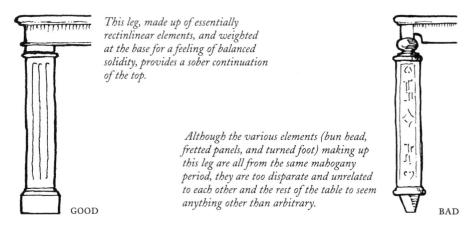

This leg, made up of essentially rectinlinear elements, and weighted at the base for a feeling of balanced solidity, provides a sober continuation of the top.

Although the various elements (bun head, fretted panels, and turned foot) making up this leg are all from the same mahogany period, they are too disparate and unrelated to each other and the rest of the table to seem anything other than arbitrary.

GOOD

BAD

FIG. 33 MISMATCHED ELEMENTS

A BRIEF HISTORY OF LEG STYLES

THE FOLLOWING CHRONOLOGICAL LOOK AT SOME OF THE major periods of Western furniture provides not only a broad outline of the more important styles, but also shows what to look for when trying to determine if a particular idea will be appropriate for the given situation.

1. Gothic–Medieval

Apart from various esoteric pieces from antiquity, such as Pharaonic chairs found in the Egyptian pyramids, and Greek and Roman furniture known primarily from artistic representations, furniture from the 14th and 15th centuries constitutes the first period from which actual examples are readily found. These were vigorous, if not violent, times, and the furniture that remains is accordingly decidedly sturdy, and largely made of durable hardwoods such as oak and chestnut.

Early tables were frequently placed upon trestles for mobility, and these proto-legs were often ecclesiastical in character, sometimes being carved with graceful gothic tracery using intersecting circles to form pointed arches and other geometrically inspired shapes, but more commonly consisting of pairs of simple slabs, occasionally made single and supported by one broad foot.

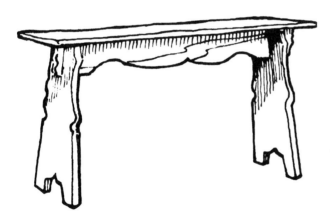

FIG. 34 15TH CENTURY SLAB TRESTLE TABLE

2. The Age of Oak

As more permanence was achieved, so-called joined tables became common. Dining tables were invariably massive affairs with large legs typically joined near their bottom by sturdy stretchers, which served not only to strengthen the legs but also to provide a place to rest one's foot — off a drafty and perhaps dirty stone floor. Early types employing a central stretcher connected to pairs of legs have the great advantage of providing plenty of space for the sitter's legs.

Square legs were frequently chamfered and cusped, and made with square stretchers mortised into them near the feet and secured with pegs. Turned legs range from basic cylinders with simple rings and square ends to those with exaggerated shapes sumptuously carved and displaying a variety of motifs from acanthus leaves to satyr's heads.

FIG. 35 LATE 16TH CENTURY JOINED TABLE

Contemporary uses for legs made in this style might include a a round dining table with a single turned and carved leg, or a kitchen or work table with simpler versions of the turned variety with square ends, as seen in much so-called English country pine pieces.

A. Simple turned leg, joined to central stretchers

B. 17th century turned leg, joined with outside stretchers

C. Kitchen table leg of pine

FIG. 36 AGE OF OAK LEGS

3. Seventeenth Century Walnut

By the 17th century, tables in general, whether large dining tables or smaller altar tables or writing tables, had become both more delicate and fanciful, and their legs, whether square or turned, are no longer merely straight but are often curved, exhibiting more pronounced turning elements such as spirals, double twists, cups, and a variety of inlay. Stetchers connecting the legs are similarly more varied with lighter, curved pieces replacing the heavy structural members found on earlier tables. There remains a distinct Renaissance influence in much of the carving, and while it is possible to divide the period into numerous categories which vary widely from one to another — such as Jacobean in Europe, and Pilgrim Century furniture in America — tables and their legs from this period are in general more sophisticated and refined than those from the Medieval and Oak periods that came before, and at the same time more inventive and decorated than the succeeding style.

This period probably presents the contemporary designer with more choices than any other, especially if he or she is not constrained by having to match or harmonize the piece with any other piece or any particular surrounding. While the construction tends to be traditional, the shape and ornamentation, as well as the material, are susceptible to infinite invention, as a visit to any museum with tables from this period will demonstrate.

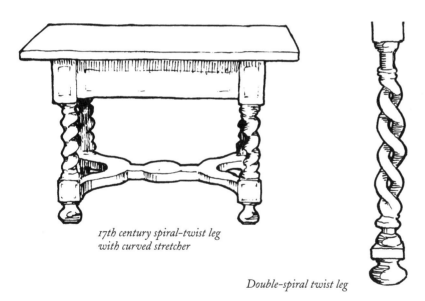

*17th century spiral-twist leg
with curved stretcher*

Double-spiral twist leg

FIG. 37 17TH CENTURY LEGS

4. Queen Anne Walnut

At the beginning of the 18th century, a marked stylistic reaction to the previous exuberance set in, and the so-called Queen Anne style (which lasted considerably longer than Queen Anne's actual reign), is typified by restraint and a lessening of ornament. More attention was paid to purity of line and elegance of design, and this is particularly typified by the Queen Anne-style cabriole leg with pad foot, and later the ball-and-claw foot, both with minimal carving.

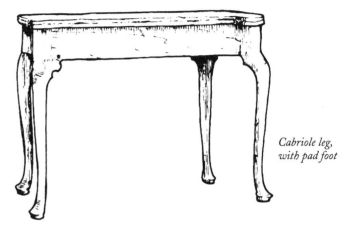

Cabriole leg, with pad foot

FIG. 38 QUEEN ANNE CARD TABLE

This was also the beginning of the classic 18th century style of furniture, represented in Britain by famous makers such as Thomas Chippendale and a host of anonymous Irish makers, and in America by such luminaries as Thomas Affleck and other Philadelphia cabinetmakers, and many other sought-after makers such as the Goddards and Townsends of Newport, Rhode Island. These men based their designs on classical paradigms

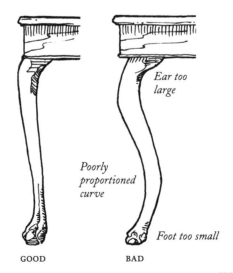

Ear too large

Poorly proportioned curve

Foot too small

GOOD   BAD

The leg on the left has been designed using one of the Orders of Architecture to determine its exact size, shape, and proportions. The leg on the right, while the individual details are correct, is misshapen and unbalanced, since no underlying paradigm has been used.

FIG. 39 UNDERLYING PARADIGMS

constructed around a series of relative proportions derived ultimately from Greek and Roman architecture. If you wish to design in this style it is important to learn something about the underlying proportional system known as *The Five Orders of Architecture* (see chapter 1) that dictates fundamentals such the ratio of height to width.

5. Mahogany Furniture

As the 18th century wore on there was a return to increased ornament, and by the time of Chippendale, table legs were once again being heavily carved with lions' feet, fretwork, flutes, and all manner of brackets.

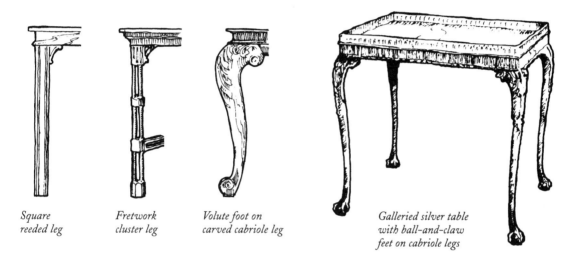

Square reeded leg

Fretwork cluster leg

Volute foot on carved cabriole leg

Galleried silver table with ball-and-claw feet on cabriole legs

FIG. 40 CHIPPENDALE-STYLE LEGS

Although succesful design in this style requires at least a passing awareness of basic underlying design principles, there are also important details identifying separate varieties, such as the markedly different ball-and-claw feet made in the various centers of furniture production. Random mixing and matching in an attempt to reproduce the general look of the

Philadelphia: flattened ball

New York: tall, squarish ball

Newport: undercut claws

FIG. 41 REGIONAL VARIETIES OF BALL-AND-CLAW FEET

period will therefore often fail and look silly. Nevertheless, choosing elements — such as a particular foot, a certain stretcher type, an overall shape or proportion — if done with an eye to overall balance, both in terms of weight, as implied by the actual size and dimensions of various parts, and form, as constituted by color, wood species, and ornamentation such as carving or inlay, can produce something new and exciting from ideas that have stood the test of time.

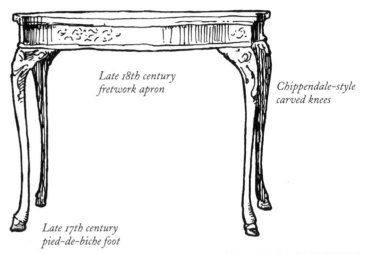

Late 18th century fretwork apron

Chippendale-style carved knees

Late 17th century pied-de-biche foot

FIG. 42 FELICITOUS MIXING OF ELEMENTS

The important thing is to avoid trying to replicate a particular style exactly, such as a New York side table from 1790, and then, from of lack of familiarity, giving it something entirely incongruous, such as a Boston foot. Remember that details, while important, should always be subservient to the whole. However much a particular element may appeal to you, do not hesitate to alter or adjust it for the sake of the leg as a whole.

6. Late Eighteenth Century

By the end of the 18th century, designers such as the Adams, Sheraton, and Hepplewhite had introduced even more classical elements, such as stretcherless tapered legs, architectural details such as classically inspired spandrels, pilasters, and fluting, and a great deal of inlay in the form of shells, urns, and stringing and banding. This was, of course, possible since cabinetmaking techniques based mainly on veneered construction had largely superseded the older forms of solid-wood joinery.

Realizing this, you will avoid the use of these techniques on legs destined for a table designed in an earlier style. Put another way, it is invariably better to restrict your design vocabulary to those elements which go hand-in-hand with the type of construction being employed. Structural logic is another aspect of form following function.

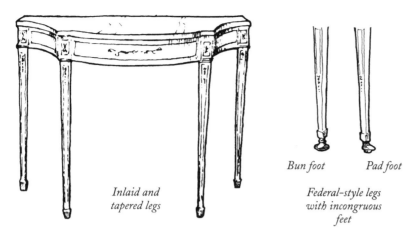

Bun foot   *Pad foot*

*Federal-style legs
with incongruous
feet*

*Inlaid and
tapered legs*

FIG. 43 LATE 18TH CENTURY SIDE TABLE

7. Nineteenth Century

The 19th century saw the general introduction of powered machinery, and with it the development of furnituremaking concerns larger than the one-master-several-apprentice shops that had previously been the norm. The increased competition led to a period much given to stylistic revivals. Consequently, there are as many distinct forms, fads, styles, and schools originating in this period as in practically all preceeding centuries.

Nevertheless, a close look at some of these styles can be instructive. The perennially popular Shaker style, for example, is well known as a model of simplicity and unadorned sobriety. Construction is honest and straightforward, and very little is added that does not have an essential structural purpose. This results in simple turned or plainly tapering legs, sufficient for the job of supporting the table, made from the most practical

FIG. 44 SHAKER SEWING TABLE WITH PLAIN TAPERED LEGS

material to hand, eschewing the use of rare and exotic species that might otherwise require additional work to make them fit for the job. Try using these principles by designing a leg that represents the minimum possible construction for sufficient support.

In sharp contrast to Shaker simplicity is much mass-produced Victorian furniture which sought to embody whatever fantastic element was the fashion of the day. This included applied veneer pieces, pressed patterns, gilded incised designs, spindled galleries, machine fluting, and coarse carving, often on two-dimensionally shaped members. One well-known example of revivalist fashion is furniture inspired by the designer Charles Eastlake who was responsible for introducing the principles of the English design reform movement to America. Originally conceived as a reaction against the melodramatic red plush and extravagant furniture of much mid-century furniture, this resulted in a series of more simplified styles drawing upon earlier models, such as Modern Gothic and Queen Anne Revival.

An eclectic mix of Gothic, Tudor, and Romanesque elements

FIG. 45 VICTORIAN TABLE LEG

Much of this furniture can today seem still excessively busy, but it can serve the contemporary designer as a model of how earlier elements can be reinterpreted. Although some of the results may be seen as a travesty of the pieces that inspired them it is instructive to observe how when reinterpreted and incorporated into new pieces they nonetheless present a coherent identity. This is another important idea to bear in mind: a well-designed leg, of whatever style, will stand on its own merits if you have fulfilled the structural requirements and have conceived the leg and the table as a whole.

8. Twentieth Century–Contemporary

By the 20th century, several factors converged to create a superficially even more confused landscape so far as the designer was concerned. On the one hand the 19th century fondness for reinventing old styles had produced an almost limitless number of confused and riotous vernaculars. On the other hand the severe reaction to everything overly ornamented and complicated, as represented by the Arts & Crafts movement's return to simple craftsmanship, had produced a spartan and four-square approach that foreshadowed the later Bauhaus movement of mid-century. Added to these diverse approaches, the continued increase of machinery, new methods of production, and greatly changing market conditions, not least the far-reaching effects of the Great War, all provided an extremely fertile ground for a variety of new styles.

Some lines of development continued the simple approach. Out of the Arts & Crafts movement came designers concerned with honesty, simplicity, and good workmanship. People such as Edward Barnsley, Allan Peters, and even James Krenov have continued to embody this approach.

FIG. 46 KRENOV-STYLE SILVER TABLE WITH SPLAYED-ENDED LEGS

At the other end of the design spectrum a more purely artistic spirit produced the more fluid and nature-inspired shapes of the Art Nouveau movement, which merged with the increasingly modern ideas of the Art Deco movement. This resulted in the exciting use of new and different materials, including sharkskin, aluminum, and multi-plies.

More recently there has been a flowering of talented new designers with a renewed interest in high-quality woodworking. Schools in Britain and America now exist where the making of both well-constructed and well-designed furniture is taught, both contemporary and traditional.

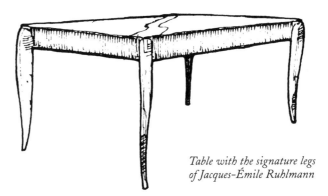

*Table with the signature legs
of Jacques-Émile Ruhlmann*

FIG. 47 1920 ART DECO TABLE

As we move into the 21st century, the result is more choices than ever for the designer. Now it would seem that anything goes. But for all the apparent variety, the fundamentals of good design — overall harmony, structural sufficiency, and balance — remain and cannot be ignored. James Krenov's furniture may be well known for its sensitive and delicate attention to overall harmony of color and grain, George Nakashima can be appreciated for his use of natural forms, and the Memphis style may stand out by virtue of its uncompromising and radical approach to color and geometrics, but all three of these superficially different approaches succeed because their fundamental concern is with the given piece as a balanced whole. Each of the various elements represented by successful pieces from the past, as illustrated above, is still important. No matter what constructional course you follow, no matter what style you prefer, strive always to design a leg that bears these in mind, remembering above all, so far as the leg — or any other element — is concerned that it constitutes an integral part of the whole piece.

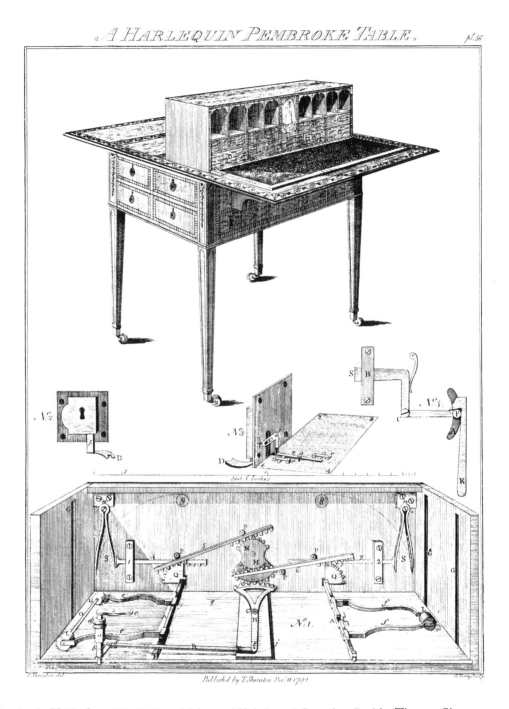

Pembroke Table from *The Cabinet-Maker and Upholsterer's Drawing-Book* by Thomas Sheraton, 1793
(see page 42)

4

DETAILS
of STYLE

A Close Look at Arts & Crafts

S TYLISTIC AUTHENTICITY CAN BE A VERY IMPORTANT ELEMENT IN SUCCESSFUL DESIGN, AND AS SUCH WAS MENTIONED IN THE PREVIOUS CHAPTER. THIS examined just one part, namely the leg, of the table we have been using as a vehicle to discuss the overall design process. In order to show how detailed an understanding of any particular style must be to be useful, this chapter examines more closely the so-called Arts & Crafts style previously mentioned under the subhead: TWENTIETH CENTURY: CONTEMPORARY.

This particular style has been popular for a hundred years: there are examples in every antique and secondhand furniture store, reproductions abound, and it is a perennial favorite with woodworkers, but what exactly is it that defines a piece as Arts & Crafts?

Ask anyone familiar with the style known variously as 'Mission Furniture', 'Craftsman Furniture', 'Crafts Style', 'Cloister Style', and even 'Quaint Furniture' — but perhaps most often as 'Arts & Crafts' — how they identify it, and you will get answers that typically contain words such as 'foursquare', 'straightforward construction', 'exposed joinery', and 'quartersawn oak'.

Such elements make this style especially inviting to many beginning woodworkers, who, attracted by its apparent simplicity, may feel less intimidated by it than by more sophisticated styles. It is, however, just as easy to get wrong as it is to fail at your first cabriole-legged Chippendale style piece — unless you understand what the underlying design philosophy is and how the various characteristic details work together.

HISTORICAL BACKGROUND

AT THE SAME TIME AS VICTOR HUGO WAS POINTING OUT in 1831, in *Notre-Dame de Paris*, that it was the invention of the printing press that had resulted in architecture ceding its role to the book as the chief demonstrator of humanity's 'soul', a similar change was occurring in the world of furniture: the individual craftsman was being supplanted by factory production as the leading influence of style. Once again, driven by strictly commercial concerns, mechanization was overtaking what up to that point had been a craft with an esthetic founded on tradition, training, and individual craftsmanship. The result was an abuse of style and an excess of indiscriminate decoration that took the form of a series of attempted revivals produced primarily for the sake of novelty in an attempt to capture the market.

What eventually became known as the Arts & Crafts movement developed primarily in opposition to this trend with the writings of influential art critics, philosophers, architects and designers such as John Ruskin, 1819–1900, and William Morris, 1834–1896. It lasted well into the 20th century with commercial furniture and other accessories produced by people like Gustav Stickley and his brothers, the noted Californian architects Charles and Henry Greene, and British designers and furnituremakers such as Ernest Gimson and the Barnsley brothers

Initially, at least, the Arts & Crafts movement was more about what not to do rather than about a clearly defined new style. But equally as important as concerns about the shoddy quality of much mass-produced factory furniture were concerns about its effect not only on the consumer but also on the people who made it. Conceived therefore as an essentially utilitarian style affordable by all, the idea that its manufacture should be something in which the maker could take pride was also central to its underlying philosophy.

Any piece of furniture built in the genuine Arts & Crafts style is, therefore, first and foremost completely functional, solidly constructed with a minimum of superfluous ornament, unashamed yet not boastful of its joinery, and one that more often than not uses oak as a primary material because oak is a supremely appropriate wood for hard-wearing furniture and one that also harks back to that period of furnituremaking history when craftsmanship was valued more than commercial success.

This explains the philosophy behind the movement but does little to describe in any useful way the physical design elements that characterize the style. Furthermore, since the movement was so long-lasting, the range of design elements that belong to this style is, in fact, much broader than many people realize.

SIX QUINTESSENTIAL ELEMENTS

THE FOLLOWING ATTEMPT TO DEFINE ARTS & CRAFTS IN practical terms is, therefore, a good example of how detailed such an understanding may have to be in order to build something convincingly in any particular style.

1. Material
Quarter-sawn oak does indeed have much to recommend it: strength, durability, relative stability (because it is quarter-sawn), and an attractive figure characterized by the medullary rays not visible in flat-sawn stock.

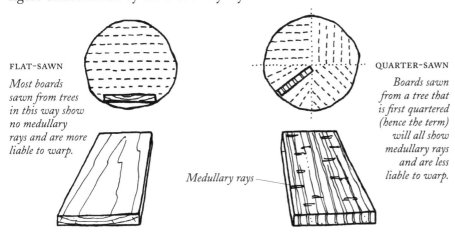

FLAT-SAWN
Most boards sawn from trees in this way show no medullary rays and are more liable to warp.

QUARTER-SAWN
Boards sawn from a tree that is first quartered (hence the term) will all show medullary rays and are less liable to warp.

Medullary rays

FIG. 48 FLAT-SAWN & QUARTER-SAWN OAK

Although a hardwood, it is not excessively difficult to work (it is easier, in fact, to produce a crisp surface with a less than perfectly sharp tool on a piece of oak than on a piece of softwood), it is not in the least toxic, and may have a wide range of color depending on the exact species (red oak, white oak, brown oak, for example), as well as taking stain well — not to mention the technique of fuming, which can produce a wonderful aged look. Nevertheless, there is little reason not to use almost any decent furniturewood. Although most factory-made Arts & Crafts furniture was made of oak, many well known designers have used other species such as walnut, mahogany, and cherry.

2. Construction Techniques

Although many designers and makers of the style occasionally used cabinet construction with veneered surfaces to provide the body of a piece, the majority of the mass-produced pieces — especially those marketed under the somewhat erroneous name of 'Mission Furniture' (so-called for its supposed similarity to the earlier American-Southwest Spanish style) — were made using solid wood and frame-and-panel construction. Consistent with the directness and honesty that is the hallmark of this style is the use of slats where a solid piece or a frame-and-paneled section would be overkill. Turned elements are rare. All this is in keeping with the principle of using the simplest possible methods of work for the most honest and unpretentious use. Simple does not, however, mean sloppy. In fact, since the aim was to design furniture of which the worker could be proud, a nice execution, particularly of exposed joinery, is absolutely essential.

3. Joinery

Without a doubt, the mortise-and-tenon is the king of Arts & Crafts joinery. Dovetails, dowels, lap joints, and housed joinery are also used where appropriate, but, in keeping with the strict demands of strength and honesty, the mortise-and-tenon joint plays the major role in most Arts & Crafts pieces. Several varieties are used, including blind, stub, through, and tusk, but each is only used when and where necessary for maximum strength without compromise. What this means is that if, for example, a through tenon is the strongest possible form in a given situation then the design will make a virtue of the necessity by not attempting to hide

Blind tenon

Stub tenon

Through tenon

Tusk tenon

FIG. 49 MORTISE-AND-TENON VARIETIES

or disguise the joint. This results in the ends of through tenons frequently being finished a little proud of the surface, often nicely chamfered, and with any wedges thoughtfully arranged with an eye to a pleasing visual pattern as well as the most efficient use.

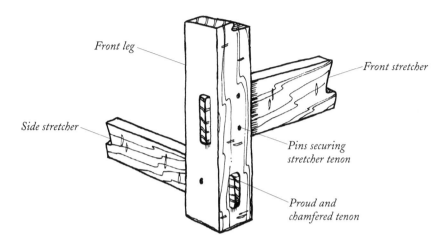

FIG. 50 TYPICAL ARTS & CRAFTS LEG DETAIL

4. Design Paradigms

There is often, especially in American Arts & Crafts pieces, whether of the less-expensive, mass-produced variety typified by Gustav Stickley's *Craftsman Furniture* or the higher-end custom-designed output of many designers like the Greene brothers, a predominating impression of squareness. This is most evident in the profiles of tops, edges, and other flat surfaces such as broad chair arms. Moulding is almost completely absent, sharp edges may be gently relieved but rarely rounded, and overhangs are kept to a minimum.

More than merely in the treatment of edges, the impression of squareness extends to overall shapes. But although many details are, in fact, square — such as in paneled framing, where a bottom rail wider than

Standard paneling typically has a frame consisting of different width stiles and rails, often moulded on the inner edges, surrounding a fielded or raised panel.

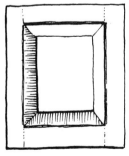

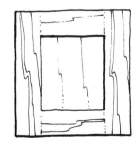

Arts & Crafts paneling is typically square, with equal width stiles and rails. Panels are sometimes carved or inlaid, but more often plain and flat in unmoulded frames.

FIG. 51 SQUARE PANELS

other frame members is rare, and in the design of glazed doors, where all panes are equally square (see FIG. 52) — absolute squareness is largely illusory, and slopes and curves are common. It is not that the style is inelegant — many pieces can be found based on sophisticated design paradigms such as the Golden Proportion — but the strength and utility of a piece always dominates.

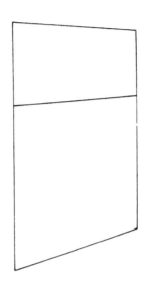

The superficial squareness and rectilinearity of this piece are actually based on the Golden Proportion: 1 : 1.618, since the overall height is 1.618 times the overall width, and so by squaring the bottom of the cabinet a second Golden Rectangle is produced, defining the glazed portion of the doors.

FIG. 52 A DESIGN BASED ON Φ

Both gently and boldly formed curves are common in aprons, chair rails, and the lower edges of cabinet sides, but they are invariably simple, and rarely compound, except for occasional tight cut-outs on stool bases. Such shapes — ogees and intersecting arcs — are nods to the influence of medieval Gothic oak furniture much valued for its craftsmanship and honesty by leaders of the Arts & Crafts style.

Geometric cutout on a stool

Ogee-profiled cutout on a magazine-stand side

FIG. 53 CURVED CUTOUTS

Similarly, curved albeit square-edged brackets are another common feature of many pieces.

Curved brackets under a chair arm

Curved brackets on a table leg

FIG. 54 BRACKETS

Another detail that belies a general apparent squareness and angularity is the frequent use of tapered legs. The tapers, however, rarely extend the length of the leg, but instead are usually limited to a short section near the base. To taper legs like this prevents the piece from seeming too heavy, but since the tapers are invariably equally formed on all four sides of the leg, a general feeling of squareness persists.

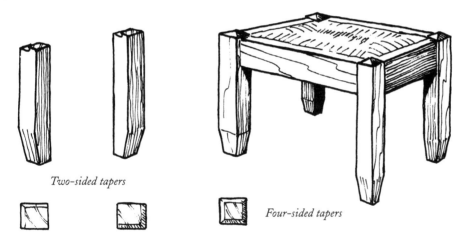

Two-sided tapers

Four-sided tapers

FIG. 55 TAPER-LEGGED FOOTSTOOL

5. Decoration

Despite a superficial plainness characterized both by square edges and the lack of moulding, together with the use of a relatively homogenous material and the flatness of panels (raised or even fielded panels are extremely rare), much Arts & Crafts furniture is often decorated with a variety of techniques ranging from simple curved cut-outs to delicate floral inlays. The influence of the more flowing, nature-based Art Nouveau style made itself felt in many Arts & Crafts pieces, as for example in the products of various so-called utopian workshops, such as the Byrdcliffe community in New York, in the form of pastel-colored painted sections, tulip inlays, and lily patterns.

A very important feature central to the principal of craftsmanship in this style of furniture is the use of other natural materials, such as reed and rush for seats, leather upholstery, and hand-wrought hardware made of iron or hammered brass. The hardware, principally as a result of the method of its manufacture, is often as square and sturdy as the furniture it serves, and stands in complete contrast to the elegant and finely wrought shapes found on many 18th century pieces or the overworked fantastic shapes common on much 19th century furniture.

A completely gratuitous form of decoration, at least in terms of structural function, but one which remains consistent with the use of natural materials, is the frequent use of a row of hand-wrought nails as an edge decoration.

6. Finish

Last but not least is the subject of finishing. It would be completely inappropriate to finish an Arts & Crafts piece with a glossy lacquered finish. But while natural finishes such as simple oiling and waxing may predominate, various other process such as filling, staining, and fuming are common.

The correct color for genuine oak Mission furniture was at one time much discussed, the relative virtues of so-called 'golden oak', 'mission brown', 'antique grey', etc., being argued, but more important than color, especially since you need not be limited to oak alone, is a careful surface preparation. In the case of an open-grained wood like oak this consists in the use of a properly colored wood filler.

If oak is first filled it may be simply waxed, or perhaps lightly oiled and then waxed. Sometimes, if wax alone is used, the wax may be colored so that wax-filled pores do not show white.

Fuming, which is the process of exposing oak to the fumes of ammonia, was a common method of turning oak darker, and one that avoids the irregular color often produced by careless staining. While the effect may be appreciated for its own sake, it is interesting to note that its popularity, especially with early proponents of Arts & Crafts furniture, was originally the result of the misconception that genuine Gothic furniture was extremely dark. That much of it is, comes from centuries of exposure to smoky atmospheres. What was not appreciated, however, was that most Gothic furniture when new was brightly painted or valued precisely for its light golden color.

INDIVIDUAL MAKERS

ANOTHER WAY TO UNDERSTAND THE CHARACTER OF A particular style is to examine the work of those regarded as practitioners of it. That each of the following examples is individually recognizable demonstrates the difficulty of achieving a single short definition, but at the same time provides an insight into how certain philosophical concepts and particular design elements can be almost infinitely manipulated to produce something that while new and original is still identifiable under a common rubric.

1. Charles Rolfs

A leading figure in the American Arts & Crafts Movement, and a friend of Elbert Hubbard, the founder of the Roycroft Colony at East Aurora, NY, Charles Rohlfs, as well as being influenced by more modern designers such as Charles Rennie Macintosh, and in common with many other Arts & Crafts designers, also looked back to the Gothic period in his use of oak, as exemplified by the drop-front desk shown below.

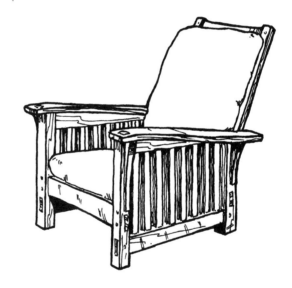

FIG. 56 DROP-FRONT DESK BY
CHARLES ROHLFS, 1883

FIG. 57 ARMCHAIR BY GUSTAV STICKLEY, 1902

2. Gustav Stickley

Regarded by many as defining the style, Gustav Stickley's mass-produced pieces were the most commercially successful manifestation of Arts & Crafts furniture. Although his are among the most simple examples of the style, Stickley drew his inspiration from more sophisticated designers, such as Voysey and Lethaby in England.

    DETAILS *of* **STYLE**

3. Byrdcliffe

The stained poplar cabinet shown below with a carved and polychromed door is a typical product of the Byrdcliffe workshops in Woodstock, NY, founded by the wealthy Englishman, Ralph Whitehead, who had been a student of the eminent Victorian art critic, John Ruskin, the generally acknowledged father of the Arts & Crafts movement. Simplicity of design as well individual craftsmanship in a communal environment informs this version of Arts & Crafts style.

FIG. 58 BYRDCLIFFE WALL CABINET, 1904

4. Frank Lloyd Wright

Although not an avowed member of the movement, the architect Frank Lloyd Wright, like the Greene brothers, designed furniture for his houses — such as this extremely rectilinear chair with exposed joinery — which although typically Wrightian is also distinctly in the Arts & Crafts style.

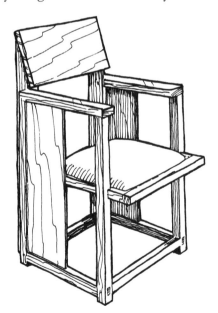

FIG. 59 ARMCHAIR BY FRANK LLOYD WRIGHT, 1904

5. Ernest Gimson

In its rectilinearity, simple lines, use of native wood (chestnut), and restrained use of minor ovolo moulding on the legs, the sideboard at FIG. 60 by Ernest Gimson, one of the chief figures of the Arts & Crafts movement, is an expression both of the values of the movement as directly expounded by William Morris, as well as of the related attempt to reintroduce traditional country crafts to high-quality furniture.

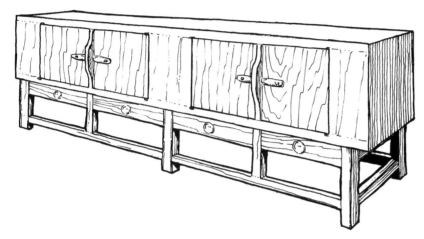

FIG. 60 SIDEBOARD BY ERNEST GIMSON, 1905

6. Charles Voysey

Voysey was another admirer of William Morris and a leading exponent of the British Arts & Crafts movement. His particularly sparse style — a Shaker-like simplicity complemented by more flowing and elegant details such as the heart-shaped cutout and square legs that taper to octagonal feet — was the direct precursor to the American 'Mission Style', which was popularized by makers such as Gustav Stickley.

FIG. 61 DINING CHAIR BY CHARLES VOYSEY, 1902

7. The Roycrofters

In contrast to the previous one-of-a kind piece by Charles Voysey shown at FIG. 61, the Roycrofters, founded by Elbert Hubbard, who was an ardent believer in many aspects of the Arts & Crafts movement not limited to furniture alone, produced extremely simple and unsophisticated 'factory-made' pieces that nevertheless belong equally to this style.

The distinctive 'Roycroft' trademark, used on every piece —

FIG. 62 MAGAZINE RACK FROM THE ROYCROFT SHOP, 1910

8. Sidney Barnsley

Made of walnut with holly and ebony stringing, the cabinet on stand is in many ways far removed from the output of the Roycrofters and the

FIG. 63 CABINET ON STAND BY SIDNEY BARNSLEY, 1914

Stickley shops, but nevertheless owes its essential design to the same principles of honesty of purpose and design shorn of superfluous decoration. Together with his son, Edward Barnsley, and Ernest Gimson, these three craftsmen constitute the Grand Old Men of the Arts & Crafts movement of which they were the leading influences.

9. Greene & Greene

Well known as architects, the Greene brothers designed Arts & Crafts furniture recognized for uniquely distinctive details such as the 'cloud lift' lines seen on various members of the dining table shown below, and plugged mortises on bread-boarded tabletops. Their work represents some of the highest expressions of the American Arts & Crafts movement.

Dining table, 1929

Dining-room serving table, 1910

FIG. 64 GREENE & GREENE FURNITURE

PART TWO

THE PROJECTS

Dressing Drawers.

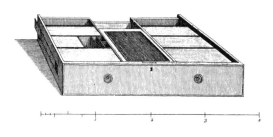

London, Published Oct.r 1.st 1787, by I. & J.Taylor, N.o 56, High Holborn.

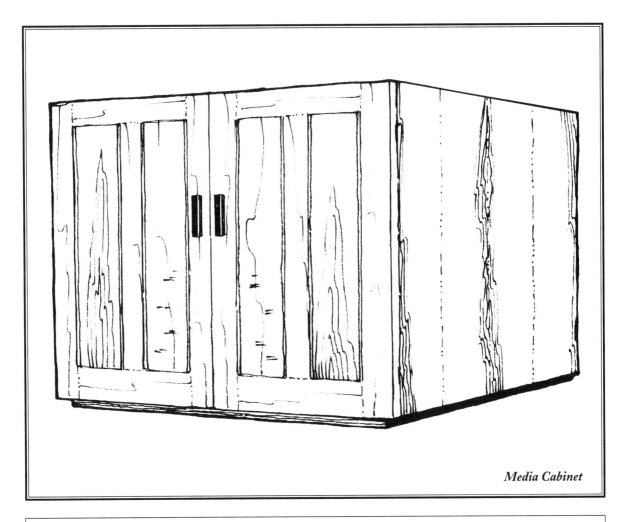

Media Cabinet

5

MEDIA CABINET

The Importance of Design

NINE TIMES OUT OF TEN THE FIRST THING THAT HITS YOUR EYE WHEN YOU LOOK AT A PIECE OF FURNITURE, EVEN IF YOU DO NOT THINK OF IT IN those terms, is the design. The shape, the proportions, and the color are what you react to first. As a woodworker you then undoubtedly get closer, assuming you like the piece, and begin to investigate how it was put together, usually with a critical eye regarding the exactness of the joinery and the niceness of the finish. For many people the technical considerations are everything, and their assessment of the piece is based solely on the maker's technical skill. These are not bad reactions but they ignore another extremely important element in a piece's overall success or failure: its design. This is partly because the elements of joinery are there in plain view for all to see while the elements of the design, all those small but important decisions that were taken along the way, are lost in the effect of the finished whole. It is much harder to trace the importance of the exact width of a stile or a rail in relation to overall length than it is to see how closely two surfaces are joined. And even if attention is paid to these things the logic behind their creation can be missed entirely by the untrained eye.

It is a big step towards becoming a successful furnituremaker when you start to ask questions about internal proportions as well as about overall dimensions. But the answers are harder to find than those to technical questions. They tend to be buried in generalizations found in books on design theory and art history. It is often difficult for the beginner to relate purely theoretical ideas to the piece in hand. This chapter describes the logic behind the design of a media cabinet; the process may be applied to numerous other projects.

You should always bear in mind the overall design of a piece and its constituent parts. Even if you are working from plans, no matter how detailed, there will always be decisions to be made that will affect whether the finished piece looks right. This is meant in an esthetic sense: does the piece have any soul, any sense of balance, any feeling of fitness or grace? Is it charming, assertive, or intrusive, or does it just sit there looking nondescript, evoking no emotional response whatsoever?

Paying attention to grain direction is an obvious example of how small decisions can affect the finished piece. The joinery may be perfect and the plans may have been followed exactly but the piece will not be as successful as it might have been if the figure of the various parts is not complementary.

The ability to appreciate the difference that such decisions can make is inherent in almost everyone, even if the reasons be not clearly understood. If the piece has been built with esthetic as well as technical care, people will be moved to talk about its 'sublime beauty' — or some similar and equally vague phrase — for lack of the ability to recognize what constitutes the bricks and mortar of that sublimity. Rarely is sublime beauty completely fortuitous; the bricks and mortar of all the small internal design considerations will have been laid with great care.

DESIGN VERSUS GIVENS

THERE ARE USUALLY A NUMBER OF SO-CALLED GIVENS WITH any project about which no discussion is allowable. Such givens may appear very complete as when, for example, you are provided with detailed drawings and specifications. But even in the absence of exact plans the client — even when you are the client yourself and you are about to make something on speculation — has usually expressed certain ideas that already determine much about the piece. It may be the function it is to fulfill, it may be the location it is to occupy, or it may be the material out of which it is to be made, but few pieces spring into being out of a total design vacuum.

The successful designer takes whatever is given and sensibly considers all the other factors that go into a piece's creation, orchestrating these elements into a cohesive whole. The responsibility is always there, if only as a result of the fact that no two pieces of wood are identical, although in reality there are usually many more decisions than material ones.

In the case of the media cabinet (a class of furniture soon destined to become obsolete as technolgy invents ever new forms of delivering entertainment, but which remains a useful example for other pieces) described in this chapter, the material, which was to be cherry, and the exterior dimensions and the interior arrangements were all clearly and exactly specified by the client. The design as given did not greatly appeal to me and there did not appear to be much room for tasteful invention on my part, but I needed the work and reluctantly accepted the commission.

The specified outside dimensions were 5 ft. wide, 3½ ft. high, and 2 ft. 6 in. deep. This created no particular feeling either way, but what did immediately concern me was that there was to be no base to this cabinet, no pediment, no moulding, and no ornament of any kind. It was to sit directly on the floor and, seen from the front, to consist solely of two identical doors which were to open onto two identical compartments, one for a television and one for a stereo receiver. It was to be a perfectly rectangular volume with no subtle or graceful curves, no base to anchor it to the ground or elevate it with grace, no ornament to focus the eye, no moulding or shaping to delight one's sense of proportion, and no crowning pediment to give it direction; a simple geometric volume without even the opportunity to play with different woods, for it was to be made of solid cherry throughout

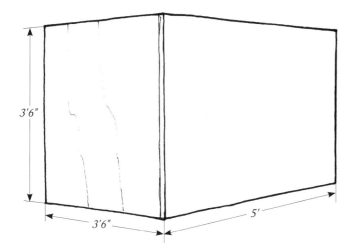

FIG. 65 GIVEN DIMENSIONS

MATERIAL PROBLEMS

I CHAFED FOR A WHILE AT SO MANY RESTRICTIONS BUT finally resigned myself to getting the job done as expeditiously as possible in order to move on to more promising projects. I ordered the lumber and prepared to start.

When the lumber arrived it was radically different from what I had expected. I had hoped to obtain wide boards of roughsawn cherry but there were none available. Instead, I received several hundred feet of very narrow boards, almost all containing some white sapwood, and all cupped and warped. By the time I had dressed the material ready for working, instead of the four-quarter cherry I had envisaged at the start of the job I was looking at a pile of narrow two-quarter-thick boards. The dramatic difference between what I had expected and what I actually had forced the first major design consideration.

I had previously thought I would build a rather bland cabinet, perhaps joining two or three quartersawn boards to obtain the necessary width of relatively homogenous material. Now I was faced with the necessity of matching numerous flatsawn boards.

Whatever the extra labor involved in obtaining the required width for the cabinet's carcase from a larger number of narrow boards, I was determined to save the widest boards for the panels of the front doors. These would constitute the most striking feature of the cabinet and it was important that they appear as consistent as possible, rather than being made up from several narrow boards, which would give them the character of randomly joined widths of cheap plywood doors. Since there was only one board available wide enough to form a front panel, the height of these panels was determined by dividing this board into four equal lengths. The board was about 10 in. wide and slightly less than 12 ft. long. Bearing in mind the ¼ in. tongue that would be needed around each panel to fit it into its framing, this fixed the panels' finished visible surface at 9½ in. wide by 34½ in. long.

The board had a little sapwood, but only on one side, and a small area of curl towards one end. The remainder of the board, being flatsawn, exhibited a pronounced flame pattern. I therefore cut the board into four lengths and arranged the pieces so that the two lengths from the curly end became the central panels, flanked by two flame-patterned outer panels. A little experimentation revealed which way round the panels looked best: the curly ones bookmatched and the flame-patterned ones with upward pointing flames. The effect was not very pronounced but definitely interesting and balanced. After checking that there was nothing glaringly unpleasant on the reverse sides as arranged, I marked the pieces with chalk triangles to show front, top and relative position as shown in FIG. 66 opposite.

A further given which was to prove problematical later was that the doors should open so that they might rest against the sides of the cabinet when the television or the stereo unit, both of which were to sit on slide-out shelves, was in use. This meant that the insides of the doors would frequently be in full view, unlike most cabinet doors whose insides

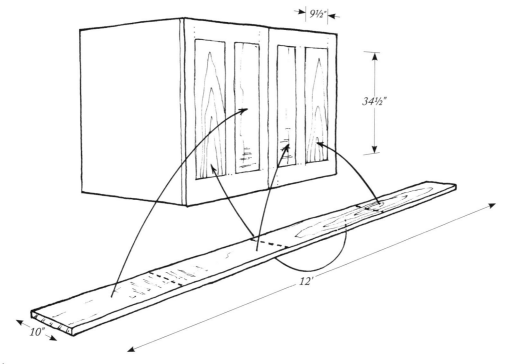

FIG. 66 THE ONE WIDE BOARD

are only seen occasionally and momentarily. These then ought to be made with a little more care than usual, and it was necessary to pay attention to the pattern of the panels on the inside as well as the outside, albeit only in pairs — since it would be impossible to see the insides of both doors at the same time. Because of the unequal distribution of sapwood and the positioning I had already determined I now had a problem: one panel definitely cried out to be reversed end-for-end. But to do so would have ruined the front view. Play as I might with new arrangements there seemed to be no way to make all panels look equally good. I was even unable to discover an acceptable compromise, which is often forced by this kind of design. I finally took refuge in the fact that the only time the unhappy panel would be visible would be when something else, such as the television or the stereo, was the focus of attention.

Since the panels were together 40 in. wide there remained only 20 in. to account for to produce the required finished width of 5 ft. for the entire cabinet. Each door would require two stiles and a muntin, making a total of six vertical framing members. This suggested an average width for these pieces of a little less than 3½ in. Having plenty of 6 in.-wide boards on hand I did not anticipate any stock selection problems and set about choosing boards for the carcase. I took the widest remaining boards for the top and sides so there would be the fewest number to join and the fewest choices to make regarding which edge looked best to which edge, construction and esthetics sharing equally in the design process.

Since every board was flatsawn and appeared to have been converted from very small trees there was a lot of white sapwood and pronounced grain. Constructing a wide area of discrete homogeneity was not an option. In much cabinet construction interest is frequently focused on elements such as doors and panels, leaving the carcase as restrained as possible, usually by making it out of bland, straight-grained material typically produced by quarter sawing. But this carcase was not going to be polite enough to stay quietly in the background, and so something had to be done to tame the wild excesses of each board's loud and obtrusive grain.

By arranging the various boards so that sapwood abutted sapwood and heartwood abutted heartwood, I avoided much jarring of disparate grain and even established a certain visual rhythm. The alternating light and dark was not exactly regular nor even particularly well balanced, but the transition from heartwood to sapwood was more natural within each board since the line of demarcation at least followed the curve and sweep of the grain rather than being arbitrarily interrupted by the straight lines of the boards' joined edges.

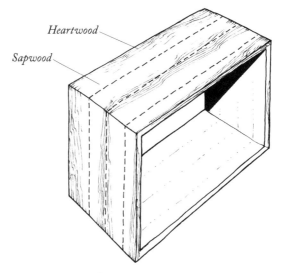

FIG. 67 ARRANGEMENT OF BOARDS COMPRISING CARCASE

I left the least desirable boards for the bottom of the carcase. The underneath would never be seen and the top surface of the bottom would be hard to see beneath the sliding shelves and whatever was stored. Some of these boards were whole boards and some were ends of other boards I had chosen for the top and sides in an effort to achieve as much continuity from side to top as possible.

MECHANICAL PROBLEMS

THE PROBLEM CONCERNING THE WAY THE DOORS WERE TO
open now made itself felt with what seemed like unending ramifications.
The solution is typical of the way in which technical problems and esthetic
considerations must be sensitively juggled if satisfaction on all counts is to
be achieved.

I had assumed that the doors would be hung inside the case rather than
be face-mounted. The primary reason for this assumption lay in the fact
that the cabinet was to have no base, and to guarantee easily operated
doors on a possibly uneven floor or thick carpet some space should be left
beneath the doors. This in turn meant that the front edges of the carcase
would be visible making their appearance important. Sure enough, the
omnipresent sapwood glared out at various points around the perimeter.

My first response was to face-mount the doors, thus hiding the front
edge of the carcase, but this returned me to the problem of doors possibly
scraping an uneven floor or a thick carpet. My second idea was to set the
doors back ¼ in. all round. But then where would the hinges be mounted?
In fact, what about the hinges?

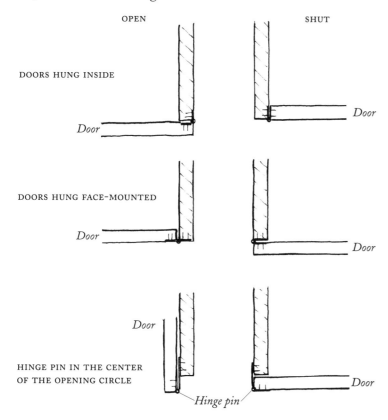

OPEN   SHUT

DOORS HUNG INSIDE

Door

Door

DOORS HUNG FACE-MOUNTED

Door

Door

Door

HINGE PIN IN THE CENTER
OF THE OPENING CIRCLE

Door

Hinge pin

FIG. 68 HINGING PROBLEMS & SOLUTIONS

MEDIA CABINET

Had the doors been set within the case as was the original assumption what kind of hinges would have allowed the doors to open a full 270°, out and around the edge of the cabinet? Invisible hinges, Soss™-type hinges, and European-style hinges open a maximum of somewhat more than 180° but less than the required 270°. Knife hinges might be found that allow the necessary opening, but they would require the door to be hung within the frame — the very thing I was trying to avoid! The principle of leaf hinges became glaringly clear: to open fully the pivot point must be in the center of the circle around which the arc of the door's opening is described. Put more simply, the hinge pin must be at the extreme outside edge of door or frame. If door and frame were not flush then the pin must be positioned in the right spot by means of variously bent leaves, similar to the offset hinges designed for face-mounted kitchen cabinet doors — which do not, however, open a full 270°.

Concern about the appearance of the front edge of the cabinet now became subservient to the problem of how to hang the doors so that they could be opened flat against the sides. The answer was not only to use surface-mounted hinges but surface-mounted doors as well. This still left the problem of how to achieve a flawless/floorless operation of the doors.

ACCEPTING DEFEAT

THE JUGGLING BETWEEN CONSTRUCTION AND ESTHETIC consideration that plays such a large part in the design process may less charitably be described as compromise. In this case the compromise involved accepting a small defeat with regard to the initial givens; my client agreed to a small base, abandoning the idea of having the cabinet rest directly on the floor.

The addition of a narrow recessed base about 1 in. high not only allowed the doors to operate unimpeded but also improved the look of the piece enormously, demonstrating how often good form follows function. I now had a large rectangular volume that floated nicely just above floor level. The effect gave a certain delicate definition to the whole. It no longer appeared hunched, hulking uncompromisingly on the ground. This is, of course, largely a subjective point view but it illustrates another aspect of design, namely that design is frequently a personal, subjective matter. Certain absolute principles do exist that upon investigation are found to rest on demonstrable scientific or mathematical logic, but much good design is mere opinion, hopefully informed and felicitous, but subjective just the same.

The carcase could now be joined with its constituent boards in the manner described and then, when in the requisite sections, sides to top and bottom. Here was another opportunity: to use the actual joinery to enhance the design. Several structurally appropriate methods suggested themselves: mitered biscuit-joints; locked rabbet joints; or dovetailed joints. But dovetailing offered the moſt opportunity for intereſting detail in an otherwise unintereſting area of casework, and despite the extra labor involved in joining what amounted to ten lineal feet of dovetailing, I decided it was worthwhile for the design's sake.

INTERNAL RHYTHMS

THE CABINET CONSISTED OF TWO EQUAL COMPARTMENTS separated by a vertical divider. There was nothing to think about here. Had the doors been set within the case, a choice would have been possible between a recessed divider againſt which both doors would have ſtopped or a divider the front edge of which would have finished flush with the front edge of the case, thereby forming an extra vertical member visible between the closed doors. However, the only design choice that remained concerned the two compartments. Each was to be fitted with a sliding shelf, the one for a television and the other for a ſtereo receiver. The size of the two units dictated the approximate location of the shelves but some leeway was possible. It could have been simply a matter of measuring off the height needed by each unit, allowing an inch or two for access, and positioning the shelves accordingly. But something more satisfactory was possible. The cabinet measured 3 ft. 6 in. high by 5 ft. wide. The central vertical divider produced two vertical rectangles, each closely approximating a Golden Rectangle, in which the ratio of height to width was approximately 5 : 3 (see chapter 2); a nicely balanced proportion producing compartments neither too narrow nor too wide. By positioning the shelves so that the one was as far from the floor of the cabinet as the other was from the cabinet's ceiling the feeling of comfortable balance was maintained, albeit asymmetrically.

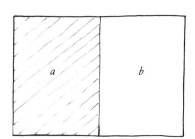

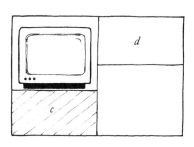

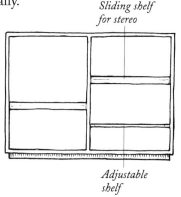

Sliding shelf for stereo

Adjustable shelf

Rectangles a, b, c, and d are all approximate Golden Rectangles.

FIG. 69 INTERNAL DIVISIONS

This decision led to another idea. The left compartment was to hold the television and was the one with the lower shelf. The compartment on the right was to have the higher shelf for the ſtereo unit, thus leaving the lower area empty. This seemed not only a little uncomfortable but also somewhat inefficient, since the space was really too high for the storage of things usual to such a cabinet, namely record albums, compact disks, videocassettes, DVDs, and other audio-visual paraphernalia. An additional shelf was needed, not one that could slide in and out but one that could be raised or lowered. Here was something added to the design, something not originally called for in the plans but dictated by constant sensitivity to both form and function.

OUTSIDE APPEARANCES

TO RETURN TO THE DOORS WHICH, FORMING THE ENTIRE front of the cabinet, constituted the main design event, it was necessary to proportion their framing as elegantly as possible. The mass of the cabinet as seen from directly in front presented a large and somewhat squat bulk. One way to overcome this oppressiveness was to emphasize the verticality already suggested by the four tall panels already cut. Accordingly, instead of making the bottom rail the widest member, as is usually done in order to provide a feeling of weight and groundedness (something this cabinet was not lacking), I made it the same width as the stiles.

The top rail, which is commonly the same width as the stiles, especially when these are narrower than the bottom rail, was made ½ in. narrower. Thus the framing was equal all the way around until it came to the top, where it was narrower. This produced a feeling a lightness. I further emphasized this top-lightness by making the central muntin of both doors the same width as the top rail. The muntin and the top rail gave the impression of being pushed upwards and outwards, and out of the surrounding, heavier, frame.

By making the difference in width between the stiles and the muntins a mere ½ in. I had tended to equalize all the vertical elements, further enhancing the dominant feeling of verticality. That the horizontal elements — the top and bottom rails — were decidedly insignificant by virtue of the fact that they were nowhere wider than any of the vertical members underlined the verticality even more.

The point where the two doors met produced, of course, double stiles. Their combined width nearly equaled the width of a panel, and in order to reduce this central weightiness I designed a pair of narrow, vertical handles, one for each stile. These formed a focus in the vast expanse of the flat front and which also pointed upwards.

One last effect designed to aid in the general upward movement was the finishing of the sides of the panels with a ¼ in. bead. This was both functional and decorative. Functionally, the bead and its quirk disguise the gap that may appear between panel and frame should the panel shrink with seasonal dryness. Decoratively, it formed the only motif in an other

The top rails and the muntins are equally wide.

Thin vertical door handles

The panels are beaded at both sides.

The stiles and the bottom rails are equally wide, and wider than the top rails and the muntins.

FIG. 70   EMPHASIZING THE VERTICALITY

wise plain geometric shape, defined only subtly by the proportions of the flush framing and paneling.

FINISHING TOUCHES

THE SLIDING SHELVES WERE TO BE SIDE-HUNG ON SLIDERS screwed to stiffening pieces fixed to the bottom of the shelves. A face piece, the top of which was level with the top surface of the shelf, was fixed across the front, providing a way to pull out the shelf and at the same time hide the sliders. The width of these pieces was determined by the width of the shelves. Their height was determined by the necessity of providing at least enough wood to cover the front of the shelf and the stiffeners with their attached sliders.

Slide

Stiffening piece

Beaded face

FIG. 71   SLIDING SHELF

The result was a substantial front that called out for some shaping or relief. Relieving the bottom at the center produced a nice line but defeated the purpose of having somewhere to grab in order to pull out the shelf. The solution was to run a ¼ in. bead across the front, about two-thirds of the way up. This lightened the heavy effect of the plain front and united the inside of the cabinet with the outside by repeating the only decorative motif, the beading that ran up and down the sides of the panels. The fact that the beadings on the inside and outside ran perpendicular to each other emphasized the difference between the closed cabinet as an anonymous volume and the inside as a utilitarian space.

The final result possessed infinitely more appeal than the original design although the specifications had been followed almost exactly. What made the difference was the attention to detail and a continuous awareness of a variety of design opportunities, elements that should be part of every project.

PARTS LIST *for the* MEDIA CABINET
(All measurements in inches)

Carcase:

1 top	60 x 30 x 1	
2 sides	42 x 30 x 1	
1 bottom	60 x 32 x 1	
1 partition	41 x 32 x 1	
1 back	60 x 42 x ¼ *(luan plywood)*	

Base:

1 front	58 x 1 x 1
2 sides	29 x 1 x 1
1 back	58 x 1 x 1

Shelves:

3 shelves	28¼ x 28 x 1
4 stiffeners	28 x 4 x 1
2 fronts	28¼ x 5 x 1

Doors:

4 panels	35 x 10 x 1
4 stiles	42 x 3½ x 1
2 muntins	35 x 4¼ x 1
2 top rails	24 x 3¼ x 1
2 bottom rails	24 x 4¼ x 1
2 handles	4 x 1 x 1

Hardware:

- 4 hinges
- 2 pair sliders
- 2 bullet catches

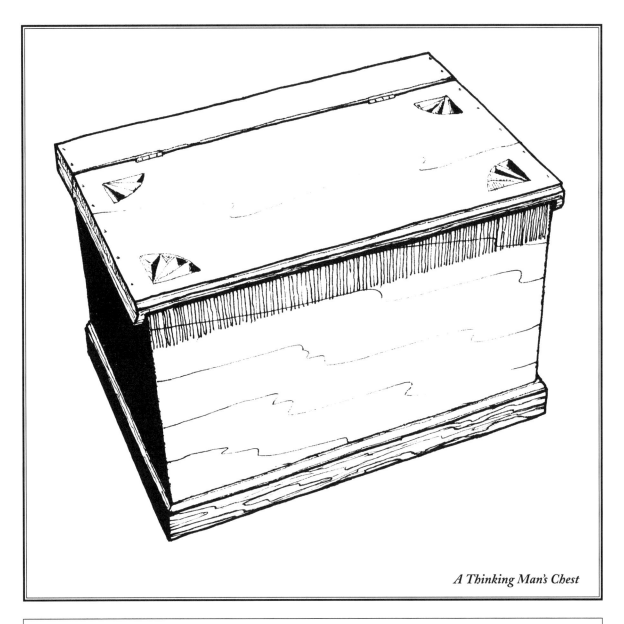

A Thinking Man's Chest

6

A THINKING MAN'S CHEST

Working with What is Available

THIS CHAPTER, WHICH MIGHT ALSO BE SUBTITLED 'FREEDOM FROM THE CUTTING LIST', ADDRESSES ONE OF THE MOST COMMON PROBLEMS FACED BY woodworkers attempting to build published projects: how to proceed if the cutting list for that particular project cannot be duplicated.

I have made many chests over the years, starting with simple toolboxes and storage chests, progressing all the way to elaborate constructions with moving parts. The construction techniques have ranged from basic six-board chests with rabbeted corners to frame-and-panel designs held together with a variety of sophisticated dovetail joints. Similarly, the materials I have used include common lumberyard material such as pine, fir, and even spruce, as well as more expensive and exotic materials ranging from oak and walnut to amaranth and angiko.

Building repeated examples of the same type of piece is enormously instructive. Each variation has its own problems, the solution of which makes subsequent problems easier to solve. But you will not learn much if having figured something out you repeat the procedure blindly or, even worse, unthinkingly follow someone else's instructions and someone else's cutting list. It is better to keep an open mind so that even when repeating a design you remain alive to the possibility of doing something better here, something faster there, and maybe even changing a major aspect of the design. This may not only produce a better constructed piece, both from the structural as well as the procedural standpoint, but can also enrich the woodworking experience.

AN AMERICAN ORIGINAL

THE DESIGN AND FABRICATION OF THE THINKING MAN'S Chest are very straightforward. Apart from the carving, this chest is identical to one built towards the end of the 19th century, and which has been in my family for years. This chest, still bearing traces of the original green milk-paint, had long impressed me with the rightness of its proportions. The construction seemed simple enough, and the fact that it had lasted so long was proof of the soundness of the design. My original intention had been simply to make a companion copy, changing neither proportions, dimensions, nor construction techniques, but when the piece was finished I had indeed done more than simply copy someone else's design; I had gained a deeper appreciation of a chest considerably more sophisticated than had been at first apparent, and along the way had also learned invaluable lessons for constructing subsequent pieces.

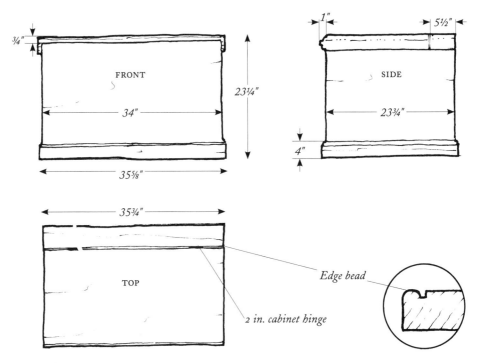

FIG. 72 CHEST DIMENSIONS

THE MATERIAL

ALTHOUGH PAINTED ON THE OUTSIDE, IT WAS EASY TO identify the material of the original as pine by looking closely at slightly damaged sections of moulding and examining the dusty and discolored interior. But using the same species was as close as I was going to get. The original was clear pine, now much too expensive for the budget I had in mind for this project, and moreover the front, back, and top were made from single boards. It is extremely difficult to find pine boards today wider than 16 in., and so bang went my original idea of an authentic copy, correct to the last detail.

It is at this point, right at the beginning of a project, that many people will give up and look for something else to make; something for which they can find the exact material indicated in the cutting list. But unless you are out to make an absolutely authentic reproduction there are often many alternatives. Your basic intention will determine the course you take. In this case I was endeavoring to follow the original builder's intent as well as my own. There were enough inconsistencies and small details to make it apparent that this was a handmade piece rather than the product of a factory, and so it was fair to assume that the original builder had used what was most efficiently to hand. If this builder (let us call him Silas, for convenience) had believed that single-width boards were absolutely necessary he would have used them on all four sides or not made the chest at all. But the existence of the chest suggests that Silas compromised and used whatever was easiest and best suited to the job from whatever was available.

I am guessing that he compromised, since the underlying design here is that of the so-called Six-board Chest type. Often made from a single length, the sides, top, and bottom were simply cut to length, each part already being of the desired width, and were then joined together to create a container with the minimum of fuss. This is both fast and structurally sound. Since the sides are all joined with the grain running in the same direction, any expansion or contraction takes place equally all the way round and is consequently usually unnoticeable. The top, being fixed only at the hinged edge and being given a 1 in. overhang at the front, is also free to move without any dimensional change being too apparent. Only the bottom is potentially troublesome, but being hidden does not present too large a problem.

Silas apparently did not have enough sufficiently wide stuff to hand to be able to get all six pieces from a single length, as would have been the ideal procedure, but nothing deterred, he did the best he could with what he had and used wide boards where they would work to best advantage. Similarly, not having anything wider than nominal 12 in. boards at my disposal, and clear stuff not being affordable, I did the best I could, and made up the requisite width by piecing narrower boards together.

A THINKING MAN'S CHEST

Far from regarding the inability to proceed along ideal lines with dismay and abandoning the project, both Silas and I achieved sufficient length of stuff capable of being finished to the required width of 22½ in., and carried on. Moreover, my open-mindedness had provided me with advantages unavailable to Silas. He, no doubt, had felt constrained by the need to take advantage of the economies of time that using wide boards made possible, while I was able to regard the use of scraps and smaller pieces as a necessary virtue, and enjoy the patterning possibilities that result from using several pieces to make a single board.

CARCASE CONSTRUCTION

ANOTHER ECONOMIC AND ESTHETIC DISADVANTAGE OF slavishly following the cutting list or abandoning the project if this is not possible deserves to be mentioned here. Simply providing oneself with the necessary parts as specified in the list, and not regarding them as a whole, will hardly ever produce happy results. It would be far better to saw all six parts of the chest from two 16 ft. lengths of one-by-twelve (a standard dimension available in most lumberyards), as shown in FIG. 73, thereby allowing the grain to run harmoniously around the entire chest. But whether you possess sufficiently wide or long material to obtain the six basic parts from a single board (or, as is more likely, from two boards as shown below), or whether you have to piece together various odd sections, do so with an eye to how all joined parts will eventually match.

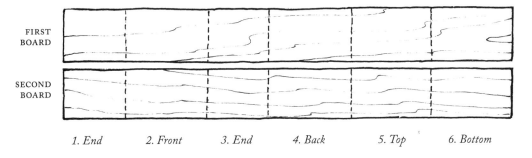

FIRST BOARD

SECOND BOARD

1. End   2. Front   3. End   4. Back   5. Top   6. Bottom

FIG. 73 THE SIX PARTS OBTAINED FROM TWO BOARDS

Assuming that each, or any, of the six basic parts needs to be formed from one or more pieces, this may be done with a simple butt joint, with doweled joints, or splined, tongue-and-grooved, or even biscuit-joined, as shown in FIG. 74.

Plain butt joints require that the edges to be joined be absolutely flat and true, and it is perhaps easier to accomplish this if you are working

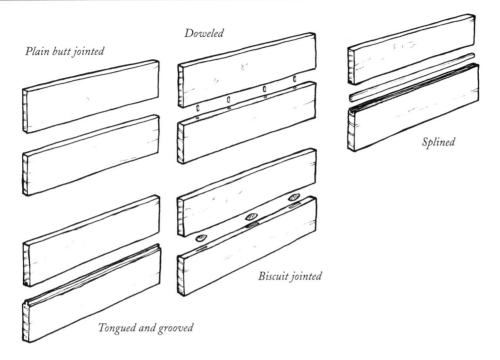

Plain butt jointed

Doweled

Splined

Biscuit jointed

Tongued and grooved

FIG. 74 FIVE METHODS FOR JOINING BOARDS

with shorter rather than longer lengths. For this reason, even if you start with two 16 ft.-long boards, as shown in FIG. 73, it might be better to saw out the parts first, being very careful to mark everything so the top of the front gets joined to the bottom of the front, etc., and so that the order of the parts around the chest is not confused.

If you decide to use dowels or biscuits make very sure that these do not coincide with corners, or you will be in for an unpleasant surprise when the sections are sawed apart.

My preferred method is to produce a flat face, then square as many edges as will have to be joined to achieve the needed width, and only then address the problem of thickness. If you have started with pre-thicknessed material such as one-by-twelve dressed stuff from the lumberyard, and work very carefully, nothing more than a light finishing on both surfaces will be needed.

The cutting list specifies 1 in. by 12 in., 1 in. by 4 in., and 1 in. by 6 in. material, and gives the finished thickness as ¾ in. Dressed 1 in. material is usually close to an exact ¾ in., so if all your material is bought at the same time it should all match, even if it is not, in fact, exactly ¾ in. Silas's chest is made of stuff that is closer to 1 in. thick; the chest I made is a fraction thicker than ¾ in.; the cutting list specifies an exact ¾ in.; and I have just said that stuff somewhat thinner than ¾ in. would be fine — so what does all this mean? It means that once again it is the intention rather than exact duplication that is important. The intention is to produce a chest with certain given outside dimensions, that can be constructed in a sound manner.

A little forethought is necessary before deviating from any given measurement, but only enough to ensure that joints can still be cut as specified or in such a way that their structural integrity is preserved, and that any hardware such as hinges and handles will still fit where planned. While many projects may start from some absolute given, such as the need to build something to fit a particular space exactly, it is usually possible to exercise considerable discretion when interpreting cutting-list dimensions. It is true that a change in one part can often domino throughout the rest of the piece, and after thinking the effect through you may discover that at the very end of the chain you run up against another immutability, but more often than not merely contemplating a change will bring other possibilities and improvements to light. People who build kitchen cabinets and spacecraft may have to stick to rigid specifications, but the making of free-standing furniture is a less exact science. An open mind can produce serendipitous improvements. It is in the nature of the material itself to surprise you, quite apart from unexpected errors that may force adaptation on the fly, since no two pieces of wood are exactly alike.

The corners of the original carcase are simply rabbeted, glued, and nailed. This is a relatively unsophisticated way of constructing a carcase but perfectly adequate if done well. I describe the process here, explaining a few less-than-obvious subtleties, but there is no objection to other methods if you have a good enough reason. A good enough reason can be almost anything from a structural need, such as might be occasioned by the intention to carry an extremely heavy load, to a decorative impulse, such as the desire to show off Bermuda dovetails or some other unusual joinery, or simply the impetus to indulge in some tricky technique for the pure pleasure of exercising your woodworking skills. Silas, no doubt, was primarily concerned with getting the job done in the most workmanlike fashion. My original impulse was to fulfill my need for a chest with something whose overall proportions appealed to me. Someone else may be trying to satisfy other demands. The method adopted will depend on the intention.

RABBETING

THE DIMENSIONS OF THE RABBETS AS SHOWN IN FIG. 75 assume the use of material that is ¾ in. thick. Obviously, the width of the rabbet should equal the actual thickness of the piece it is receiving, although a hair wider is useful if you plan on planing the end grain of the rabbet flush with the surface of the sides after glue-up; the depth of the rabbet is a function of providing the merest step for the ends to butt up against, and

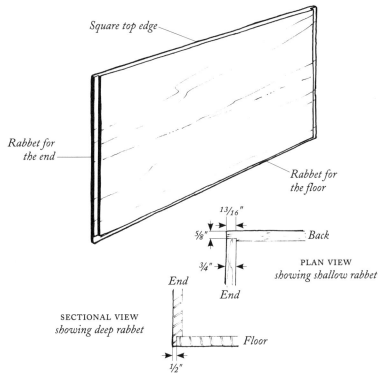

Square top edge

Rabbet for
the end

Rabbet for
the floor

13/16"

5/8"

Back

3/4"

PLAN VIEW
showing shallow rabbet

End

End

SECTIONAL VIEW
showing deep rabbet

Floor

1/2"

FIG. 75 RABBET DIMENSIONS

is not much affected by any change in the thickness of the stuff. It is true
that a deeper rabbet will provide more of a shoulder and make it easier
to keep everything square when gluing up, but since you will be using
clamps, which are easily manipulated to achieve perfect squareness of
the carcase during this operation, it is more important to leave as much
thickness as possible at the bottom of the rabbet the better to hold the
fasteners, nails or screws, that enter from the outside of the front and back.

So far as the walls are concerned, it is only the front and back that
are rabbeted, but to accommodate the floor of the chest you must also
rabbet the bottoms of all four sides. Since the floor is liable to shrink
and expand against the grain of the end pieces, it will help to make the
rabbet in which it sits somewhat deeper than the rabbet provided in the
front and back for the ends. This is still not an ideal solution. Silas did
not worry about this, probably for two reasons: First, his material was
better seasoned than today's lumberyard pine, which although kiln-dried
to national standards is by no means as stable as was his air-dried stuff,
the proof of which is the minimal amount of shrinkage that has occurred
over the last ninety or more years, and in any event the piece was painted,
which helps a lot in reducing changing moisture-content and the resultant
dimensional changes. Second, although the chest was built in a very

workmanlike fashion — it is very neatly executed and exhibits several very caring touches described later — I doubt that he was building for posterity; his intentions were certainly not for woodworking perfection.

This raises another issue connected with slavishly following instructions rather than keeping the purpose of a piece clearly in mind. It is unlikely that we all share the same reasons for building any given piece, and so while technical information such as how to saw to a straight line or manipulate a router through a tricky maneuver may be vital, many other aspects, such as the exact depth or type of rabbet, may well be irrelevant.

Bearing this in mind, if your goal is cabinetmaking perfection, you may prefer to cut a rabbet in the floor in the form of a tongue, with a matching groove in the insides of the sides, as shown below. This will allow the floor to expand and contract without conflicting with the ends. You will, however, lose the extra support and strength that the fasteners used in the original would have provided. If securely nailed in place, the original floor runs the risk of splitting if it contracts, or even worse, pushing the sides apart if it expands, but it gains substantial strength, useful if the chest is to be carried around with heavy loads, and also serves to guarantee the rectilinearity of the bottom of the chest. Moreover, you may not be able to cut sufficiently deep grooves in the sides to accommodate all possible movement of the floating floor, and the floor might shrink so much that it drops out! There are ways, of course, to provide for these eventualities, such as raising the floor and fixing a substantial ledger beneath it, attached to the sides with slotted screws at the ends to support it, or even by making a frame-and-panel floor, but this would all be inconsistent with the plain rabbet joints used on the sides; a bit like carpeting a cheap car with the finest Persian rug.

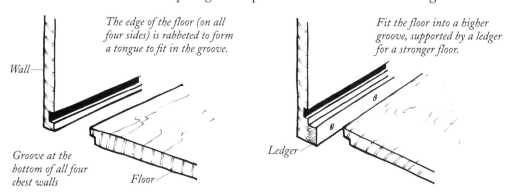

The edge of the floor (on all four sides) is rabbeted to form a tongue to fit in the groove.

Wall

Groove at the bottom of all four chest walls

Floor

Fit the floor into a higher groove, supported by a ledger for a stronger floor.

Ledger

FIG. 76 FLOATING FLOOR JOINERY

Nevertheless, if this is your intention then go ahead, but if, like Silas or myself, you simply need a sturdy and well-proportioned chest built as efficiently as possible, accept the compromise. The point is not to feel locked into the instructions, but to keep your own goals in mind.

GLUING UP

HOWEVER YOU MAY HAVE PREPARED THE PARTS OF THE carcase, the time will come for assembly. Unless you have used some form of self-supporting joinery, such as dovetails or locking corner joints, you must prepare for this, possibly with an additional pair of hands.

The easiest method is to assemble the sides first, upside down, with glue in the rabbets and held together with just a couple of bar-clamps or pipe-clamps running from front to back. Before nailing or screwing, set the floor in place, since this will make the corners square, providing it has been cut out carefully and checked for squareness. Silas's chest was simply nailed with what are now regarded as rather handsome, period cut-nails. I chose to use countersunk screws and plug the holes. With a little planning, attractive patterns can be created by grouping the screws and using contrasting wood as plugs, but do not bother with this if you intend painting the chest.

Even with the floor in place it is a good idea to check the squareness of the top and adjust if necessary by a little judicious repositioning of the clamps. Placing the clamps out of parallel with the sides will skew the box (or remove any skew). Be aware that if you tighten the clamps too much, especially when using pipe-clamps, which can deflect out of straight under pressure, you will not be able to check squareness by placing a framing square on the corner since the sides may be bowed. A better method of checking squareness is to check that the diagonals across the top of the chest are equal.

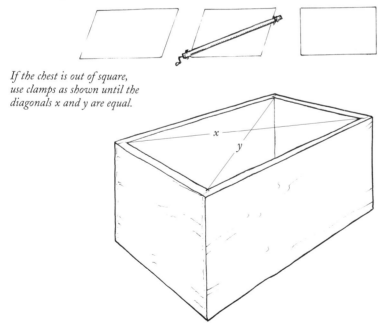

If the chest is out of square, use clamps as shown until the diagonals x and y are equal.

FIG. 77 CHECKING RECTILINEARITY

A THINKING MAN'S CHEST

THE PLINTH

WHEN THE CLAMPS HAVE BEEN REMOVED, ANY EXCESS glue cleaned up, and the end grain of the rabbets planed flush as suggested earlier, it is time to make the plinth.

The structural purpose of the plinth is to protect the bottom of the chest and cover the nails holding the floor. Esthetic considerations are more subtle. A plinth of a certain size may function adequately so far as structure is concerned but look poorly proportioned. To some extent this is subjective, and if you like the way the piece looks as made according to the cutting list then follow these measurements. Otherwise, express yourself how you will, but do so in an informed way. To help you do this I give here detailed instructions on the hand method probably followed by Silas, since this is no longer the commonest method.

The simplest form for plinths on chests this size is usually one about 4 in. high. It is usually finished with a moulded top edge, even if this moulding is nothing more than a simple chamfer. The reason is very practical: a moulded edge has less of an extreme arris and as such is less likely to be damaged or collect dust; even a simple chamfer will provide less of a shelf for dust than a square-edged plinth.

Silas's plinth was finished with a common ovolo, a profile common on wooden window sash, and was undoubtedly made with a sash moulding plane. The same moulding is used for the front edge of the lid. These details suggest that Silas was more of a carpenter than a cabinetmaker, since carpenters were more likely to make windows than furniture, and had less use for the fancier profiles favored by furnituremakers.

While the modern method might be to use a router or a shaper fitted with the appropriate bit, sash ovolo planes are by no means rare and can often be found at fleamarkets and in antique shops for the same price as a good router bit. Their use is quiet, easy, and pleasant. If you use the modern tool, nothing more is required than to choose an appropriate bit and take care to avoid any chattering, burning, or routing of knotty material. But if the nicer feel of a hand-planed moulding is decided upon, the following points must be borne in mind: First, since the moulding plane is a plane like all other planes, you should try to plane with the grain. And since you are planing on an arris you must take into account not only the grain on the face of the wood but on its edge as well. Second, a moulding plane is commonly used in the reverse direction from a bench plane. That is to say, you do not start at the back end of the wood and plane towards the front, but rather you must begin at the far end of the wood and, while still planing in a forward direction, gradually work your way backwards starting each stroke closer to the near end until the entire length has been worked.

It is also necessary to prepare a length of moulding somewhat longer than the actual length required, since you will lose a certain amount of the length when cutting miters for the corners, and since it is difficult to plane the extreme ends of a piece to an exact shape.

Clean up the moulding with a small rabbet plane or a wooden rubber cut to shape. Cut the pieces to length using a miter box, holding the back of the miter against the back of the box to avoid a ragged edge at the front of the miter. Remember that the measurement you take along the bottom edge of the chest is the inside measurement of the plinth piece, not the measurement from the end of one miter to the end of the other.

Be sure to cut on the waste side of the line when sawing the miters. Trim down to the line for a perfect fit using a block plane and a donkey's-ear miter shooting-board. This is an easy piece of shop equipment to make, similar to a bench hook, and guarantees exact miters, especially when they are tall in relation to their width.

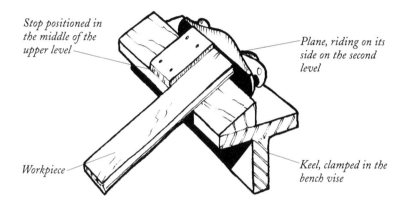

Stop positioned in the middle of the upper level

Plane, riding on its side on the second level

Workpiece

Keel, clamped in the bench vise

FIG. 78   DONKEY'S EAR SHOOTING BOARD

Make the front piece first and fix it with finishing nails. In this way, if the chest is still slightly out-of-square, you will be able to adjust the side miters to fit, which is an easier business than vice-versa.

THE LID

ALL THAT REMAINS IS THE LID, WHICH COMPRISES THREE parts: the hinge jamb, the top, and the cleats. The hinge jamb is a very simple idea not often seen but very useful. It provides an additional guarantee of squareness for the back and sides of the chest, and solves the problem all too often encountered with chest lids that are hinged directly to the back of the chest, whereby the weight of a carelessly opened lid pulls the lid off the hinges.

The hinge jamb is nailed directly to the top of the back and the ends. Its front edge is finished with a ¼ in. bead, which softens the edge and turns

A THINKING MAN'S CHEST

the unavoidable gap between the lid and hinge jamb into a nice, moulded feature. The back is made flush with the back of the chest, but the sides extend past the ends enough to accommodate short pieces continuing the line of the cleats that will be fixed beneath the outside edges of the top. Note that a little clearance will be necessary between the inside edges of the cleats and the ends of the chest; you should not fix their mates under the hinge jamb close against the sides of the ends of the chest, but leave a similar gap of no more than ⅛ in.

Once again, the only vital part of the above from a structural standpoint is the existence of the jamb itself. Even its exact width is not an absolute; as given it reflects the standard width of a nominal one-by-six as sold in today's lumberyards. All other details may be changed or even omitted. As described, they are witness to Silas's sensitivity to a level of work consistent with an age that produced joinery and millwork to a standard considerably higher than much of today's. But there are other ways to achieve the same effects, such as making the continuation of the end cleats from five-quarter stock and being able thereby to fix them tightly against the side of the chest while still having their outside face be flush with that of the ¾ in.-thick cleats. There is also no reason why the front edge of the lid should not be finished with a common thumbnail moulding. Do not take for granted the unalterability of the cutting list.

The lid itself in its simplest form is one piece, deep enough to span the distance from the front of the hinge jamb to a point 1 in. past the front of the chest, and wide enough top accommodate one-by-two cleats at each side.

The overhang at the front serves the purpose of providing somewhere to lift the lid easily and also to disguise any expansion or contraction. Its exact measurement is a matter of taste and how the moulding looks in profile. Silas's ovolo looks best if its top fillet is more or less in line with the outside face of the front, as shown below. A more usual moulding, such as the thumbnail moulding, might happily protrude a little more; a chamfer might require less of a protrusion. Before you decide, consider the given measurements and any alternatives that come to mind.

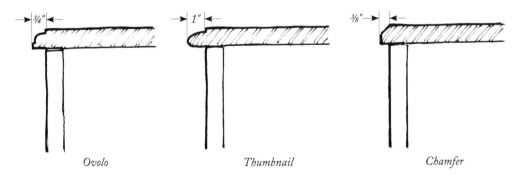

| Ovolo | Thumbnail | Chamfer |

FIG. 79 OVERHANG PROFILES

The cleats not only help keep Silas's single-board top flat — which might not be so necessary if the top were made from a number of pieces whose orientation with respect to the center of the tree from which they were cut was alternated — but also provide a measure of airtightness and dust protection when the lid is closed, and would be useful even if the top were made in a manner that required no help to ensure flatness.

The profile of the front ends of the cleats echoes the profile of the moulding formed on the front edge of the top; yet another sensitive detail adding to the overall harmony of the piece.

LAST DETAILS

SUBSTANTIAL HANDLES FIXED TO THE ENDS ARE NO doubt indispensable if the chest is to be moved easily, but the carving is entirely optional. I love simple chip carving in pine, and find it especially useful for taking attention away from knots. Of course, the pieces that constitute the various parts of my chest were assembled with an eye to the best arrangement of these unavoidable features of number 1 pine — knot-free pine is graded as 'clear', and a few small, tight knots constitute number 1 — larger knots constitute number 2, etc.), and in turn played a part in dictating the type and location of carving used, since I had chosen not to paint my chest like Silas's but rather to finish it with a coat of linseed oil.

This kind of decision has to be unique to each piece, and while it may be necessary at first to follow instructions in order to learn the various processes and understand their rationale, it is a final example of the initiative we must practise if we are to be anything more than kit assemblers.

PARTS LIST *for the* **THINKING MAN'S CHEST**
(All measurements in inches)

Carcase:

1 front	34 x 22½ x ¾
1 back	34 x 22½ x ¾
2 ends	22½ x 22½ x ¾ *(assumes ⅛ in.-deep rabbet in front and back)*
1 floor	33 x 22¾ x ¾ *(assumes ¼ in.-deep rabbet in sides)*

Plinth:

1 front	35⅝ x 4 x ¾
1 back	35⅝ x 4 x ¾
2 sides	25¼ x 4 x ¾

Lid:

1 lid	35¾ x 19¼ x ¾
1 lid jamb	35¾ x 5½ x ¾
2 cleats	19¼ x 1½ x ¾
2 lid jamb cleats	5½ x 1½ x ¾

(All the above parts may be made from standard number 1, nominal ¾ in. pine.)

Hardware:

1 pair chest handles
1 pair 2 in. cabinet hinges

Jewelry Box

7

JEWELRY BOX

Making the Most of Exotic Material

THE JEWELRY BOX ILLUSTRATES A SIMILAR FORCE ON DESIGN AS DID THAT OF CONSTRUCTION IN THE PREVIOUS CHAPTER, NAMELY THAT OF FUNCTION. 'Form follows function' is repeated so often we tend to lose sight of its importance as one of the great pillars of wisdom upon which good design rests. Furniture is distinguished from other constructions by its need to fulfill a useful function. Not merely an esthetic or expressionistic function but a truly utilitarian function. It must, for example, contain an object, support a person, or provide a work surface. If it has no other purpose than to delight the senses it may be a work of art, a masterpiece, or a dazzling tour-de-force but it is not truly furniture. Furniture must function. Function, therefore, is an indispensable part of furniture design which if ignored can result in the piece's failure no matter how beautiful or how well constructed it may be.

Whatever else the jewelry box may be, it is a functioning piece of furniture, and its functioning — the capaciousness of its interior, the division of its interior into separate spaces — is central to its design. To design a piece successfully requires, among other things, that it function adequately for the purpose for which it is designed. Although this may sound dangerously close to tautology it is surprising how much furniture is produced that fails miserably in its avowed purpose: chairs that collapse if anyone heavier than a child sits on them, tables that you can not get your legs underneath, or boxes whose bottoms fall out when anything heavier than a telephone directory is carried in them. These failings may be the result of poor construction, but all too often they are the result of the wrong construction. A butt joint used in the box's carcase may be made well and neatly executed but simply be the wrong joint for the purpose.

Understanding all this, if we develop a design bearing in mind its function we will necessarily include construction techniques that will exert their own influence on the design. The jewelry box must be of a sufficient size to hold at least average pieces of jewelry. This is not very large, so a top may be made that consists of a single board or panel. A larger area might require additional construction techniques such as several panels to provide sufficient stability. Since additionally the jewelry box is by its very nature more special than a box designed, for example, to hold potatoes, it makes sense to use a better material than commonplace pine or even plywood. Both of these could be used with constructional success but they would less successfully result in something special or beautiful. These functions are also important.

Like many woodworkers I find it difficult to keep the ever-growing scrap pile under control. One solution is to use up these odd pieces on smaller projects after a big job is finished. Having just completed a set of dining chairs made of amaranth (the South American relative of African purpleheart), I found myself with numerous ½ in. by 4 in. lengths of this attractive but very hard material. I had also been saving two small pieces of ebony for possible use as accents on a larger piece. The black of the ebony, although waned with a blond area, was very attractive next to the rich purple of the amaranth, and I decided to make a jewelry box.

Although only ½ in. thick, the denseness of the amaranth — it is so dense it will barely float — makes it extremely strong and more than sufficiently sturdy for a box measuring 1 ft. by 1 ft. 6 in. Laying out the 1 in. by 4 in. strips on the bench suggested a box large enough to contain two sliding interior compartments covering a lower area as large as the entire box. The only problem was how to maximize the material, especially the ebony, and at the same time produce a coherent design and a construction with sufficient integrity.

MIRROR IMAGING

AMARANTH IS NOT NOTED FOR UNUSUAL GRAIN PATTERN, but for its striking color, which although greyish, almost bonelike, when first cut, quickly deepens to a rich purple on exposure to the air. Unlike padauk, also known as vermilion, which is brilliantly red when first cut but which can slowly turn to an undistinguished brown on exposure to the light, amaranth or purpleheart remains intensely colored. Its color is so unusual that I often have to explain to people unfamiliar with the wood that it has not been stained. With such a species there is little need to fuss over which piece might look better in which position; the grain pattern is not obtrusive, it is the color which constitutes the main design element.

This is not always the case with ebony. Although certain species are valued for their homogenous blackness, areas of lighter wood can occur. Such was the case with the small 6 in. by 9 in. piece I had. Having decided to use the piece as a contrasting panel in the lid of the proposed box, I found that whichever way I oriented the piece, the area of lighter wood spoilt the design. Fortunately the piece was almost a full 1 in. thick. Careful resawing on the bandsaw produced two pieces that were mirror images of each other. By edge-joining these two pieces a single piece was created whose grain pattern was now strikingly symmetrical. This useful trick is well-known to users of veneer, who often arrange successive leaves of veneer to produce symmetrical patterns known as bookmatching, quartering, diamond, and herringbone.

When next faced with a growing scrap pile of pieces too precious to throw away, bear these design principles in mind. Many species, such as oak, Philippine mahogany, elm, ash, and much maple, can be used for their color alone. Other species with more dramatic grain can be used as effective contrasts in combination with their quieter cousins. A little judicious resawing can produce striking but balanced effects. To duplicate the illustrated jewelry box follow the directions but use your own scrap pile to best effect.

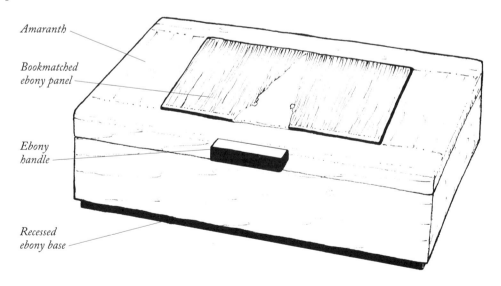

Amaranth

Bookmatched
ebony panel

Ebony
handle

Recessed
ebony base

FIG. 80 JEWELRY BOX

THE SIDES

START WITH THE SIDES, WHICH ARE MITERED AND SPLINED, preferably cutting all four sequentially from the same board in order to continue any grain pattern around the box, similarly to the way in which the sides for the Thinking Man's Chest of the previous chapter were cut, as shown in FIG. 73. After preparing such a board, or individual lengths, to exactly ½ in. thick by 4 in. wide, cut the front and back pieces to measure exactly 17⅜ in. long, and cut the side pieces to measure exactly 12 in. long from the outside of the miters. Cutting the miters is most easily done on a tablesaw or a radial-arm saw, but a backsaw can be used with a miterbox, if one is available.

Before cutting the slots for the splines in the miters, rout a ¼ in. rabbet at the bottom of the inside face of all four sides. This rabbet will receive the bottom of the box. You may prefer to cut this rabbet before the sides are cut from the single board — if indeed you start with a single board — but be sure to mark the piece so that the top edge and the face side are clearly visible to avoid confusion.

If the miters have been cut on the tablesaw you need do no more than lower the blade half its height, flip the individual pieces over, and make a second pass at each end to cut the slot for the spline. Unless you are using a super thin blade, the typical ⅛ in.-wide kerf will form a sufficiently wide slot for a spline.

The spline itself can be cut from the edge of a strip of the same material as the sides. Opinions differ as to the best grain orientation for maximum strength, but in a construction this small a long-grain spline is easiest to prepare and quite adequate. Just make sure the fit is snug.

Glue lengths of spline in one end of each piece, and then glue the sides together, clamping them so that perfect rectilinearity is maintained. Measure diagonally from corner to corner to check that the sides are square, as was shown in the previous chapter in FIG. 77. Do not tighten the clamps excessively, since the ½ in.-thick material may bend, thereby rendering any attempt to test the right-angledness of the corners with a trysquare impossible. It also helps to reference the entire assembly off a known flat surface, such as your benchtop or the tablesaw table, in order to ensure that the top and bottom edges of the assembled sides lie in the same planes.

THE BOTTOM

THE BOTTOM MAY BE MADE UP FROM AS MANY PIECES as are necessary to produce the required length and width. Orienting the strips so that the grain runs from side to side rather than from front to back will require the fewest joints, as well as producing the narrowest

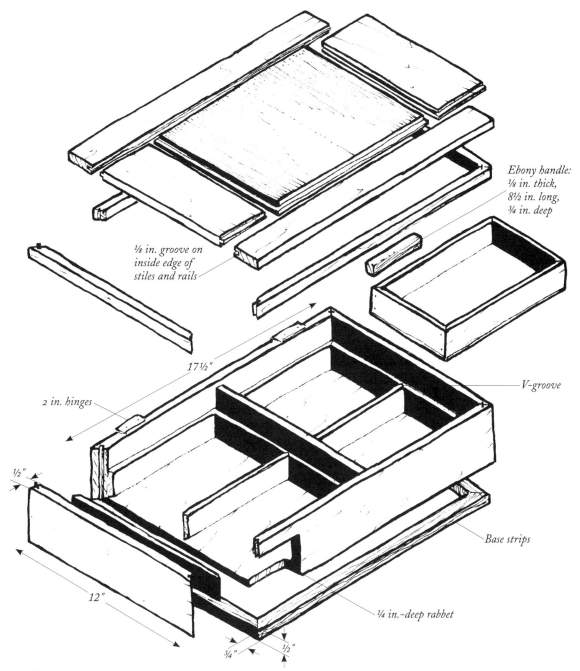

Ebony handle:
⅛ in. thick,
8½ in. long,
¾ in. deep

⅛ in. groove on
inside edge of
stiles and rails

V-groove

17½"

2 in. hinges

Base strips

½"

¼ in.-deep rabbet

12"

¾"   *½"*

FIG. 81 JEWELRY BOX

width across which the grain can shrink, as it inevitably will. Do not worry
about any possible shrinkage, however, since this will be hidden by the
recessed base strips. Trim the prepared bottom to fit nicely in the rabbet
at the bottom of the sides, and then glue it in place.

The joint between bottom and sides is covered by the addition of mitered base strips ½ in. thick and ¾ in. wide, which are fixed in place ¼ in. in from the face of the sides. These pieces are screwed into the bottom with ¾ in. number six countersunk flathead woodscrews, arranged so that there is one at the end of each strip and one in the center of each strip.

THE LID

THE TOP OF THE LID CONSISTS OF A SIMPLE FRAME AND panel, the panel being the contrasting piece. The frame does not need to be mortised-and-tenoned, as is usual for larger framework, but merely provided with a ⅛ in.-wide groove in its inside edge. This groove will not only hold the matching tongued edge of the panel but will also provide sufficient gluing area to keep the short side pieces firmly aligned to the longer front and back pieces of the frame. The elimination of mortises and tenons is possible since the entire frame and panel assembly will be glued to a narrow section of the sides, separated from the rest of the sides later by sawing, to form the lid proper.

Prepare the rails and stiles of the frame to the correct thickness, length, and width, and rout the ⅛ in. groove in what will be the inside edge. The width of the rails and stiles is a matter of design, and in the case of the illustrated box was largely determined by the size of the central panel. Since this was the focus of the design, and the idea was to use the ebony to maximum advantage, the rails (the end pieces) were made twice as wide as the stiles, both to accommodate the ebony as well as to emphasize the front-to-back grain direction. The stiles were run from side to side rather than into the sides of the rails as is normal. In practice you may make the width of the frame members whatever is convenient and most attractive. Remember that running the stiles entirely across the box avoids any end grain showing from the front. This is more attractive than the more usual arrangement of rails and stiles.

In order to set the panel in its frame so that it is slightly proud of the surround, form the tongue around its edge by rebating only its top edge. The advantage of positioning the panel this way is to attract attention to it and minimize the otherwise distracting effect of any shrinkage that might occur across the panel's grain.

Glue the rails and stiles together, with the panel in place but not glued to the framework, for this could cause it to split should it shrink later, and then glue the frame to the top of the sides.

When the glue has set, plane or sand the joint between the frame and the sides perfectly smooth, and saw off the lid from the sides by running the box across the tablesaw one side at a time — but leaving always just the ends of the sides unsawn. The top being thus connected to the sides by its corners, the tablesaw operation will be safe and the sawcut remain consistent. When all four sides have been thus partially sawn, finish the cut by hand, taking care to use the handsaw (a backsaw is fine, a Japanese backless saw perhaps even easier) so that its kerf is centered exactly in the tablesaw's kerf. The two kerfs are unlikely to be of the same thickness, and a little planing with a block plane will be necessary to trim the edges of the lid and sides, but if you have finished the handsawing as suggested this should present no problem.

The severed lid is now hinged to the back of the box with 2 in.-long, ½ in.-wide (when closed) brass hinges mortised into the top of the sides and the bottom of the lid equally, and to a depth that will allow the lid to close tightly on the sides. The depth required will be found to be exactly half the distance from the bottom of one hinge leaf to the top of the other when both leaves are held perfectly parallel. Note that simply closing the hinge does not always place the leaves parallel to one another. Much older work is often found where the edge of one leaf furthest from the knuckle is flush with the surface of the wood in which it is set, thereby necessitating a sloping-bottom mortise. There are advantages to mortising hinges this way, mainly stylistic, but it is considerably easier to mortise the hinge so that the knuckle is perfectly centered over the joint between the two hinged pieces and the hinge leaves are set parallel.

When screwing the hinge in place start by making one pilot hole in each leaf, and make this pilot hole only big enough to receive a steel screw one size smaller than the brass screw that will ultimately secure the hinge. This will allow for some adjustment should the pilot hole not be perfectly located, and also ensure that the brass screw will still have enough wood to grip after the steel screw has been removed. Do not try to adjust brass screws for they are very easily broken, especially when being screwed into such hard wood.

The handle for the lid is a simple ½ in.-thick piece, 3½ in. long by ¾ in. wide, glued to the center of the lid front. Although ebony is oily, and as a result sometimes difficult to glue, it should not be necessary to secure the handle by screwing through from the inside of the lid, although this remains an option. Wiping an oily wood like ebony with mineral spirits before gluing can be helpful.

THE INTERIOR

CUT A ONE-HALF INCH THICK STRIP TO FIT FROM THE back of the box to the front of the box ¼ in. below the level of the sides. Now prepare ¼ in.-thick strips half as wide as the interior height of the sides and miter their ends so that they hold each other in place around the inside walls of the two partitions formed in the box by the ½ in.-thick center piece first made. In the center of each of those strips destined for the sides, both of the box and the center piece, cut a 45° V-groove that

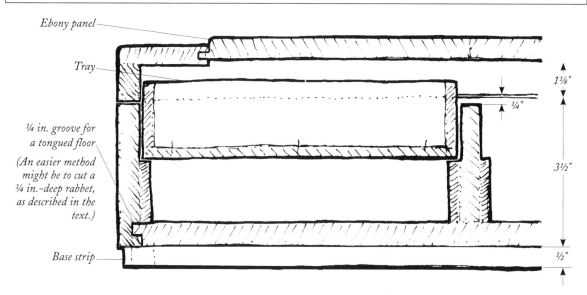

Ebony panel

Tray

¼ in. groove for
a tongued floor

(An easier method
might be to cut a
¼ in.-deep rabbet,
as described in the
text.)

Base strip

1⅛"

¼"

3½"

½"

FIG. 82 CROSS-SECTION THROUGH THE INTERIOR

runs from top edge to bottom edge. A small, V-bottomed moulding plane known as a partition plane is ideal for this job, but the job can be equally easily done by scribing a line with a marking knife and trysquare and then planing the sides of the scribed line to a V-groove using side rabbet planes or even a knife. If you use a mitered piece of scrap as a fence against which to guide the plane or the knife you can guarantee the exactness of the 45° V-groove.

Two more ¼ in.-thick strips, with double-mitered ends as shown in FIG. 80, are cut to form the partitions either side of the center partition, and all strips can be placed in position with no glue or fixing needed.

The two small trays that run backwards and forwards on top of the strips, on either side of the center partition, are themselves made by mitering ¼ in.-thick pieces. Bottoms are glued onto the bottom edges of the tray sides, and small brass pins to hold the trays together are inserted from the sides and bottom only.

FINISHING

SOFTEN ALL EDGES WITH A BLOCK PLANE AND SANDPAPER, especially the edges around the lid, the edges of the center panel, box corners, and base strips. Make sure the trays slide easily in the partitions. Clean up any extruded glue with a sharp knife or chisel from any inside corners.

Cut pieces of card ¹⁄₁₆ in. smaller than the interior of the trays, and cover these cards with a suitable material such as felt or velvet, gluing the neatly trimmed edges of the material to the underside of the card and then press the covered cards into the trays.

Apply the finish of your choice — oil, urethane, wax, or lacquer — and polish till ready.

PARTS LIST *for the* JEWELRY BOX
(All measurements in inches)

Case:

2 fronts	5⅛ x 17⅜ x ½	
2 ends	5⅛ x 12 x ½	
base	16⅞ x 11½ x ½	
base moulding:		
	2 strips	17⅛ x ¾ x ½
	2 strips	11¾ x ¾ x ½
handle	½ x 3½ x ¾	

Lid:

2 rails	17⅜ x 1¾ x ½
2 fronts	5⅛ x 17⅜ x ½
2 ends	5⅛ x 12 x ½

Interior:

center divider	10⅞ x 2¾ x ½
tray supports:	
4	10⅞ x 2¾ x ½
4	7⅞ x 2¾ x ½
2	7¾ x 2¾ x ½

Legless Coffee Table

8

LEGLESS COFFEE TABLE

Minimal Production, Maximum Result

SOMETIMES A DESIGN MAY BE THE RESULT NOT SO MUCH OF REALIZING A PRE-CONCEIVED PICTURE OF A PARTICULAR PIECE, BUT RATHER THE RESULT OF A pragmatic, trial-and-error approach worked out for other reasons as you go along. Good design should always take construction into account, but construction alone should never be allowed to determine the design. The opposite is more usually the case: we stretch our construction abilities in order to realize a better design.

The legless coffee table resulted from a need that I attempted to satisfy with the minimum of effort. I needed to replace the coffee table that I had co-opted as a piano bench. It had to be fairly large and, most importantly, it had to appear almost immediately. There was no time for another lengthy project that would take weeks to germinate, days to execute, and further days to finish. I sat in the shop and gazed unhappily at my small store of coffee-table grade lumber. I was loathe to waste such precious material on a quick knock-up, but how else to construct something that could be completed in a couple of days? Then I remembered the two planks of baywood a friend had brought me from Oregon.

THE PATH OF LEAST RESISTANCE

EACH PLANK WAS OVER SIX FEET LONG AND ROUGH-SAWN to about 2½ in. thick. The planks were not straight-sided but interestingly curved, wider at one end than at the other. I had been thinking I would have to carry them over to a friend's shop and run them through his large resaw bandsaw and then saw them into straight boards and then joint and surface them before I could use them for anything. The prospect of so much work had so far dissuaded me from using them. But one of them looked suspiciously like a possible coffee table top . . .

I laid the plank across the sawhorses and stared at it. It was almost the perfect width for a coffee table, and its length closely matched the couch in front of which it was needed. Its gentle curves and gradually increasing width would also complement the way in which the couch was arranged at right-angles with a neighboring armchair. Best of all, its massive presence would harmonize well with the large stone fireplace that dominated the room it would occupy.

THE PROBLEM OF SUPPORT

PLEASED WITH WHAT APPEARED TO BE AN IMMEDIATE solution to my need for an instant coffee table I started to think about how the top might be supported. Cutting out legs from the second plank and joining them to an aproned frame was not too much work but would involve making sure that the top was perfectly flat so that it would fit securely. Since the top would be about 6 ft. long and almost 2½ in. thick, the supporting frame would have to be similarly massive to restrain any possible warping and provide a solid base. Visions of Flintstone furniture that would require two elephants to move flashed before my mind's eye and I rejected the standard construction. Perhaps I could saw the base plank into two slabs that would support the top transversely, one at each end. I played around with this idea for a while, making several drawings and even taking some chalk to the second plank to mark out where these slabs might come from. It was not, on the whole, a bad idea, but even if the supporting slabs were mortised into the underneath of the top, the extreme length and weight would still demand some extra form of connecting support such as a connecting trestle-like member, either high up under the top or lower down, at the level of a foot rest. Or perhaps two connecting members, one on each side of the slab, let into the edge, and perhaps even supporting an additional shelf for magazine storage and other items. But each solution involved more work. Every time I got close to structural sufficiency I found I had created a project that would take just as long as a more conventional approach. The point here was to create something quickly.

Finally I realized the second plank, from which I had been thinking about sawing out various legs, slabs, and other forms of support, was massive enough to be ſtood on edge and support the firſt plank as is — almoſt. It was about the right height when ſtood on edge, and it was certainly thick enough to provide all the support necessary. Furthermore, using juſt one support like this would leave the top plank completely free to shrink or expand with no fear of anything being ſtressed or pulled apart. Additionally, the extra space for ſtretched-out feet that a legless conſtruction would provide promised to be very useful for a coffee table. The only remaining problem was how to get the supporting plank to ſtand securely on edge.

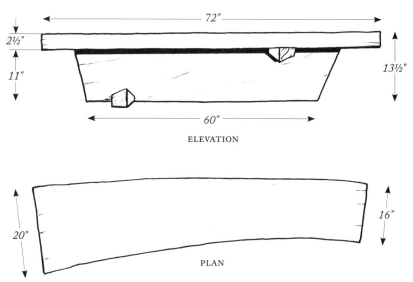

ELEVATION

PLAN

FIG. 83 COFFEE TABLE DIMENSIONS

It was while thinking about how to trim the ends and sides of these two planks that the solution presented itself. Although I wanted to keep the overall curve of the top plank, I would ſtill have to saw off a certain amount to produce the moſt felicitous shape, especially since I was now viewing the two planks as a whole and was trying to see how the one might beſt balance the other, both visually and ſtructurally. Since my chief aim was to produce something with as little work as possible, I planned on removing the smalleſt amount I could get away with. This turned out to be a ſtrip barely 3 ft. long that tapered from about 3 in. thick to 1½ in. thick. I realized that by sawing this piece in half I could use one piece housed in the bottom of the supporting board to keep it upright, and the other piece housed in the top edge to provide a pair of arms that would support the top. Both the top and the base would thus be supported at three points. Since one of the advantages of tripods over four-legged objects is that they will not rock no matter whether the surface they are resting on or their own individual lengths are uneven, this provided me with an excellent solution to the problem of leveling an object as massive as this coffee table.

THE TOP & BASE

WITH A DESIGN THAT CALLED FOR ONLY FOUR PIECES and two joints I felt I had successfully dealt with the structural part of the problem. All that remained was to use the chalk to mark exactly where I would trim the two planks. I wanted to keep the natural texture of the wood and, after brushing the surfaces thoroughly before sawing to remove any edge-damaging grit or dirt, I was pleased to discover that the rough-sawn surface was attractive enough to be left unplaned, thus further reducing the amount of work necessary.

The planks had been sawed out of the tree with a chainsaw mill, and the irregular series of fan-shaped marks left were not too excessive and presented an interesting texture. A few very light licks with my jack plane to remove the odd hair and whisker — not enough to produce any smoothly planed patches, but just to the point that you could run your hand over the surface of the wood without fear of splinters — and the surface would be ready for use. It was ideal in more ways than one: the mild but attractive grain was visible, the rough-sawn texture was not only visually interesting but also provided a surface that would be difficult to damage the way a highly finished surface might be — ideal for putting your feet up — and slippery objects would be able to get a better grip.

To keep the edges consistent with the surface texture, I left these also as they came from the saw. The edges on the top plank turned out to be all fairly square, but the ends of the plank that became the base had been sawed somewhat out of square, both to the surfaces and the sides. I thought about this and decided the only edges that were critical were those that would bear against the floor and the top. The oddly-angled ends and edges of the ends actually added interest, especially if I positioned the base so that the shorter side was down. Since the top was 1 ft. longer overall than the base, this also added to the balance of the overall design and gave the table a profile somewhat reminiscent of an aircraft carrier.

The only finishing that was necessary was a small, ¼ in. chamfer around all exposed surfaces. This was planed by hand with a block plane small enough to be able to follow the curved edges. This small chamfer had the effect of making the rough-sawn material look nicely finished, as if the shape of the top had been purposely designed that way, rather than having been the result of a fortuitous accident on the part of the sawyer or lumberjack originally responsible for converting such a large section of Oregonian baytree into commercial lumber.

THE ARMS

I SAWED THE STRIP I HAD REMOVED FROM THE BASE INTO
two lengths. The first was 18 in. long: the width of the top at its narrow
end. The second, cut from the thicker end of the taper was only 16 in. long.
The shorter but somewhat sturdier piece I let into the bottom edge of the
base, 2 ft. in from the sloping end. The longer piece, which contained most
of the taper, running from 3 in. thick to a bare 1½ in., I let into the top
edge of the base 11 in. in from the opposite end.

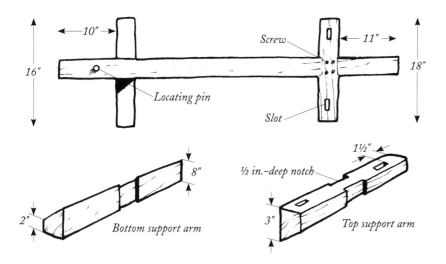

FIG. 84 THE BASE

The original strip had one edge out of square, and this angled edge was
placed downwards in the case of the top arm and upwards in the case of
the bottom arm, or foot. The arms were positioned so that the narrow
edges of both pieces faced towards the respective ends of the base, giving
the feeling of forward movement to the ship-like table as a whole.

Like the base and top, the edges of the arms were finished with a
¼ in. chamfer, and their ends were planed smooth with the block plane.
These ends were thus the only perfectly smooth surfaces, but their relative
smallness together with their inconspicuous placing lent an appropriate
finishing detail further emphasizing the appearance of a finished piece,
even though the shape was basically natural.

The actual joint used here is a form of double housing-joint. Most of
the joint is formed by notching out the respective edges of the base board,
since the notch required does almost nothing to its integral strength. But
a much smaller, ½ in. notch was made in the mating surface of the arms.
This serves the purpose of keeping the arm securely aligned by providing
two extra bearing alignment surfaces. Marking the depth of the required

notches needed to be done carefully, since the arms were neither square nor even in profile. But by making the small notch in the center of the arms first, a fixed reference was established from which the various depths of the notches required in the base could be measured. The entire process required the use of only four tools: a rule, a trysquare, a backsaw, and a 2 in. firmer chisel to pare away the waste between the two sawn lines.

The arms were set in place just a trifle proud of the top and bottom edges of the base to allow for any adjustment and guarantee the tripod effect. The bottom edge rose slightly from the end opposite that into which the bottom arm had been housed. The top edge of the base was also slightly convex and required a little judicious planing at each end and at one side of the supporting arm before the top piece, supported by the ends of the arms and the opposite end of the top of the base, would rest securely.

FINAL FIXING

ALTHOUGH THE ASSEMBLED TABLE WAS INDEED MORE than sufficiently massive to be adequately stable I wanted to avoid any disasters that might occur should anyone stand on any part of the top. Consequently, I secured both the top and bottom arms with four 3 in. number 12 woodscrews each, angled into the corners of the joint. The top was kept in place by a 1 in.-diameter locating-dowel that projected from the top of the base at the opposite end from the top arm, and fitted into a 1 in.-deep matching hole in the underside of the top. Two 3 in.-long slot-screwed roundhead woodscrews driven up through the bottom of each end of the top arm about 2 in. in from the ends completed the fixing and transformed the four parts into a single whole that when assembled did, indeed, need two people to move it.

A final check with block plane and a lightly waxed cloth to make sure all surfaces were clean and safe and pleasant to the touch completed the project. The entire process had taken less than three hours, and the need had been filled with a design that while functional and stable had not been held hostage to complicated construction techniques.

PARTS LIST *for the* **LEGLESS COFFEE TABLE**
(All measurements in inches)

Top:

tabletop	72 x 20 x 16 x 2½
support arm	18 x 3 x 2½ x 1½
locating pin	2 x 1 in. diameter

Base:

center board	66 x 60 x 11 x 2½
support arm	16 x 3 x 2½ x 2

Parson's Table

9

PARSON'S TABLE

The Essence of Simplicity

A PARSON'S TABLE IS THE NAME GIVEN TO A SIMPLE TABLE, USUALLY SQUARE, SUPPORTED BY A LEG AT EACH CORNER. IT IS HARD TO THINK OF ANYTHING more straightforward when considering the possibilities for a table: a flat surface supported at a given height, and yet there is more to such apparent simplicity than meets the eye.

Very often we make things for structural or esthetic reasons, and design our work accordingly. The acquisition of a new tool or the learning of a new technique inspires us to design and build something to try out the tool or practise our skill. As wood lovers we are often lured by our appreciation of the material into creating something simply to celebrate the exquisite grain or other properties of a choice piece of wood. What we build may be functional, and we may even have a need for the finished object, but that this is not the prime motivation is often demonstrated by the fact that need alone would hardly have dictated countless hours spent constructing something that might have been obtained ready-made far more cheaply. This is probably why we are woodworkers in the first place: we like the materials and processes, and the ability to produce something useful is only a secondary benefit. But occasionally a project comes along where function is the motive force and chief consideration. Caring about our material and the way we build things will still influence what we make, but technical excess for the sheer joy of woodworking, and clever design simply to display the beauty of the wood are no longer the name of the game. Such was the genesis of this coffee table. What was required was the simplest, most straightforward design consistent with structural integrity and the character of the material that was available to make it.

Almost by definition, therefore, a parson's table was the chief candidate for this design, but seeking to keep the design and the construction as simple as possible and recognizing the greater importance of function over form, can be far from easy. Simplicity is often quite complicated!

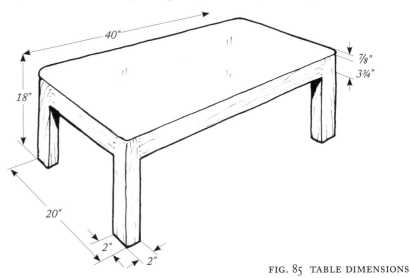

FIG. 85 TABLE DIMENSIONS

THE ELEMENTS OF SIMPLICITY

SIMPLICITY, AS JUST DEFINED ABOVE, INCLUDES SEVERAL elements that may conflict: a straightforward design serving the required function as well as possible, a structure that supports this and which at the same time is as easy to build as possible and is also possessed of sufficient integrity not to fall apart at the first use, plus the use of a given material, in this case, red oak, that is not only consistent with the two previous requirements but is also used to its own best advantage.

DESIGN

THE DESIGN OF THIS TABLE WOULD AT FIRST GLANCE SEEM to be a perfect opportunity for applying the well-known maxim 'form follows function'. The function of a coffee table represents no great mystery; all that is required is a fairly low, stable, flat surface that can be conveniently positioned in front of a couch or by an armchair. So long as flatness and height are provided, the actual shape of this surface is susceptible to a wide variety of interpretations. But since we are also looking for the simplest structure, wild or subtle outlines and complicated or ingenious supports must be avoided. We need a simple flat surface, simply supported, and simply made.

Basic geometric shapes suggest themselves: circles, squares, ovals, and triangles. Theologians have argued — and their arguments have been the basis for much architectural design, especially during the great period of cathedral building — that nothing is simpler than the circle. It was supposed to represent divinity, infinity, and perfection. But its perfection is often a great mystery, as is the construction of ovals, whose parameters are endless. It is considerably easier for most woodworkers to construct rectilinear forms. Since triangles are not the easiest form to position in front of a couch we are left with squares and rectangles. The advantage of a rectangular coffee table in front of a rectangular couch is obvious.

Having determined on a rectangular surface, we are now faced with the problem of how to support this as simply as possible. One solution would be to make the surface sufficiently thick that its top was at the right height. Nothing could be simpler than this, and both stability and ease of construction would be attained. But this would be impracticable for other reasons: it would require excessive material and no one would be able to put their feet under the table.

The next simple solution would be to provide a single, central support, but this could perhaps introduce problems of stability and consequent construction complications. As we investigate the possibilities of other leg arrangements, it soon becomes apparent that a leg at each corner is the easiest way out. And so we arrive at an elongated parson's table.

STRUCTURE

THE NEXT PROBLEM IS TO DETERMINE THE SIMPLEST WAY to connect the four legs to the rectangular surface, without resorting to nails or other crude approaches, that will provide stability and structural integrity.

There are many ways to join an upright securely to a flat surface, and choosing any one of these in combination with four legs of exactly the same length might provide the desired stability for a while, but structural integrity is a different matter. We need to be concerned not only with the engineering of the desired structure, but the nature of the material. Wood may contract and expand in response to changing ambient moisture content indefinitely, as disastrous checking in ancient pieces suddenly brought into different surroundings can prove. Moreover, wood moves differently with and along the grain. If several pieces were attached to one another with their grain all running in the same direction, any movement would result in all pieces moving in the same way, and provided the movement was unrestrained little damage would result. But when pieces of wood are firmly connected so that their respective grain directions are at right-angles to each other trouble can be expected as the different movements inexorably result in splitting or separation.

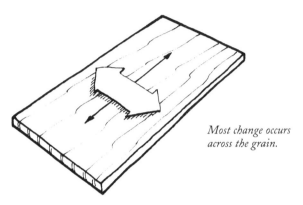

Most change occurs across the grain.

FIG. 86 WOOD MOVEMENT

It may truly be said that accommodating wood movement lies at the heart of all woodworking technique. Joinery and cabinetmaking were both developed to produce joints and wooden constructions that although sturdy and stable could accommodate the dimensional changes in the various members of any given piece of furniture. This then becomes the central structural problem of our design, which consists of various members oriented at right-angles to each other.

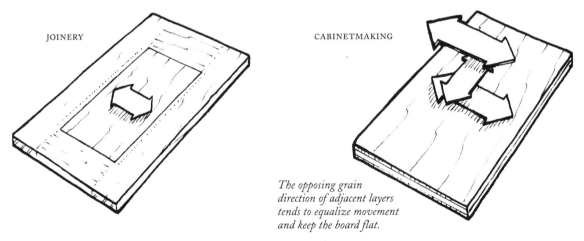

JOINERY

CABINETMAKING

The opposing grain direction of adjacent layers tends to equalize movement and keep the board flat.

FIG. 87 METHODS OF ACCOMMODATING MOVEMENT

If we can attach a single-piece top in such a way that it is free to contract and expand while remaining firmly connected to the legs we will have done much to ensure the structural integrity of our design without having to resort to more complicated techniques such as different varieties of frame-and-paneling and veneering. These are, however, considerably more time-consuming than preparing a single-piece top.

The Shakers, who were masters of simplicity, were fond of using sliding-dovetail cleats that kept a board-top flat and attached to a base without restricting its movement. But this requires a certain amount of time to make with care.

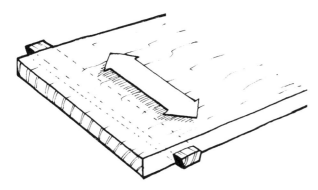

FIG. 88 SLIDING-DOVETAIL CLEAT

Slot-screwing is another technique whereby a flat surface may be held to a base and still be free to move, but this too requires several operations to accomplish. A simpler method is to connect the legs with a narrow apron, grooved at its top inside edge, and attach the top to the apron, with wooden buttons or metal hardware that slide in the grooves as needed.

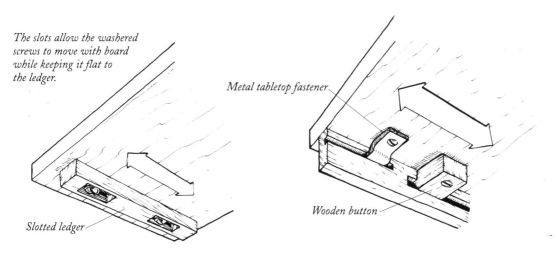

The slots allow the washered screws to move with board while keeping it flat to the ledger.

Metal tabletop fastener

Wooden button

Slotted ledger

FIG. 89 SLOT-SCREWING

FIG. 90 BUTTONS & TABLETOP FASTENERS

THE MATERIAL

LASTLY, WE HAVE TO CONSIDER THE MATERIAL ITSELF. Different species of wood have different characteristics, are better suited for some purposes than others, and behave differently under similar conditions. Using softwood for a project subjected to heavy wear would be a bad idea. Using a noticeably figured and strongly colored wood in a subdued setting might represent an unpleasant contrast. Making a relatively unimportant piece out of an extremely expensive and rare piece of wood would also be inappropriate. In this instance oak was chosen since it was available, it was certainly strong enough to be used for a coffee table, and it matched the rest of the furniture in the intended location.

At the same time it has to be remembered that oak is open-grained and has a pronounced figure. Both these points can affect a design if they are not worked with sympathetically. For example, designing something in oak with many parts requires that careful attention be paid to the grain pattern or it might overpower the structural design. While oak is good to carve because its hardness makes clean cuts easier, its open grain is not well suited to very fine detail. Once again simplicity becomes a virtue.

CONSTRUCTION

WITH ALL THE FOREGOING IN MIND, THE COFFEE TABLE was designed as illustrated and constructed as follows: the length and width of the rectangular shape having been decided upon, and enough material chosen and put aside for this purpose, attention was first given to the base, since it is easier to adjust the finished size of the top to the base than vice-versa.

THE LEGS

THE LEGS WERE MADE FROM A SINGLE LENGTH OF eight-quarter oak. Since this particular piece of 2 in.-thick oak was a little over 4 in. wide, it needed only to be as long as the combined length of two legs, since it could then be resawed to make four pieces.

It was first planed flat and straight on one face. A jointer might have been used for this, or even the tablesaw, but 3 ft. is not too much to plane, and a nice surface is left from the plane iron. Next, one adjacent side was planed not only flat and true but also perfectly perpendicular to the finished face by checking frequently with a trysquare. The remaining face was now planed perpendicularly to the first side.

Using a marking gauge set at a little over 2 in., lines were scribed down both faces and connected around one end to serve as a guide for resawing by hand, although once again there were other options available, including the tablesaw or the bandsaw. After resetting the marking gauge to exactly 2 in., all four sides of both pieces were scribed, and then planed where necessary to these lines.

Now the two pieces were sawed in half to produce four, care being taken that each end was first marked perfectly square with a trysquare.

Finally, before laying out the legs for joining to the apron, they were looked at from all sides to determine which way round and which way up the grain would look best. This is a subjective procedure and ultimately depends on what looks best to you; different arrangements are likely to be preferred by different people. It is extremely unlikely, however, that if the process is omitted an arrangement will result that is acceptable; leave the orientation of such strongly figured wood to chance and one or more pieces is certain to stand out oddly.

The legs had been sawed from a piece of rift-sawn stock. This is a method of sawing whereby the growth rings of the tree are left diagonal to the section, and normally results in legs all of whose sides display relatively similar figure rather than the markedly different face grain and side grain pattern that flat-sawn or quarter-sawn pieces would show. Consequently, no side displayed the characteristic medullary rays of quarter-sawn oak. There were, nevertheless, sides marked more strongly than others, and these were oriented towards the inside in an effort to present the most regular faces to the more visible outside. The legs thus arranged were grouped together and their top ends marked as in FIG. 92 so that this order would be clear throughout subsequent construction.

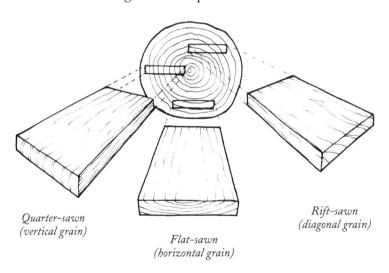

Quarter-sawn
(vertical grain)

Flat-sawn
(horizontal grain)

Rift-sawn
(diagonal grain)

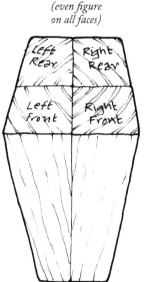

Rift-sawn
(even figure
on all faces)

Quarter-sawn boards stay flattest but usually have less figure on their face; flat-sawn boards have better figure but may warp the most; rift-sawn boards show even figure on all four sides.

FIG. 91 BOARD CONVERSION

FIG. 92 LEG ARRANGEMENT

PARSON'S TABLE

THE APRONS

THE NARROW APRONS THAT CONNECT THE LEGS, AND TO which the top is connected, were prepared in a similar manner to the legs. Starting with a piece twice as wide as the required finished width, and as long as the combined length of one front apron and one side apron, the outside face side was planed first, then one edge was finished exactly square to the face, followed by the inside face. Finally, the two pieces were ripped down their centers. The four resultant pieces were considered for the best grain orientation, designated accordingly, and then marked to the finished width and planed carefully to his line.

The width had been determined carefully to balance the thickness of the legs, taking into account the expected finished thickness of the top. Anything less and the aprons would have had an appearance too insubstantial; anything more and they would have looked too heavy. That what looked just right also left enough width for the biscuit-joinery planned to connect them to the legs, and for the groove to be made on their upper inside surfaces was also confirmed. But what was immaterial was the exact thickness: provided there was a minimum of ¾ in. to secure a single biscuit and provide for a safe groove about ⅜ in. deep, each apron might in fact be a different thickness. Additionally, the inside face need be only roughly finished since it would never be visible.

The groove for the table fasteners was made by setting the tablesaw fence ⅜ in. from the inside face of the sawblade, and setting the depth of cut to ⅜ in., and then running a couple of saw kerfs, adjusting the fence after the first cut, along the inside faces of the aprons near their top edges.

For successful biscuit-joinery, mating surfaces must be perfectly flat and square. To guarantee that the ends of the aprons met this criterion, each pair of aprons was trimmed together on a very carefully adjusted tablesaw. A slower method would have been to square off the ends with a trysquare and trim to this line with a block plane, always working in from the edges, and ideally using a shooting block if one was available.

If several attempts had been necessary to obtain perfectly square-ended pairs, consequently shortening the length each time, no great harm would have been done since the top had not yet been made and could easily be adjusted to fit.

Number 2 biscuits were used with a plate-joiner to join the aprons to the legs in pairs, each pair being glued, assembled, clamped, and left to dry before both pairs were assembled together.

This sounds straightforward, but implicit in successful assembly is perfect alignment of all parts. This may be achieved by assembling each pair, and finally both pairs together, on a known flat surface, making sure that all four legs touch the ground and that the rectangle formed by the apron-connected legs is indeed a rectangle and that the diagonal measurements taken from opposite corners match exactly, adjusting the positions of the clamps if necessary to achieve this.

THE TOP

NO MATTER HOW MANY PIECES MAY BE NECESSARY TO make the top large enough to cover the base exactly, they must all be arranged as felicitously as possible. Once again, this is largely a matter of personal choice, but almost any thought given to this matter will produce a happier result than if none is given.

There are various opinions about how the grain should be oriented in adjacent pieces forming a flat surface. This stems from the fact that an unrestrained flat-sawn section will tend to cup towards that side which, when it was still part of the tree, faced the outside. Some people recommend joining pieces all the same way so that any cupping will result in a single large cup, which can perhaps be easily controlled at its center or edges. Others recommend alternating pieces so that cupping is spread out between the components, creating a washboard effect, but an overall smaller deformation. You can avoid the problem entirely if you join wood so that its cross-section most closely resembles quarter-sawn lumber, even if this means sawing up the available stock and regluing it as shown below. By doing this you will, of course, end up with side grain forming the surface, a happy effect in this case where we are aiming for simplicity and regularity.

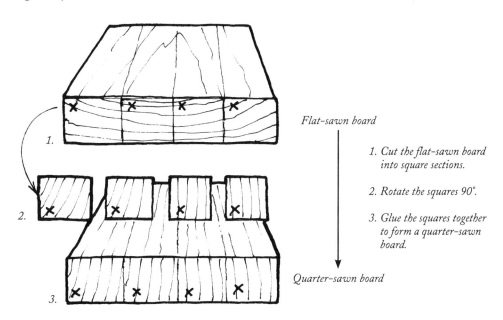

Flat-sawn board

1. Cut the flat-sawn board into square sections.

2. Rotate the squares 90°.

3. Glue the squares together to form a quarter-sawn board.

Quarter-sawn board

FIG. 93 CONVERTING FLAT-SAWN STOCK TO QUARTER-SAWN STOCK

PARSON'S TABLE

In any event, no matter how you glue up the top, cupping should not be too great a problem providing the top is surfaced flat and then attached to the base properly. The finished thickness as given is also not critical providing it looks right.

Before rounding the edges, cut the top to size simply by scribing round the base placed upside down on the top, leaving an extra ⅛ in. all round.

EDGE TREATMENT

IN ORDER TO KEEP THE TOP AS SIMPLE AS POSSIBLE AND allow for movement without periodic unsightly misalignments between the edges of the top and the base, the edges of the top were rounded to form an almost complete half- circle, and the top edge of the base was also rounded. Do this with appropriately sized round-over bits in a router, by chamfering the corners with a block plane and then completing the round by planing additional facets and sanding, or by running the various sections through a shaper. This effectively disguises the exact point at which the top meets the base, so that any changes in this relationship are hard to detect. In order to impart a feeling of integral consistency to the whole piece, the outside corners of the legs were rounded to the same degree as the top of the base. All other edges were merely softened slightly.

ASSEMBLY & FINISHING

WITH A COUPLE OF CLAMPS POSITIONED JUDICIOUSLY TO hold the top in position on the base, table fasteners were attached to the underside of the top so that their offset end engaged the slot in the aprons. Remember that the top is liable to change size most across the grain, and that fixing a screw at the center of each end will force this movement to take place equally on both sides.

Finishing consisted simply of multiple coats of a danish oil, applied thinly and rubbed well at daily intervals. Four coats will be sufficient for average protection; more coats afford more protection and also increase the shine.

PARTS LIST *for the* **PARSON'S TABLE**
(All measurements in inches)

Top:

1 piece	20 X 40 X ⅞
2 short aprons	16 x 3¼ x ⅞
2 long aprons	36 x 3¼ x ⅞
6 buttons	1¼ x ¾ x ¾ *(or 6 table fasteners)*

Legs:

4 pieces	18 X 2 X 2

Sound Shelving

10

SOUND SHELVING

Designing to a Need

THE MOST SATISFYING PROJECTS ARE OFTEN THE RESULT OF A SERENDIPITOUS FIND AND AN URGENT NEED. IN THIS CASE IT WAS THE HAPPY MARRIAGE of a couple of cherry boards I had inherited by chance and the pressing need for a better way to house my ever-increasing collection of stereo components. The cat's habit of jumping on the unprotected record turntable was doing it no good, and the compact disc player stacked on top of the amplifier, in turn stacked on top of the receiver, was also bad for the health of these expensive items. I did not want to build an entire entertainment center, which might include the flat-screen television, cablebox, DVR and speakers, but I did need to get the audio components off the coffee table and shelve them somewhere convenient and protected.

The cherry consisted of two irregular, 6 ft. boards. Both boards were considerably narrower at one end than at the other, and it occurred to me that by removing a tapered section from the narrow end of each board, reversing it, and joining it to the wider end, I could produce a pair of well-proportioned, sloping sides, as shown below in FIG. 94. The resulting shape had several advantages of which the most appealing was the feeling and look of balance. The last thing wanted when designing shelving for electronic equipment is something that might tip over. These sides were sufficiently broader at the base than the top to be almost as stable as the pyramids. The sloping font also made access to the different components equally easy, and the sloping back provided room for all the wires and connecting cables while still permitting the unit to be pushed, at its base, securely against the wall.

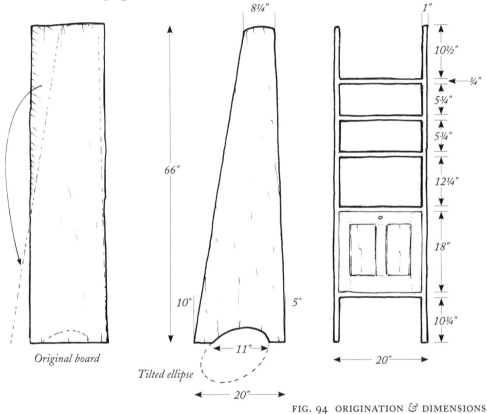

Original board

Tilted ellipse

FIG. 94 ORIGINATION & DIMENSIONS

Since much of the shelving is necessarily covered by what sits on it, buying extra cherry seemed a little wasteful. Pine is cheaper and readily available at most building-supply houses. The color also provides a pleasant contrast to cherry. All that was needed was a single 14 ft. length of one-by-twelve (a nominal dimension that typically measures closer to ¾ in. by 11½ in.). By careful cutting it was possible to avoid most of the small knots that are usually found in what is commonly called 'number one' grade. Those that were left were in places that would not be visible. Buying clear pine would have been considerably more expensive, although probably still cheaper than cherry, quite apart from the fact that in many parts of the country it can be hard to fine cherry as wide as pine.

THE DESIGN

SINCE AUDIO COMPONENTS NEED TO BE CONNECTED together, the shelves were designed to be backless. A backless shelf unit, however, poses problems of side-to-side stability. One way to solve this problem is to add a diagonal brace. A better way is to provide at least a partial back. By designing the shelving to start at waist level, thereby enabling each component to be reached without excessive bending, adequate space for a small cupboard was left beneath the lowest shelf. The back for this cupboard provides the needed sideways stability, and the cupboard itself forms a useful storage area for various accessories, such as record-cleaning equipment, headphones, and manuals.

One last consideration in this era of transience influenced the design: the need for easy transportation. Knock-down furniture is much easier to move or store than are solid pieces that take up more space and remain vulnerable to damage while being manhandled in and out of apartments and moving vans. Joining the shelves to the sides with sliding dovetails accomplished this, as well as making assembly easier. None of the shelves is permanently fixed in place. The dovetails are stopped 1 in. short of the front edge of the sides as shown. This allows the shelves to be pushed firmly into position, and guarantees that all are equally aligned. The paneled front is hinged to the bottom shelf and can be easily disassembled by unscrewing the hinges, or transported folded against it. The paneled back, which is the key to the entire unit's stability, is secured between the two bottom shelves by two screws through each shelf.

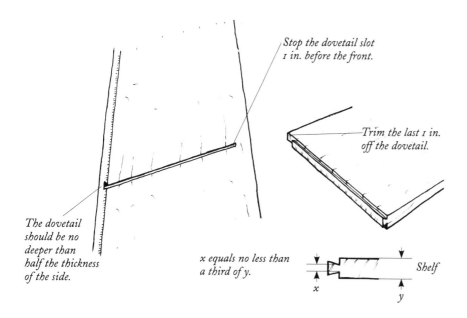

Stop the dovetail slot 1 in. before the front.

Trim the last 1 in. off the dovetail.

The dovetail should be no deeper than half the thickness of the side.

x equals no less than a third of y.

Shelf

x

y

FIG. 95 SLIDING DOVETAIL DETAILS

DIMENSIONS & METHODS

THE MEASUREMENTS GIVEN HERE MAY BE ALTERED TO SUIT individual preferences, bearing in mind that the size of audio components is relatively standard. Use these measurements as starting points, and aim for a pleasing shape while maintaining stability. The exact shape of the sides will depend on the material available.

The dimensions of the sides as shown above in FIG. 94 were largely the result of the size of the original boards. One important fact that made the construction of sliding dovetails easy was the 1 in. thickness of the finished material, but with a little care the same dovetails may be cut using standard material that measures ¾ in.-thick.

It is much faster, and the results are more likely to be evenly accurate, if the sliding dovetails are cut with a router or on a shaper, rather than by the traditional hand method, but all other operations and procedures needed to build this unit are equally easily undertaken using either handtools or powertools, according to your preference and the tools at your disposal. Do not feel bound by any particular method.

THE SIDES

PREPARE THE SIDES FIRST BY CUTTING AND JOINING WHERE necessary, and then surface both sides to be as flat as possible. Cut out the slightly off-center half-oval in the bases, using a thin lath to fair the curve on one side and then using this side to lay out the curve in the other side. Ideally, this curve should be part of a tilted ellipse whose dimensions bear some relationship to other dimensions of the piece. The bottoms of the sides are left flat but the top, front, and back edges may be given a shaped profile. A 1 in. round plane was used on the piece shown, working to lines drawn ¼ in. in from the edge, a file being first used on the top before the plane was employed, to produce a gently rounded profile. Other methods include using a block plane to produce a chamfer, or a shaped bit in a router, or even leaving the edge flat.

The exact shape and angles at which the front and back slope are not critical, but it is important to make both sides identical. Should you decide on dimensions other than those given, remember that most audio components are around 10 in. deep; leave at least this depth for the top shelf, or whatever stands on it will hang over the edge. Since turntables are the most variable in size, and in any event are at least large enough to accommodate a 12 in. record, it is best to design the lowest shelf to be deep enough to hold this component. Most components average 17 in. in width; when deciding how wide the shelves should be, include an extra 1 in. on either side of your widest component. It is also important to leave at least a 1 in. air-space above each component for ventilation. You will need more space above the turntable, if this is part of your system, to permit its lid to be raised or removed.

Having worked out the dimensions for all the above, design the bottom of the cupboard so that it looks proportionately well while being as big as possible for greatest stability, and finishes at a height above the floor that gives the unit the right overall appearance of balance. Rather than trying to do this by eye, use some proportional paradigm, as explained in chapter 1. I like a little space beneath the cupboard to complement the space between the sides at the top of the unit, but you may even prefer to omit the cutout at the bottom of the sides and have the cupboard reach all the way to the floor.

Whatever dimensions you settle on, lay out the positions of the shelves on the insides of the sides as accurately as possible. Double-check by comparing both sides to each other. Use a sliding bevel set to the angle of the slope to determine true horizontality, but remember that you may have different angles at the front and back.

Mark a line parallel to the front edge of the sides across the shelf layout lines, 1 in. in from the front. The female section of all the dovetails will be stopped at this point, guaranteeing equal alignment of all shelves. Insert a ½ in. dovetail bit in the router and clamp a guide across the side so that the bit cuts exactly in the middle of each shelf. Make sure at least half the side's thickness remains at the bottom of the dovetail slot.

A final sanding of the sides at this point is useful to remove any slight feathering that may have occurred along the dovetail slot, and then the sides may be considered finished.

THE SHELVES

PREPARE AS MANY SHELVES AS ARE NECESSARY TO THE required width, joining pieces where needed to produce the right depth. Bevel their front and back edges to match the slopes of the front and back of the sides. With the dovetail bit in the router at the same depth as was used to cut the female portion of the dovetail cut the male portion of the joint in the ends of the shelves. This requires two passes, one on each side. Use two pieces of scrap clamped either side of the ends to provide a stable bearing for the router's base, as shown over in FIG. 96. Make sure these pieces are perfectly level with the end and mark them so the same piece is always used on the same side. Lay out the position of the male dovetail on the end of the shelf, and after the two scrap pieces are clamped in place adjust the router's fence to cut the bottom side first. Cut the bottom side on all shelf ends before cutting the top side, making sure you keep the scrap pieces clamped to the same sides. This will guarantee that even if the first complete dovetail is less than perfect all shelves will at least be at the same height. Making a trial joint on a piece of scrap that is the same

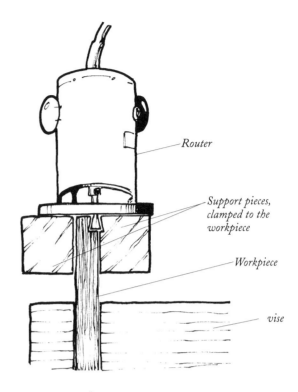

Router

*Support pieces,
clamped to the
workpiece*

Workpiece

vise

FIG. 96 CUTTING THE DOVETAIL IN THE SHELF ENDS

thickness as the shelves will make obvious any adjustment that may be necessary to the router's fence when it comes to cutting the top half of the dovetail.

Finally, pare back the first 1 in. of the dovetail from the front edge of every shelf and test every shelf in its matching slot in both sides. Plane, scrape, or plane, according to your preference, every shelf to finished perfection, and assemble everything. Although the joints should be tight enough to require light malleting home, using a piece of scrap to protect the beveled edges, the unit will doubtless wobble somewhat from side to side. The back will take care of this.

THE CUPBOARD BACK & DOOR

MEASURE THE DISTANCE BETWEEN THE BOTTOM TWO shelves and make a mortise-and-tenoned frame to fit, as shown in FIG. 97. Allowing an extra ⅛ in. all round is a good idea, since the finished frame can then be trimmed to fit perfectly, especially by beveling the top and bottom edges. This is necessary since the back should slope at the same angle as the back of the sides (see FIG. 98). To avoid having to join

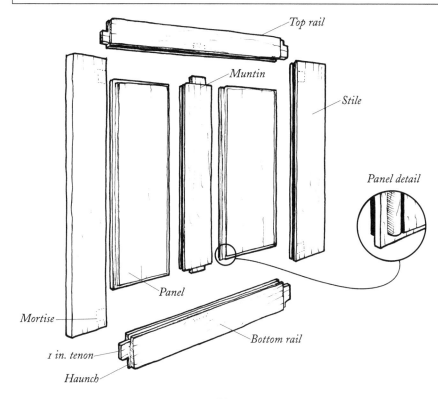

Top rail

Muntin

Stile

Panel detail

Panel

Mortise

1 in. tenon

Bottom rail

Haunch

FIG. 97 EXPLODED VIEW OF THE DOOR & THE BACK PANEL

material in order to make a single panel wide enough to fill the frame, and also because I felt it looked better, I fitted a central muntin in the frame and made two smaller panels.

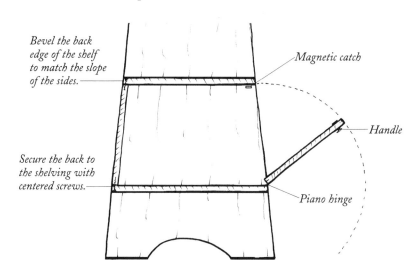

Bevel the back edge of the shelf to match the slope of the sides.

Magnetic catch

Handle

Secure the back to the shelving with centered screws.

Piano hinge

FIG. 98 FITTING THE DOOR & THE BACK

After the various framing members have been cut to length and width, plough a groove in all inside edges to accommodate the panel, or panels. The job is much easier if the groove is centered and also made the same width as the mortises. If working with handtools, this means using the same width plough iron as mortise chisel, keeping the mortise gauge set to the same width when marking mortises, tenons, and the panel groove, and being sure to use the mortise gauge always from the same face. If you are using ¾ in.-thick material, ¼ in.-centered tenons work well.

Center the ¼ in. tongue formed around the edge of the panel, and allow a little space for the panel to expand should its moisture content increase, but not so much that should the reverse happen and the panel shrink across its width it will not pop out of the frame. Since a certain amount of movement is inevitable, forming a bead and quirk down both long-grain sides on the face side of the panel will mask any variation in width. A ¼ in. wooden beading plane is an extremely easy tool to use, and not too hard to find at fleamarkets or antique shops. The same effect can also be produced with an easily made scratch stock: simply file a scrap piece of steel, such as an old scraper blade or piece of bandsaw blade, to the desired shape, secure it in a stock as shown below, and run it down the panel until the bead and quirk have been scratched out. It is also possible, of course, to use a router or shaper bit to produce the require profile, but this is a noisy and dusty way to proceed.

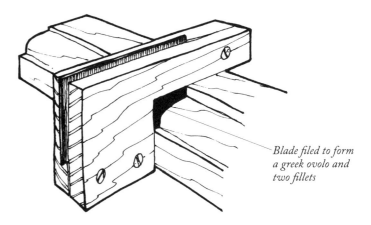

Blade filed to form a greek ovolo and two fillets

FIG. 99 SCRATCH STOCK

Clean the panels and framing members before assembly. Glue only the mortise and tenons, being careful that no excess glue escapes into the panel grooves, since the panels must remain free to float. After the frame is out of clamps, plane away any irregularities at the joints and trim the assembly to fit between the shelves, securing it with two countersunk screws through both shelves.

The door is made exactly the same way, except that when completed there should be ¹⁄₁₆ in. to ⅛ in. space all round so that it will open and shut easily. The door is hinged with a strip of piano hinge along the entire width of its base. There is no real need to mortise the hinge into the bottom of the door, but you may want to do this in the shelf for the sake of a better appearance. Attach a simple handle at the top of the door, and adjust its closing by fixing a magnetic cabinet catch to the underside of the top shelf.

FINISHING & FURTHER POSSIBILITIES

ALL THAT REMAINS IS ANY FINAL SCRAPING OR SANDING and the application of any finish. The cherry had been hand-planed to perfection and required only a light, well-rubbed coat of oil. The pine was similarly treated before the entire unit was waxed. In time, pine treated this way will darken to a very close match to the cherry. There is no reason why almost any other finish, or none at all, may be used. The only real considerations are how much sheen is desired and whether any protection against grubbiness is necessary.

Similarly, depending on the size of the cupboard and what you might store in it, some adjustable shelving might be provided. In keeping with the piece's knock-down character this should also be made removable, perhaps resting on movable shelf supports inserted in a series of holes bored in the inside walls of the cupboard section.

PARTS LIST *for the* **SOUND SHELVING**
(All measurements in inches)

Case:

2 sides	66 x 20 x 8¼ x 1
1 shelf	19½ x 18 x 1
1 shelf	19½ x 14½ x 1
1 shelf	19½ x 12 x 1
1 shelf	19½ x 11 x 1
1 shelf	19½ x 10 x 1

Door and back panel:

4 stiles	18 x 2¾ x ¾
2 bottom rails	14½ x 3½ x ¾
2 top rails	14½ x 2½ x ¾
2 muntins	15¼ x 2 x ¾
4 panels	14½ x 5¾ x ¾

Hardware:

1 piano hinge	17 x ½
1 knob	
1 magnetic catch	

Traveling Trestle Table

11

TRAVELING TRESTLE TABLE

Designing for Convenience

SIX HUNDRED YEARS AGO IN EUROPE ONLY THE RICH HAD FURNITURE. EVERYONE ELSE SLEPT ON THE FLOOR, SAT ON CRUDE BENCHES, AND GENERALLY led a life bereft of much that we would today consider essential furnishings. This state of affairs was not just the result of the general level of sophistication enjoyed by people in the 14th century, it was also due to relatively unstable social conditions. Even the rich were forced to carry their furniture around with them from castle to castle if they wanted to keep it in one piece. Such requirements had a strong influence on design. Many pieces were made to carry and store goods as well as provide seating, and most were made with portability in mind. This was the age of iron-bound chests and large box-chairs. Tables were no exception to the demands of the times, and a large and relatively immobile piece would have been out of the question. Consequently, collapsible units consisting of boards supported on removable trestles were very much the order of the day. Times may be a little more secure now, but given the rate at which many people change addresses an easily disassembled and transported table remains an idea whose day is far from over.

TRESTLES OLD & NEW

A TRESTLE IS ESSENTIALLY A SUPPORT. IN FURNITURE THE trestle is understood as a pair of diverging legs, joined at their upper end, and commonly used to support a table or bench. They are typically used in pairs and are frequently capable of being folded up and easily moved. But a trestle may have other forms. So long as it retains the ability to support a superincumbent structure it remains a trestle. The trestle design used in the traveling table actually consists of three pieces: two uprights and a connecting horizontal beam known as the stretcher. The stretcher is, in fact, the piece originally meant by the word 'trestle'; it derives from the Latin: *transtellum*, meaning something 'placed across'.

Despite the general interpretation of the word 'trestle', the term 'trestle table' most often implies something slightly different: specifically a table that is supported neither by a single central column or pedestal, nor the more usual four corner legs. In addition, many contemporary trestle tables are not collapsible, hence the need to distinguish this particular table, which is particularly easy to dismantle, transport, and reassemble.

THE TRAVELING TRESTLE

OVER THE YEARS I HAVE MADE SEVERAL OF THESE TABLES, each one slightly different from its predecessor, but all with the same basic framework. The first one was designed in response to the problem of how to build a table larger than could be negotiated up stairways and through doors that were too small to admit the finished piece to its intended location. Subsequent tables were made in a similar fashion purely to take advantage of the ease of transporting a piece of furniture that might be readily disassembled into conveniently small pieces. This is still, however, a substantial piece of furniture, which when assembled is rock steady and gives no impression of impermanence. It is not the same as a folding card table or a picnic table, the very essence of which is their temporary nature and almost instant erection, for it takes half an hour or so to take apart and reassemble each time. But nevertheless, unlike more monolithic structures, it is possible to move this piece in a medium sized automobile if necessary.

Since this table comes apart, it may also be thought of as modular, and as such is capable of being built with differently sized parts to fit different areas. The same trestle may be used to support tops of different sizes, and even parts of the trestle may be built to different measurements depending on your needs. The measurements given here may be thought of as resulting in the standard model, but there is no reason why, when the structure is understood, it may not be built to different dimensions. As a table it is, of course, subject to certain limitations: the top should be around 29 in. high if it is to be used for writing, and lower still if a keyboard is to be accommodated. If its main function is as a dining table, 30 in. will be a better height. Any construction attached to the underside of the top should allow sufficient knee room for someone sitting on an average 18 in.-high chair, which means a lower limit of around 24 in. And the width of the top, if intended as a dining table for facing diners should be at least 30 in. wide. Each use will dictate its own set of dimensions, as will the requirements and physical size of the owner.

If you bear all this in mind, make sure you understand the minimum requirements of the individual structural components, and remain flexible; it will be perfectly all right to change any of the dimensions given here. I have rarely made two pieces with identical dimensions except, of course, when building sets of chairs or purposely matching units. The top of this table, for example, as finished is 76⅛ in long by 31⅜ in. wide, although the original intention was for something 76 in. by 32 in. The slight variations are of little importance and result from other considerations that occurred during construction.

THE TOP

IN LIEU OF OTHER GIVENS AND REQUIREMENTS THE TOP IS often a good place to start, since it is the most visible. It is also the part most easily varied. A straight-sided top can have advantages if the piece is to be placed against a wall, but there is no reason why some other shape might not be used.

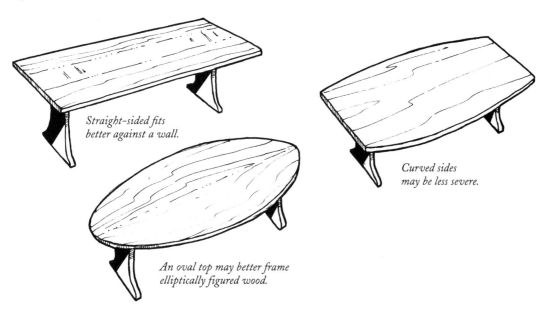

Straight-sided fits better against a wall.

Curved sides may be less severe.

An oval top may better frame elliptically figured wood.

FIG. 100 ALTERNATIVELY SHAPED TOPS

All other things being equal, let the material decide the size and shape. The boards I had available for the top of the traveling trestle table, three particularly nice pieces of mahogany, were long enough, but when joined did not give me the required width. It was an easy matter to rip an 8 in. piece of padauk into two 3½ in. boards and thereby increase the width and add a little extra complementary color to the design.

The actual process is an exercise in careful jointing. All five of my boards were simply butt-jointed. No splines, pins, biscuits, or tongues and grooves should be necessary if the stock is prepared carefully. Jointers and planers can save a lot of handwork when preparing perfectly flat and equally thicknessed boards, as well as then also obtaining perfectly square and true edges, but surfacing may also be done by hand if you are equipped with properly conditioned planes and winding sticks. So far as surface preparation is concerned, it is often safer to use handplanes when dealing with figured or cross-grained material, since this avoids the dreaded tearout often encountered with powertools.

When the boards to be joined are all of the same thickness and are perfectly flat, with no winding, twisting, or cupping, prepare their edges for butt-joining. To do this successfully and without having to depend on splines or pins or clamps to pull the boards together in perfect alignment requires that the edges be shot perfectly square and true. Very careful use of an exactly adjusted power jointer may achieve this, but more control is possible by using a plane. The ideal tool is the longest tryplane or jointer at your disposal, used in conjunction with a machinist's straightedge. A machinist's straightedge is a precision instrument and if, when placed on the top of the edge, does not rock or show any light between it and the wood, will show that the edge is flat enough for a perfect butt joint — provided it is also square.

To joint an edge by hand takes a little practice, but when the skill is acquired you have more control over the vagaries of grain and density. The plane iron should be very sharp, sharpened with the merest crown,

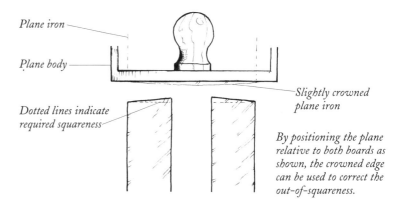

Plane iron

Plane body

Dotted lines indicate required squareness

Slightly crowned plane iron

By positioning the plane relative to both boards as shown, the crowned edge can be used to correct the out-of-squareness.

FIG. 101 CORRECTI NG FOR SQUARENESS

and set with the smallest possible mouth so that if one side of the edge is too high, planing with the tool off-center will produce the required uneven shaving as shown in FIG. 100. Use the straightedge and the trysquare frequently, and make every inch of every pass count. When adjacent edges have been prepared as perfectly as possible in this way, proceed by testing the fit with the boards themselves, adjusting with the plane by taking the slightest shavings possible. The aim should be two edges that fit so well together they almost create a suction effect when you attempt to separate them. Such joints need only to be glued on one side to form joints stronger than the wood itself.

When the entire top has been thus assembled, both the underside and the top should be planed clean. The best finished surface will then be obtained if you use a well-tuned smooth plane rather than abrading and filling the grain with dust by the use of sandpaper. If the grain is too difficult to manage by hand a scraper may help, but this also needs to be extremely sharp.

I had originally planned on a top 1 in. thick, but by the time I reached this stage the actual thickness was slightly less than ⅞ in. To give the top a fatter look I finished the edges with an upward-facing bevel. If the top had been too thick, a downward-facing bevel would have achieved the opposite effect, making it appear thinner. If the top is just right, consider other edge treatments from perfectly square to rounded over or moulded into quarter-rounds, thumbnails, or ogees, as shown below.

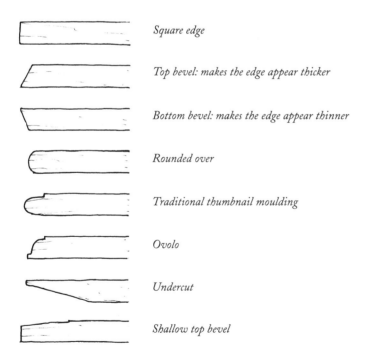

Square edge

Top bevel: makes the edge appear thicker

Bottom bevel: makes the edge appear thinner

Rounded over

Traditional thumbnail moulding

Ovolo

Undercut

Shallow top bevel

FIG. 102 EDGE PROFILE EXAMPLES

Moulding such a large piece is most easily done by hand, using a plane with an angle guide or a specific moulding plane. An electric router is another choice, but extreme care must be taken not to chip away the corners, burn the surface, or slip. Furthermore, when you have finished you still have to clean up the surface to remove the cutter marks, whereas the surface left by a plane is a single facet, already partly burnished by the plane's wooden sole.

THE TRESTLE ENDS

THE TRESTLE CONSISTS OF TWO ENDS, A CROSS BAR HELD in the ends by removable wedges, and a substructure that connects the tops of the two ends. This substructure (FIG. 108) takes the form of a shallow framework holding three drawers. The drawers may be omitted (although they are useful for holding cutlery and table linen if the table is to be used for dining, and for holding pens and pencils if the table is to be used as a writing desk), but the basic framework of the substructure is the key to the table's integrity and rigidity when assembled.

Make the ends first. Each end consists of three pieces: a top, a bottom cross piece, and a vertical piece. The vertical pieces are 20 in long, and may be prepared from two-by-eight material. The horizontal cross pieces are 28 in. long but may be prepared from two-by-six material. The idea is to make the top horizontal piece a couple of inches or so shorter than the width of the top, thereby providing the maximum amount of support necessary to keep the top flat. Whatever the width of this top piece, the

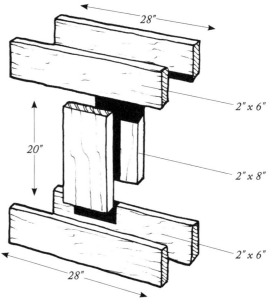

FIG. 103 THE ENDS

bottom piece should be an inch or so wider to preserve the proportions of the ends. All three pieces are first prepared to thickness and left rectilinear so that the mortise-and-tenon joint that connects them may be more easily made.

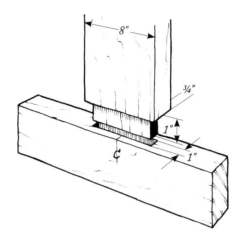

FIG. 104 STUB MORTISE-AND-TENON DIMENSIONS

After assembling both ends trace the actual shape required (FIG. 105) from a template made of cardboard, masonite, or even stiff paper. I make these full-size patterns for any curved work I do and, carefully labeling them, keep them for possible future use. Nevertheless, refinement is always possible, and indeed is sometimes demanded by the presence of a knot or some other peculiarity of the material.

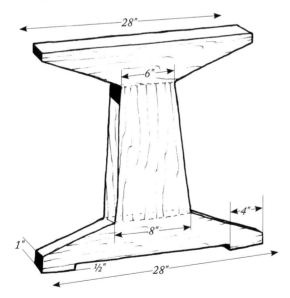

FIG. 105 DIMENSIONS OF THE END BEFORE ROUNDING

The traced outline may then be cut out with bow saw or bandsaw, the resultant surfaces and curves smoothed with files and spokeshaves, and all arrises except those that will abutt the underneath of the top and those that will rest on the floor rounded over. This final rounding over, which should produce a curve equal to a quarter of a circle measuring an inch or so in diameter, is one place where careful use of an electric router fitted with a sharp round-over bit may prove easier than traditional handtools. Take great care to preserve the shape of the inside curves, and watch the direction of the bit when working the corners.

THE STRETCHER

PREPARE THE STRETCHER FROM A SINGLE PIECE, TWO inches wide by 3 in. deep, and 59 in. long. Both ends of the stretcher are then reduced to 1¼ in. by 2 in. for a distance of 4 in., as shown below. Cut corresponding through-mortises in each of the end pieces, assemble stretcher and ends, and mark the location of the wedge mortises in the ends of the stretcher.

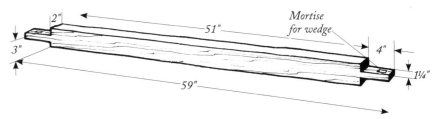

FIG. 106 STRETCHER DIMENSIONS

This is all straightforward work, but a few tips are worth bearing in mind: Firstly, the location of the mortises in the end pieces must be carefully considered. If they are too low the stretcher is liable to get in the way of your feet when sitting at the table; too high, and it will be uncomfortable to rest your feet on it. The lower the stretcher, the more strength it provides, but you do not want to weaken the joints connecting the upright and bottom parts of the ends, so the position as shown, just above the joint, is perhaps ideal.

Secondly, it will prove easier to mark out these mortises while the ends are still rectilinear, before they are sawn to shape. But in any event work first from the outside of each end, since the inside face will be partly covered by the shoulders of the tenon on the stretcher, and any slight misalignment may be hidden. It is bad practice to make allowances in advance like this for expected errors; you should anticipate and strive for exactness at all parts of the job. At the same time a little insurance is always prudent!

Thirdly, bevel the ends of the tenon and the edges of the mortise on the inside face of the ends so that there is less risk of splitting out the edges of the mortise every time the crossbar is removed and replaced.

Lastly, make sure that the inside face of the wedge mortise is positioned a little inside the outside face of the ends, as shown in FIG. 107. It is better thus to create a slight draw-bored effect than to cut this mortise so that no matter how firmly the wedge is pushed in it can never make contact with the outside face of the end.

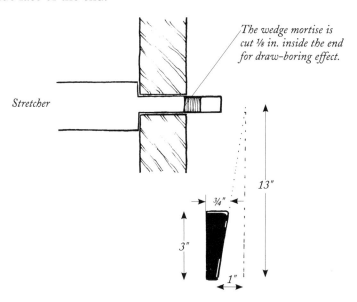

The wedge mortise is cut ⅛ in. inside the end for draw-boring effect.

Stretcher

13"

¾"

3"

1"

FIG. 107 STRETCHER WEDGING

STRETCHER WEDGES

THE WEDGES, ALSO KNOWN AS KEYS, THAT HOLD THE stretcher to the ends are best made of something somewhat harder than the rest of the table. It is better that the ends be slightly deformed by the wedges than to allow the wedges to become deformed. Their shape is critical. If the angle is too steep the wedges will be inclined to work loose; if the angle is too shallow it will be difficult to remove them. Therefore cut the wedges with a slope on the outside face only at a pitch approximating one in thirteen.

THE SUBSTRUCTURE FRAMEWORK

WHEN THE LOWER PART OF THE TRESTLE ASSEMBLY IS complete make the top part, known as the substructure, to match. The outside length of the substructure must equal the distance between the tenon shoulders on the stretcher, which should have been 51 in. If there was any variation, adjust the length of the substructure accordingly.

A shallow framework, no more than 3 in. deep, that fits between the ends and that is somewhat less than the width of the top is required. Centered across the length of the top is a 3 in.-wide member that overlaps the framework and is cut to the shape of a dovetail at each end. These dovetailed ends drop into matching mortises cut in the top of the end pieces. Together with screws inserted into the end pieces from the inside of the framework's ends, this dovetailed center member holds the end pieces together at the top in the same way that the stretcher holds them together near their bottom.

In addition to being fixed through slot-screw mortises in the upper parts of the end pieces (as described a little further on), the tabletop is also secured by three screws inserted through this central member. This procedure has the added advantage of ensuring that the substructure itself cannot sag should it be fitted with heavily loaded drawers.

If drawers are to be fitted, proceed as directed below, but should you elect not to include drawers all that need be done is to construct a simple framework as shown in FIG. 108, making sure to leave access to those parts through which screws are to be inserted into the end pieces and the top.

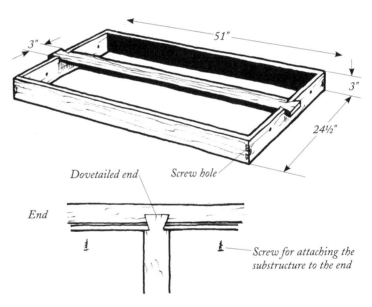

FIG. 108 DRAWERLESS SUBSTRUCTURE FRAMEWORK

SUBSTRUCTURE WITH DRAWERS

THE TRAVELING TRESTLE TABLE AS ILLUSTRATED HAS three drawers which fit flush with the front of the framework. They are carefully made to slide on small runners fixed to the sides of the four main front-to-back members of the substructure. Make these four pieces first to the dimensions shown in FIG. 109, and then cut housings in the center of each to accommodate the central member so that it may be fitted flush with their top surface. Four pieces 51 in. long and measuring at least ¼ in. thick by 4 in. wide are now secured by gluing and screwing to the front and back top and bottom edges of the cross pieces. Note that the top pieces should be housed similarly to the central member, but that this is not necessary for the two bottom pieces.

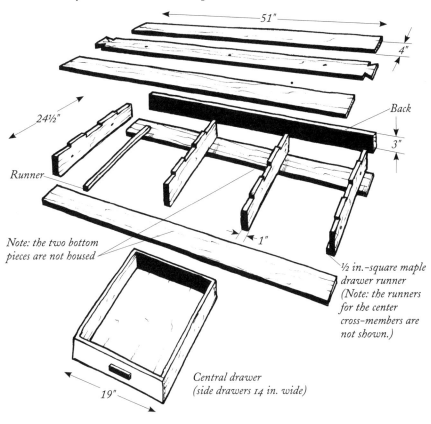

51"

4"

24½"

Back

3"

Runner

Note: the two bottom
pieces are not housed

1"

½ in.–square maple
drawer runner
(Note: the runners
for the center
cross-members are
not shown.)

Central drawer
(side drawers 14 in. wide)

19"

FIG. 109 SUBSTRUCTURE WITH DRAWERS

The central member, as explained above, is longer than the four pieces just made, in order that shallow but wide dovetails may be cut at each overlapping end. These should be no more than 1¾ in. deep so that they do not show through the end pieces. Mark their corresponding mortises directly from the dovetails and you will be assured of a perfect fit even if the dovetails have been cut a little irregularly. By doing so purposely you make it easier to see which end piece goes at the left or right end of the table, but in any event stamp or mark matching numbers on all adjoining parts so that the various parts of the trestle can always be reassembled in the same way.

At the back of the framework fix a single piece to cover the backs of the drawer compartments so that when viewed from this side the table will appear to have a normal apron. If this side is to be visible, joining the apron to the ends of the framework with lapped dovetails is a nice touch, although merely gluing is sufficiently strong.

Standard dovetailed drawers should be made to fit in flush with the ends of the cross members, to which small runners made of ½ in.-square maple or some other hardwood should be fitted, flush with their bottom edges.

If the drawers are made somewhat shorter than the width of the substructure as measured from front to back, you can create a usable secret compartment between the back of the drawer and the apron mentioned above which will be accessible from underneath the table.

FIXING THE TOP

ASSEMBLE THE TRESTLE AS FOLLOWS: FIRST, FIX THE stretcher to the ends and lightly drop the wedges into place. Next, drop the substructure into place so that the dovetails engage, and then screw through the ends of the substructure into the end pieces, taking care that the tops of the substructures' ends remain perfectly flush with the tops of the end pieces. In order that these screws do not interfere with the smooth operation of the drawers, they should be carefully countersunk below the surface. When the substructure is thus brought snugly up against the end pieces, tap the stretcher wedges in more firmly. The trestle should now be a rigidly solid unit.

Turn this unit upside down and bore slot-screw mortises into the bottoms of the end pieces' tops, as shown below. Also prepare countersunk pilot holes for the screws that will hold the cross member tightly to the underside of the tabletop.

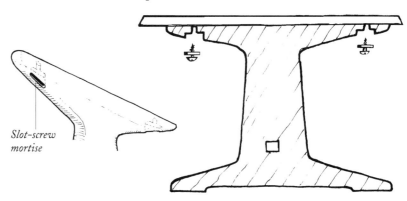

Slot-screw
mortise

FIG. 110 SLOT-SCREWING THE TABLETOP

Attaching the tabletop is most easily accomplished with the entire piece the right way up, the only difficulty being the positioning of the tabletop exactly over the trestle. To do this, take frequent measurements from various points around the tabletop's circumference to the ends of the trestles. When you are satisfied, clamp the tabletop to the substructure before starting to screw. Subsequent assemblies will be merely a matter of aligning the screw holes in the tabletop with the slot-screw mortises and the pilot holes in the central member. This process is made considerably easier if a strong light is available.

DETAILS

I HAVE SAID LITTLE ABOUT SUCH DETAILS AS FITTING partitions in the drawers, their actual construction, and the kinds of handles used, and nothing about the carving visible on the ends; all this is up to the individual. Drawermaking is a subject in itself (see *Traditional Woodworking Techniques*, chapter 18), but what material to use for the drawer fronts and their handles, in this case amaranth and ebony respectively, is largely a question of personal design preferences. I chose the amaranth since it matched the mahogany's intensity well and provided a dramatic contrast to the dovetailed white maple sides of the drawers. The ebony is especially beautiful against the purple amaranth, and used in such small pieces provided a visual connection with the ebony wedges holding the crossbar to the ends.

Finishing was accomplished with a danish oil. Many extremely light coats were applied twenty-four hours apart. Seven or more coats applied like this provides a finish that will stand up well to dining table use, including spills of water and alcohol, and although there is often a rush to get the finished piece out of the shop, there is less actual work involved than flooding the surface for twenty minutes and then wiping up the excess, as is sometimes recommended. This wiping is very hard to do and the invariable result, especially on mahogany, is a daily recurrence of new fish-eyed spots of oil leaking out onto the surface. It is true that they are easily dissolved by a fresh application of the oil but it is all too easy to miss some here and there, and I find it easier to apply coats of oil so lightly that it is only just possible to see the smear of fresh oil as you wipe the rag over the piece.

Finish the table disassembled, so that all parts and surfaces are equally treated, and when done apply a wax finish to the tenons of the stretcher to make assembly easy.

PARTS LIST *for the* TRAVELING TRESTLE TABLE
(All measurements in inches)

Tabletop:

    1 finished piece 76⅛ x 31⅜ x ⅞

Trestles:

2 top pieces	28 x 2 x 6
2 bottom pieces	28 x 2 x 6
2 vertical pieces	20 x 2 x 8 x 6
1 stretcher	59 x 3 x 2
2 wedges	3 x ¾ x ¾

Substructure:

1 back	51 x 3 x ¾
1 front	51 x 3 x ¾
1 center piece	53 x 3 x ¾
2 ends	24½ x 3 x ¾

Hardware:

4 screws	#8 x 2½ in. roundhead
4 flat washers	½ in. diameter

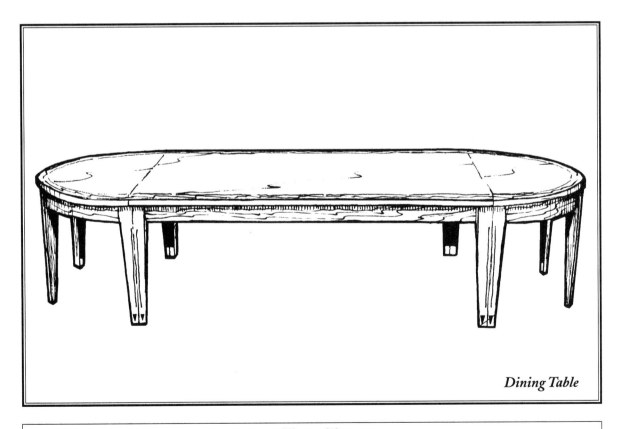

Dining Table

12

DINING TABLE

Unusual Requirements

YOUR JOB AS A DESIGNER WILL SOMETIMES REQUIRE YOU TO WORK OUT SOLUTIONS THAT CANNOT BE FOUND IN STANDARD TEXTS ON WOODWORKING or that are not duplicated in project books. This project is an example of how to accommodate unusual requirements that may require new ways to effect them, and how to get the most advantage out of what may at first seem like problematical limitations. Part of the design as finally realized — namely the substructure — calls for fairly standard construction and is described only summarily. The only unusual feature, represented by the curved apron, is actually a very straightforward procedure. This chapter concentrates on the solution to the design problem and the technique developed for constructing the solid banding.

The initial problem was how to design a table big enough for the occasional dinner party of twelve or so people, but that would not dwarf the three or four people who might use it the rest of the time. A table that expands and contracts by means of sliding, removable, or folding leaves would have been out of the question because in its contracted state it would have looked too small for the room it must occupy.

The solution was a large table with removable ends which when not required for the maximum number of diners stood separately against the wall. Such an arrangement leaves a smaller, more intimate table for three or four, and yet still fills the room comfortably.

The removable sections were designed with semi-circular tops, which become pier tables when placed against a wall. When used together they form a single round table. When situated at either end of the main rectangular part, the whole assumes the form known as a racetrack table. Besides maintaining comfortable spatial relationships between the room and the table, this arrangement also makes possible a variety of seating opportunities as shown below.

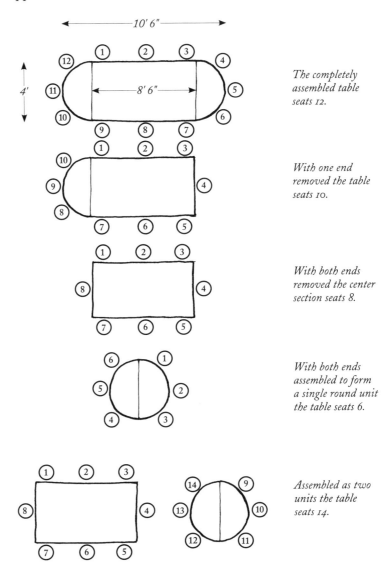

The completely assembled table seats 12.

With one end removed the table seats 10.

With both ends removed the center section seats 8.

With both ends assembled to form a single round unit the table seats 6.

Assembled as two units the table seats 14.

FIG. III SEATING OPPORTUNITIES

CONSTRUCTION

THE APRONS AND LEGS, WHICH ARE MADE AFTER THE TOP is completed, present few problems, but the top is considerably more involved. Its construction is detailed below.

The tabletop is edged in solid wood, but the central areas are veneered. Not only does veneer make the construction of a large flat surface easier than with solid wood, but it also allows the use of a patterned figure and, most importantly in this case, avoids the problems of expansion and contraction that a solid surface might have on a semi-circular solid banding.

Banding, circular or straight, is frequently veneered cross-grained onto solid or other laminated stock. This has its advantages: the grain is always perpendicular to the edge, there is little waste, and the pieces used are often small enough to minimize any wood-movement problems. Solid banding, on the other hand, also has advantages: the edge does not have to be separately veneered or previously faced, and it is easier to work any desired moulding in a solid edge than a veneered or composite edge.

If you veneer a surface all of whose edges you intend to band, it is easiest to make an oversize panel and trim it to size after the veneer has been applied. In this case, since there is no banding on the straight sides of the semi-circular ends and no banding on the matching ends of the rectangular center section (in order that the completely assembled table might present an unbroken veneered surface) the edges of the core that are not to be banded are first faced with a ½ in.-wide plain edging of solid maple. The alternative would have been to veneer the edge after the panel had been laid up and trimmed. There is nothing structurally wrong with this procedure except that it results in two additional lines of veneer, as shown below.

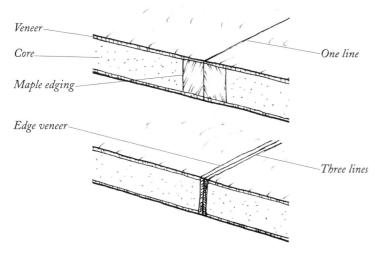

Veneer — One line
Core
Maple edging
Edge veneer — Three lines

FIG. 112 VENEER LINES

Fiddleback maple is laid up in a centered wall-match pattern onto a substrate of standard density particleboard, as in FIG. 113. This pattern ensures that the two end sections join the center section and each other with a book match that is balanced from the very center of the table. The bottom surface is simply slip-matched with plain maple; the pattern here is not important, since the underside of the table is not normally visible, but it remains extremely important to veneer both sides of any panel to equalize moisture content changes.

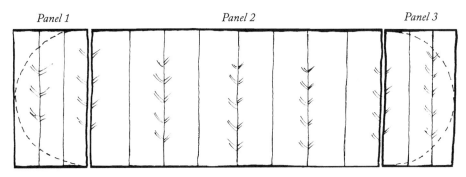

Panel 1 *Panel 2* *Panel 3*

*Three panels laid up with a centered wall-match
so that panel 1 matches panel 2 and panel 3*

FIG. 113 VENEER LAYOUT

CUTTING THE SEMI-CIRCULAR ENDS

MAKE SURE THAT THE MATING EDGES OF THE TWO ENDS do, in fact, mate perfectly, then align the veneer, and carefully establish the center of the matching edge. As a precautionary measure first describe the desired semi-circle on the panel using a pair of trammel points with a pencil attachment. Mount the router in a simple circle-cutting jig and position the jig on each panel in turn at the center mark, set to cut ⅛ in. outside the pencil line. Make several increasingly deep passes with a ½ in. double-flute up-cut bit to cut out the semi-circle. Bring the panel to size and leave a perfectly square cut by running the router around the semi-circle in the opposite direction with a light finishing cut.

MAKING THE BANDING

THE CENTER SECTION IS BANDED WITH TWO STRAIGHT pieces cut to the same width as the trimmed banding on the semi-circular ends, straightforwardly splined in stopped grooves and glued up. Banding the ends is considerably more involved.

The number of segments needed is a matter of how well you can match the grain, but for a two-part circular top the number must necessarily be even. Twelve produces a conveniently sized piece. Find the circumference using the formula: $2\pi R$ (where π equals 3.1415 and R equals the radius of the circle). Choose a board about ¹⁄₁₆ in. thicker than the top and somewhat longer than the circumference, and mark the required number of segments sequentially so that the grain will match from segment to segment. Laying out a couple of extra segments is a good insurance policy.

Make a template for the segments by marking off around one of the semi-circles the position of each of the six segments. The distance between marks will give you the inside measurement of the segment. You can trace the inside curve directly from the panel. The width of the banding is a matter of choice; 3 in. was used for the table illustrated here.

Dividing a circle into twelve parts is a simple geometric exercise that can be done with compasses or arithmetically, simply dividing 360° by twelve. The resulting angle at the center of the circle made by each of the twelve pie-shaped segments is 30°.

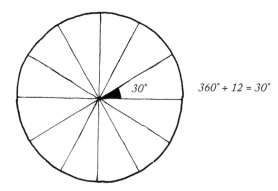

FIG. 114 TWELVE-SEGMENTED CIRCLE

Produce these lines to the circumference and measure carefully between each point. The distance between each pair must be equal. If necessary, average unequal distances and mark and measure again until each segment is exactly the same length.

In order to make clamping and final trimming as easy as possible, cut the segments from a board that is the same width throughout its length. This will also make cutting the angled abutting edges of the segments simple. What you need to know in order to be able to cut out a template (and a segment) is angle A, shown overleaf at FIG. 115 Since angle a has already been found to be 30°, angle b plus angle c must equal 150°, since there are only one hundred and eighty degrees in a triangle. If the board has parallel sides, angle b, which is half a plus b (since the triangle is isosceles) must equal angle A, that is, 75°.

This completes the information needed to make the template for laying out the segments on the board. But be sure to keep the segments marked so that you do not confuse their order.

DINING TABLE

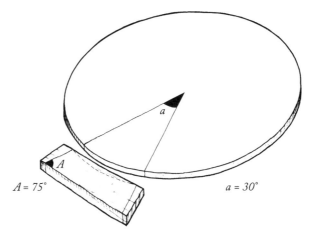

$A = 75°$

$a = 30°$

FIG. 115 LAYING OUT THE TEMPLATE

Cut the miters at exactly 75°, and so that the distance on the short side is exactly the same as the distance between the marks on the circumference of the top. This is essential if the segments are to join perfectly, and completely encircle the top. The next step is to cut the inside curve of the segments to fit the curve of the top. The hand method involves tracing the required curve directly from the top onto the segments, and then sawing to the line, smoothing the cut with a circular plane. If you use a simple circle-cutting jig on a bandsaw the labor will be considerably reduced.

The bandsaw method requires firstly that the table, jig, and segment are all perfectly perpendicular to the bandsaw blade, otherwise the segments will tilt when joined to the top. Secondly, for a perfect arc, the leading edge of the teeth must be exactly perpendicular to the exact center of the jig's pivot point. Thirdly, the distance between the center of the pivot point and the inside edge of the blade must be the same as the radius of the tabletop. Before cutting the spline grooves in the segments, lay them around the top to check how well they fit, adjusting as necessary, but remember that if they seem a trifle large, clamping will probably make them fit perfectly. Cut the grooves with a slotting bit in the router. Make sure the bit is the same thickness as the splines you intend to use. If the segments have indeed been cut from stock that is 1/16 in. thicker than the top, cut the groove in the table edge first then lower the bit 1/32 in. before cutting the grooves in the segments. This centers the segments on the top, leaving them slightly proud for easier planing and cleaning up when attached.

To avoid having the the splines show, stop the router before reaching the ends of the semi-circular tops, and also before reaching the ends of those segments that will lie at these points. Additionally, stop the groove that is cut in the mitered sections of the segments before it reaches what will be the outside radius of the banding.

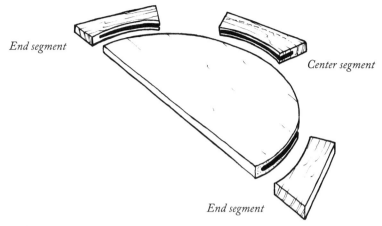

End segment

Center segment

End segment

FIG. 116 STOPPED GROOVES

You may make the splines from a variety of materials. If you use wood, make sure the grain is at right angles to the length of the spline. This will involve so many pieces that you may prefer to use a material like masonite or thin plywood. A 3 in.-wide banding can be held securely with a spline measuring 1 in. wide. Lay out sufficient strips using trammel points set ½ in. further apart than for the radius of the veneered section of the top. Bandsaw to these lines, and then use a marking gauge set to 1 in. to mark lines parallel to the inside radius of the spline, and then bandsaw to these lines, as shown below.

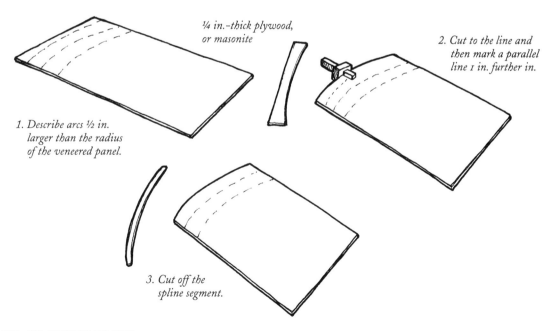

¼ in.-thick plywood, or masonite

2. Cut to the line and then mark a parallel line 1 in. further in.

1. Describe arcs ½ in. larger than the radius of the veneered panel.

3. Cut off the spline segment.

FIG. 117 MAKING SPLINES

DINING TABLE

Cut a little more spline than needed to completely encircle the top so that there will be enough to lay out in such a way that spline joints avoid the segment joints. Cut the splines joining the segments' miters from a single ſtraight section, rounding their ends to fit the rounded end of the slot, as shown below. Be sure to check that the spline is nowhere too wide before you begin to glue up.

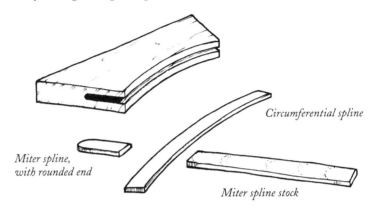

Circumferential spline

Miter spline, with rounded end

Miter spline stock

FIG. 118 MITERED SPLINE SEGMENTS

ASSEMBLY

START BY GLUING THE EDGE SPLINE INTO ONE OF THE semi-circular tops, then glue the firſt end segment and attach it. Glue and insert the miter spline and attach the next segment and so on until both halves are banded. Clamp both halves together with a band clamp, pulling together opposite pairs of segments where necessary with bar, sash, or pipe clamps.

To ensure that the end segments on both halves line up with the ends of the halves, insert a waxed ſtrip of batten between the two halves and make adjuſtments if needed with shims. Gluing up a 4 ft.-diameter top is a lot of work. White glue will give you a little more working time than yellow glue, but you ſtill need to work faſt. Position each segment exactly, for it will not want to move horizontally when its neighbors are in place.

As soon as you are sure that all segments are tight againſt the veneered panels, and that all miters are closed, make one laſt circuit before the final tightening of the band clamp to check that each segment is flush with its neighbor. Any discrepancy here can be fixed with a smaller clamp placed directly over the joint.

After the glue has set, remove the clamps, separate the two halves, and reattach the router circle-cutting jig, increasing the radius by 3 in. It will be beſt to work in small increments to avoid tearout while trimming the dodecagonal top to a circle.

Final treatment of the edge is accomplished by further routing or with a few passes of a finely set circular plane. The top and bottom surfaces may be planed flush with the veneer before a final scraping of the entire top.

THE SUBSTRUCTURE

CUT THE LEGS TO SIZE BUT LEAVE THEM SQUARE TO facilitate the mortising necessary to receive the aprons. Make the aprons for the semi-circular ends from ⅛ in.-thick strips glued together around a plywood form cut to the correct radius.

Attach the two central legs at each end with bridle joints. Attach the others with mitered blind mortise-and-tenons, as shown below.

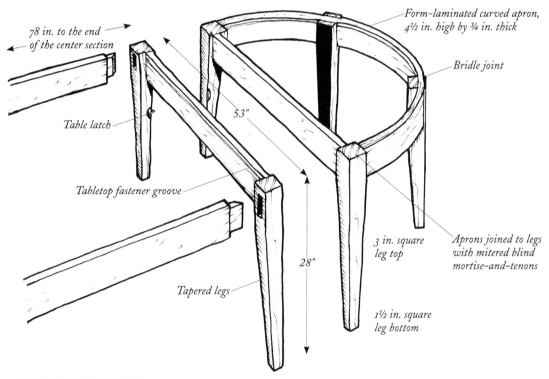

78 in. to the end of the center section

Form-laminated curved apron, 4½ in. high by ¾ in. thick

Bridle joint

Table latch

53"

Tabletop fastener groove

3 in. square leg top

Aprons joined to legs with mitered blind mortise-and-tenons

28"

Tapered legs

1½ in. square leg bottom

FIG. 119 SUBSTRUCTURE DETAILS

Before gluing the aprons to the legs, slot the top inside edge of the aprons to receive the buttons or tabletop fasteners that will secure the top, and taper the legs.

PARTS LIST *for the* DINING TABLE
(All measurements in inches)

Tabletops *(inclusive of banding)*:

        1 center section 78 x 55 x 1

        2 end sections   55 x 1 x 54 in. radius

Legs:

        8 pieces   28 x 3 in. square tapered to 1½ in. square

Aprons:

        2 long   75 x 4½ x ¾

        2 short   50 x 4½ x ¾

        2 semi-circular 54 in. radius x 4½ x ¾

Hardware:

        4 table latches

        16 table fasteners

        8 furniture glides

Standing Cabinet

13

STANDING CABINET

Contemporary Design

ENTION WAS MADE AT THE START OF CHAPTER SIX OF THE DIFFICULTY OF 'REINVENTING THE WHEEL', AND AT THE SAME TIME OF HOW CENTRAL to the human character is the desire to create something new. Designing furniture is an ideal field for this endeavor, since once the utilitarian and constructional aspects that have been stressed in previous chapters have been thoroughly understood there remains the purely esthetic side. It is not that this part of the equation can be regarded apart from the other more pedestrian concerns but that it should play an equally important part if the design is to have any artistic merit.

Without forgetting the lessons of the earlier chapters, you should simultaneously be aware of the esthetic impact of the design. This means paying attention to how the piece looks. Although to a certain extent subjective, and therefore dependent on the degree of sophistication possessed by the observer, certain values are quite straightforward and easily seen once you look for them: Is the piece balanced or does it look top-heavy or about to fall over? Does it complement its surroundings or does it somehow stand out as jarringly inappropriate — is it, for example, the wrong color or the wrong shape? Or is it perhaps built in a style so different from other pieces nearby that it seems out of place? This last consideration is often one of the first things to determine a design. Style is infinite and need not be controlled by the need to match existing styles. That a piece's style complement its surroundings is more useful an idea than that it be necessarily a member of the same club. It is, however, somewhat easier, especially if you feel a little unsure of whether something will fit in, to design in a similar style.

Our standing cabinet is clearly contemporary in that it lacks any characteristics easily identifiable with previous stylistic periods. It has no mouldings common to furniture of the 16th century oak period (as shown, it is not even made of oak, although there is no reason why you might not use oak to build it); it has none of the characteristics of 17th and early 18th century walnut furniture, even though walnut is used; and it lacks any of the many features by which we identify furniture variously classified as Sheraton, Hepplewhite, or Federal. Notwithstanding the fact that so-called contemporary furniture may clearly belong to any one of a number of distinct stylistic schools, ranging from the tonally quiet and homogenous pieces most often thought of in connexion with contemporary woodworkers such as James Krenov and Sam Maloof, to the loud and striking designs of the Memphis School, or the more visceral, sculptural creations of Michael Coffey or Wendel Castle, the standing cabinet remains undeniably contemporary by virtue of its almost total reliance upon the relatively plain, unadorned volumes constituting its superficial design. You may choose to build it from different woods, and in so doing alter its color to something whose effect is considerably louder and more glaring, or to something even quieter and more subdued. Using a soft, fine-grained material such as pear or ash or elm would produce the latter effect. Choosing highly figured and contrasting woods for its different parts would produce a startlingly different effect. In either case the piece's predominant presence is a result of its strictly rectangular form.

DESIGN CONSIDERATIONS

ALTHOUGH STRICTLY RECTILINEAR AND SIMPLE IN FORM, the standing cabinet is constructed using a variety of joints including mortise-and-tenon, several types of dovetail, splined miters, and mitered clamp joints. Despite the sophistication of the construction, the shape is the chief design element. It is contemporary in feeling, consisting of massed volumes unadorned by any moulding, carving, or surface decoration. It is the relationship of the various parts, both in terms of shape and color, that gives the piece interest.

It was designed specifically as a silver cabinet, the drawers being intended to hold cutlery and the cupboard below them to hold plate, but

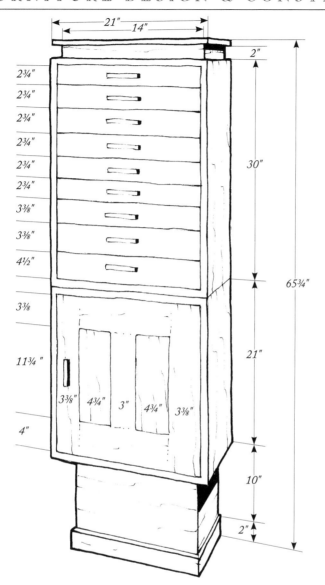

FIG. 120 CABINET DIMENSIONS

it could serve a number of other purposes equally well, such as: a carving cabinet, with the drawers fitted out to hold chisels and gouges and the cupboard forming the ideal place to keep mallets and clamps; a music cabinet, the shallow drawers being well-suited for sheet music; or as a collector's cabinet for a variety of things from coins to butterflies. Its modular construction is an additional advantage, since it can be easily disassembled and transported.

While there are no real structural reasons why the relative sizes and spacings of the various parts such as drawers and cupboard section could not be altered, care should be taken to preserve overall harmonious proportions. This might be thought to be subjective, but it should be considered carefully with the help of the various paradigms discussed in chapter 1 before function be allowed to dictate radical changes.

CHOICE OF MATERIAL

ALTHOUGH THE CONTRASTING WOODS OF THE CABINET AS built constitute much of its appeal, the same design might be duplicated using other species, or even a single species. Certain species can be inappropriate, such as softwoods for drawer runners, but very often the choice of material starts from a particular given. In this case I had long been saving a wonderful board of rare Brazilian rosewood, which I now realized would be just enough to make the drawer fronts and the door frame, and when I subsequently acquired a few pieces of amaranth that nicely complimented the rosewood the project became a reality.

Starting with rosewood and amaranth led to the choice of walnut for the carcase, since its color was sympathetic and allowed the rosewood to dominate. Maple was used for the drawer sides, since the contrast was dramatic when the drawers were opened, showing off the dovetailing to advantage, and, more importantly, because hard-wearing maple is an excellent structural choice for side-hung drawers.

Wood that is not normally seen, such as the bottoms, backs, and interior sections of a piece, is commonly referred to as secondary wood, and is normally less fancy and expensive than the primary species, but structural considerations, such as the need for a hard-wearing species for moving or rubbing parts, should always be borne in mind when choosing this secondary material.

THE CARCASE

THE BULK OF THIS PIECE CONSISTS OF TWO NEARLY EQUAL boxes, the upper one fitted with drawers and the lower one constituting a cupboard. The top, bottom, and sides of the boxes are formed by what began as two lengths of walnut, edge-jointed to provide the requisite width, which were then cut to form the four pieces needed for each box.

Although it is more convenient if you can start with boards that are long enough to form all four sides, shorter pieces may be used. Wider boards will necessitate less work, but in any event remember to match the sides of the upper box with the sides of the lower box since both will be visible in the finished piece, and strongly mismatched grain patterns will produce a discordant effect.

Since all four sides are made with the grain running in the same direction there will be no problem with uneven wood movement. The

1. Join two matched walnut boards.

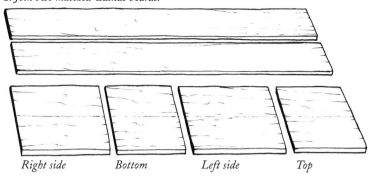

Right side   *Bottom*   *Left side*   *Top*

2. Cut sequentially to form the pieces indicated.

FIG. 121   CARCASE PIECES

front will be totally unaffected since it consists of drawers and doors not fixed to the sides, but the back poses a different problem. Cheap cabinets are typically provided with a plywood back nailed directly on the back or perhaps set in a rabbet. A solid back is a different matter, for whichever way it is oriented it will always be in conflict with the case to which it is fixed in one direction.

Frame-and-panel construction solves this difficulty. The panels, which comprise the largest area of the back, are free to move within the frames as any humidity changes cause the wood to swell or contract. The frame members, being of much smaller dimensions, constitute little threat to the carcase's overall dimensional integrity, since any change in their width is relatively minor.

It is possible to fix the paneled backs directly to the back edges of the carcases, but by setting them into a small rabbet, the sides remain unspoiled by the possibility of ill-matched side grain of the edges of the backs. Furthermore, setting the frames within the sides provides an additional way to ensure that the carcases will be square.

You do not need to do anything to accommodate the drawers or cupboard door at this stage, but before starting work on the dovetails that join the carcase sections cut the rabbet for the paneled back. This will prevent the mistake of laying out the dovetails awkwardly. The rabbet can be cut on the tablesaw or the jointer, with a router, or by hand using a rabbet plane. Whichever method you choose, mark all four pieces of each carcase carefully before you start so as to avoid any confusion regarding front and back and inside and outside. The rabbet should be formed on the back inside corner of all four pieces of each carcase. The width of the rabbet must equal the thickness of the proposed framing of the back so that it may sit flush with the back edges of the sides. The depth of the rabbet need be no more than one third the thickness of the sides, as shown below in FIG. 122 .

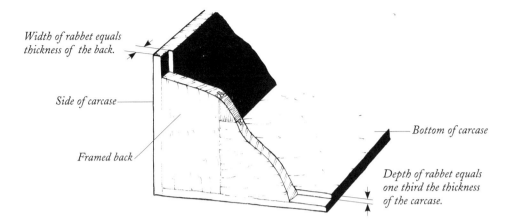

Width of rabbet equals thickness of the back.

Side of carcase

Framed back

Bottom of carcase

Depth of rabbet equals one third the thickness of the carcase.

FIG. 122 RABBET DIMENSIONS

SPECIAL DOVETAILS

AFTER ALL CARCASE PIECES HAVE BEEN CUT PERFECTLY square and to the proper width and length, and have been appropriately rabbeted, lay out the dovetails so that the square ends of the tails are visible at the sides. This provides the sides with the maximum resistance to being pulled apart.

At the front edge of the case the dovetailing is mitered (as explained in the next paragraph), since this presents a better appearance than the butted edges that would otherwise result. But the rabbet at the rear edge

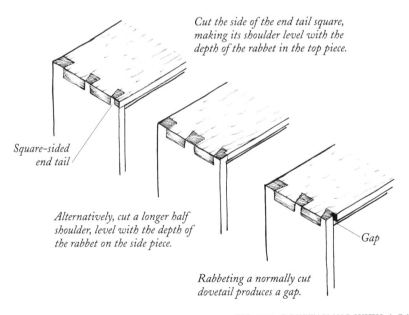

Cut the side of the end tail square, making its shoulder level with the depth of the rabbet in the top piece.

Square-sided end tail

Alternatively, cut a longer half shoulder, level with the depth of the rabbet on the side piece.

Rabbeting a normally cut dovetail produces a gap.

Gap

FIG. 123 DOVETAILING WITH A RABBET

also requires special treatment, since if a normal dovetail were formed here the rabbet would result in a gap. You can avoid this by setting the dovetail further in from the edge than usual and then making a square cut on the tail, level with the rabbet, and then cut the tail short, or by making the square cut on the tail as before but leaving it full length, removing a corresponding amount level with the rabbet from the pin.

Cut the mitered dovetail at the front similarly to the rabbeted dovetail: the end tail is cut with a square side and its whole end is mitered. When you cut the corresponding miter in the pin take care not to cut the miter deeper than the width of the tail, or a gap will result around the first pin. FIG. 124 makes this joint clear. The most important thing to remember is to cut on the waste side of the miter line, or the joint will not be tight. It is better to leave a little too much, assemble the joint, and then saw through the resultant bulging miter with your thinnest dovetail saw. The wood removed by the kerf should be sufficient to allow the joint to close tightly, since both sides of the miter will have been made by the same cut.

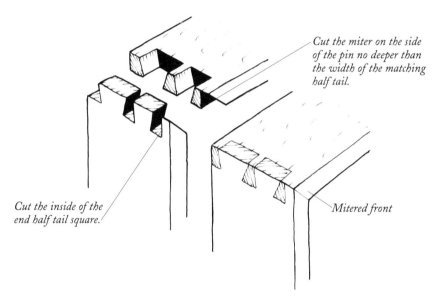

Cut the miter on the side of the pin no deeper than the width of the matching half tail.

Cut the inside of the end half tail square.

Mitered front

FIG. 124 MITERED DOVETAIL

FRAME-AND-PANELING

THE BACKS OF THE TWO BOXES AND THE CUPBOARD DOOR are made to a similar pattern, their respective overall sizes being measured directly from the assembled cases. Do not glue the cases together when taking these measurements since the finished backs will make this job easier by keeping the cases square.

Cut the frame members to length and width, and mark each piece to show its relative position. Cut a groove equal to the thickness and plane of the proposed tenons on all members in their inside edges. Whether you use the tablesaw, router, or plough plane to form the grooves, make sure they are all in the same plane by laying them out always from their face side. For maximum ſtrength, plan on centered tenons about one-third the thickness of the framing.

Whether you cut the mortises or the tenons firſt is up to you, but all joints should be made and dry-teſted for fit and flatness relative to the framing before preparing the panels. Although the grooves for the panels are cut in the center of the framing, the panels' matching tongues can be cut so that the panels fit flush with, recessed in, or proud of the framing. FIG. 87 shows two methods of preparing the panels' edges.

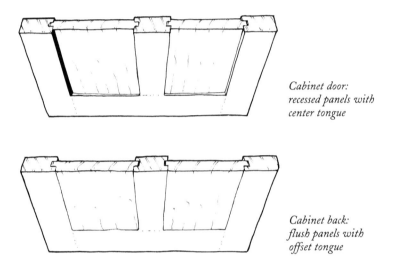

*Cabinet door:
recessed panels with
center tongue*

*Cabinet back:
flush panels with
offset tongue*

FIG. 125 RECESSED & FLUSH PANELS

After gluing up the frames, taking care not to allow any glue into the panel grooves since the panels muſt be free to float, finish-plane both backs and use them to keep the carcase square when this is glued and assembled. The cupboard door should be ⅛ in. smaller all round than its opening, and its opening edge should be beveled about 15° to allow it to open and close easily, but you need not hang it until both cases are fixed together and the interior is complete.

THE DRAWERS

THE DRAWERS FIT FLUSH WITH THE FRONT OF THE UPPER case. Since there is thus no overhang or lipping to hide any gaps, you muſt measure the drawer fronts very exaćtly, allowing no more than ¹⁄₁₆ in. gap all round.

As well as carefully preparing the stock to fit, pay attention to the effects created by arranging the drawer fronts in different orders. Not only should the color and grain of adjacent drawers look well together, but their relative sizes should also be considered. If you place the largest at the bottom, a comfortable feeling of balance will be obtained; the rate at which each superior drawer diminishes in height is also important.

After you prepare the fronts and mark them to show front, top, and their relative order, make the sides. These need not be as thick as the fronts, which have to accommodate lapped dovetails, but should still be thick enough to accommodate the ¼ in.-deep groove for the runners on which they will ride (see inset, FIG. 126). The backs of the drawers may be even thinner, although it is easier to cut the through dovetails which will join them to the sides if both pieces are the same thickness. Cut the sides the same height as the fronts, and short enough to allow the drawer front to be pushed in flush with the sides. For safety's sake leave a little extra room here, since the alignment of the fronts is managed by careful positioning of the runners in the grooves.

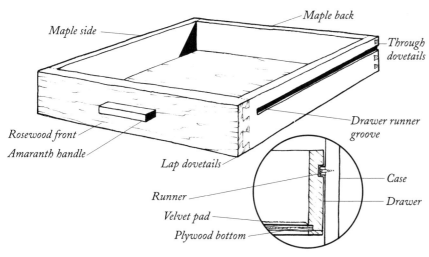

FIG. 126 DRAWER DETAILS

Make the grooves before the drawers are assembled, stopping them before they reach the front of the drawer but allowing them to run all the way out at the back. Lay out the through dovetails for the sides and back so that the groove does not hit a tail. Take similar precautions when laying out the lapped dovetails at the front, but note that here the groove for the drawer bottom should run through a tail so that its end will be covered by the drawer front.

Although the top of the back is level with the top of the sides and the front, it only extends down to the top of the groove cut in the sides for the drawer bottom.

Cut the bottoms from ¼ in plywood, to which there should be no esthetic objection, because the interior of the drawers will be lined. Furthermore, since plywood is more stable than a thin sheet of solid wood, plywood bottoms, if cut exactly, will help keep the drawers square when they are glued and assembled.

Attach the handles to the completed drawers, first locating the screw holes which hold them from the inside with all drawers stacked in the order they will occupy in the case. By subtly decreasing the size of the handles proportionately to the decreasing height of the drawers and by fixing the larger ones slightly closer to the tops of the drawers than those of the smaller drawers whose handles are more nearly centered you will produce an effect more elegant than the arbitrary centering of each handle on its drawer.

Prepare runners for the drawers from very smooth and straight strips of maple that fit snugly in the grooves cut in the drawer sides. Slot-screw the runners to the sides of the carcase so that they can be adjusted forwards or backwards to allow each drawer to close perfectly flush with the front of the cabinet and at the same time accommodate any movement of the carcase. Install the runners starting from the bottom up, projecting from the back of the drawer, with a piece of thin card as a spacer beneath the drawer resting on the bottom of the carcase.

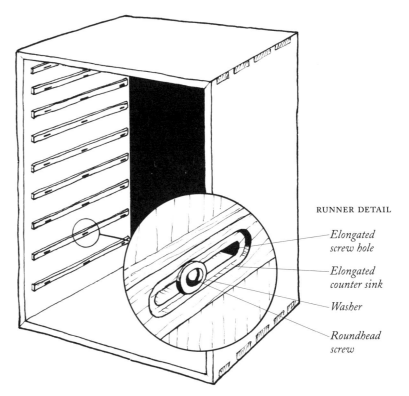

RUNNER DETAIL

Elongated screw hole

Elongated counter sink

Washer

Roundhead screw

FIG. 127 DRAWER RUNNERS

THE CUPBOARD

THE LOWER CASE CONTAINS AN ADJUSTABLE SHELF MADE
from a walnut board, breadboarded to keep it flat. There are several ways
to do this: the board may have tongues formed on its ends over which
the grooved cleat is fitted, glued only at its center; the board itself may be
grooved and the cleat formed with a matching tongue; or both board and
cleat may be grooved, held together with a separate spline.

In order to be adjustable, the shelf is supported on removable shelf
supports that may be arranged in a series of holes bored directly in the
inside of the case. Use the same boring template when boring all four
columns of holes to guarantee that all holes are aligned. Their spacing
depends on the degree of adjustability you need. Avoid boring completely
through the case walls by using a depth stop on the drill bit.

Hang the door so that its front is flush with the front of the case. For a
neat appearance use knife hinges at top and bottom, but if regular cabinet
butts are used, position them so that they relate equally to the top and
bottom rails of the door frame, setting the bottom hinge further from the
bottom than the top hinge is set from the top. This is a small detail, but
one that adds to the thoughtfulness of the design.

The door handle is similar to the drawer handles, fixed from within by
a countersunk woodscrew. A bullet catch installed in the bottom edge of
the door is the neatest way to ensure an aligned closure and additionally
provide a measure of anti-sag support to the heavy rosewood frame.

THE BASE

THE BASE CONSISTS OF A SIMPLE FOUR-SIDED BOX JOINED
with a splined miter joint and finished with a square mini-plinth of

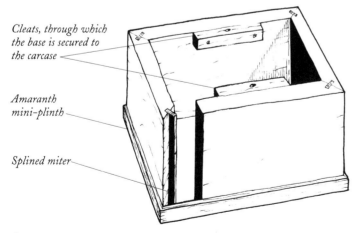

Cleats, through which
the base is secured to
the carcase

Amaranth
mini-plinth

Splined miter

FIG. 128   THE BASE

mitered amaranth. If the stock used to make the sides of the base is much thinner than 1 in., screw a thicker cleat around the entire inside top edge through which the screws that connect the base to the bottom case may be inserted, otherwise short cleats as illustrated will suffice.

THE TOP

MAKE THE TOP IN TWO PARTS: A SIMPLE CLEATED COVER similar to the cupboard shelf, but with mitered ends to the cleats at the front, as shown in FIG. 129, so that no end grain is visible, and a supporting frame of amaranth that matches the mini-plinth on the base. Bore a hole vertically through the center of each side of the amaranth frame and use this as a boring template to bore matching holes in the top of the upper case and the underneath of the cover. Glue dowels that project ¼ in. top and bottom into the frame, just enough to engage the matching holes in cover and case. The top thus forms a shallow secret compartment.

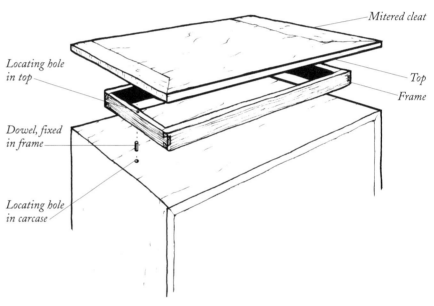

Mitered cleat

Locating hole in top

Top

Frame

Dowel, fixed in frame

Locating hole in carcase

FIG. 129 THE TOP

ASSEMBLY

SCREW THE BASE TO THE BOTTOM CASE THROUGH THE cleat or cleats provided around the inside of the top of the base, first centering the base on the case. Screw the top case to the bottom case by screwing up through the top of the bottom case, taking care to use screws short enough not to protrude into the top case.

FINISHING

ROSEWOOD AND AMARANTH ARE SUCH DENSE WOODS that not much more than a little paste wax was necessary to bring out their rich color. The walnut case may be given a well-rubbed coat or two of oil. The choice of finish is a matter of personal preference as well as a function of the wood used to construct the piece. While such a piece does not need as protective a finish as a tabletop it is still important to treat all surfaces equally in order to equalize any effect that changing moisture conditions may have, or unequal absorption will set up unequal stresses, with possible damaging results.

PARTS LIST *for the* STANDING CABINET
(All measurements in inches)

Top and bottom carcases:

2 top sides	30 x 15 x 7⁄8	
18 runners	12½ x ¾ x ¾	
2 bottom sides	21 x 15 x 7⁄8	
2 tops	21 x 15 x 7⁄8	
2 bottoms	21 x 15 x 7⁄8	
1 shelf	19 x 12 x ¾	*(inclusive of cleats)*

Top back panel:

2 stiles	29 x 2½ x ¾
1 top rail	16½ x 2⅜ x ¾
1 bottom rail	16½ x 3⅞ x ¾
1 muntin	24⅜ x 3 x ¾
2 panels	23 x 6¼ x ¾

Bottom back panel:

9 stiles	19⅝ x 2½ x ¾
1 top rail	16½ x 2⅜ x ¾
1 bottom rail	16½ x 3⅞ x ¾
1 muntin	15 x 3 x ¾
2 panels	13½ x 6¼ x ¾

Drawers:

6 fronts	19⅜ x 2¾ x ¾	
6 backs	19⅜ x 2¼ x ½	
12 sides	13½ x 2¾ x ½	
2 fronts	19⅜ x 3⅜ x ¾	
2 backs	19⅜ x 2⅞ x ½	
4 sides	13½ x 3⅜ x ½	
1 front	19⅜ x 4⅝ x ¾	
1 back	19⅜ x 4 x ½	
2 sides	13½ x 4⅝ x ½	
9 bottoms	13¼ x 18½ x ¼	*(luan plywood)*
10 handles	4 x 1 x ½	*(for drawers and door)*

Door:

2	stiles	19½ x 3⅜ x ¾
1	top rail	14½ x 3⅜ x ¾
1	bottom rail	14½ x 4 x ¾
1	muntin	13 x 3 x ¾
2	panels	12½ x 5 x ¾

Base:

1	front	16 x 12 x ¾
1	back	16 x 12 x ¾
2	sides	11 x 12 x ¾
2	plinth pieces	16½ x 2 x ½
2	plinth pieces	12½ x 2 x ½
2	screw-cleats	6 x ¾ x ¾

Top:

2	pieces	13 x 2 x ½
2	pieces	19 x 2 x ½
1	top	15 x 12 x ¾ *(inclusive of cleats)*
2	pins	2½ x ¼ in. diameter

Hardware:

1	pair 2 in. cabinet butts	
1	bullet catch	
4	shelf supports	
54	woodscrews	#8 x 1½ in. roundhead
54	flat washers	⅜ in.
12	woodscrews	#8 x 1¼ in. flathead

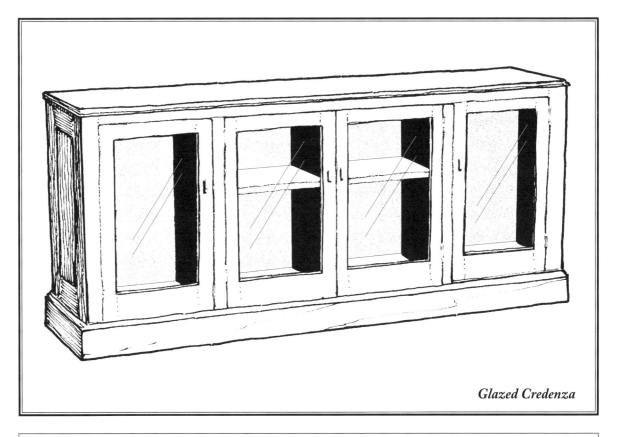

Glazed Credenza

14

GLAZED CREDENZA

New Uses for Old Furniture Types

WHEN FACED WITH THE TASK OF DESIGNING A PIECE OF FURNITURE FOR A SPECIFIC FUNCTION, YOU CAN EITHER START COMPLETELY FROM SCRATCH, evolving your own form to suit the occasion, or look to existing examples of the class of object needed to see how others have solved the problem. A third way is to adapt pieces originally developed for purposes other than yours. The glazed credenza described in this chapter was designed to house unusual and oversized books with more safety than is provided by the usual open system of bookcases while still being able to display them to better advantage than would be possible if they were simply hidden away in a locked cabinet. It was also important to provide a place where the books could be opened and examined without having to be taken to a separate table.

THE ORIGINAL CREDENZA

A CREDENZA IS NOT PRIMARILY A BOOKCASE. CREDENZAS come in a variety of shapes and sizes. The term is loosely used to describe things from sideboards to buffets, large chests, low tables, and all sorts of other cabinets. The only characteristic in common among such diverse pieces is a height greater than a table but lower than that of a standing cabinet such as a lowboy or highboy. The word is Italian, and derives from the Latin: *credentia*, meaning security given or credentials. It was originally used to describe the practice of putting a nobleman's food and drink on a sideboard or buffet to be tasted by a servant in order to make sure it had not been poisoned before being given to the nobleman. Such sideboards became known in Renaissance Italy as credenzas. The term was gradually extended to cover all sorts of buffets, communion tables, and other pieces of furniture used for fancy plate and silverware; in short, any work surface used for something special or valuable. Equally part of the definition is that, in keeping with the style of the Italian Renaissance, credenzas have no legs, but rest directly on the floor.

Our glazed credenza is essentially a waist-high cabinet measuring 7 ft. long by 20 in. deep. A cabinet is by definition an enclosed construction usually accessed by doors, drop fronts, or lids. In this case a series of four glazed doors extend across the entire front, providing complete visibility of the interior while protecting the contents.

The exact measurements are shown in FIG. 130, but there is no reason why they may not be altered to accommodate other situations, provided they remain within the broad definition of credenza. It is the overall proportions that are most important. So long as individual members such as rails and stiles remain appropriate for the job they have to do, the most important consideration is whether they look well together.

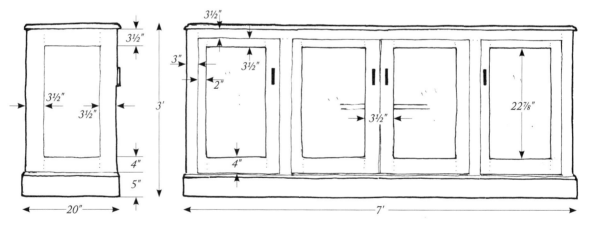

FIG. 130 CREDENZA DIMENSIONS

MATERIALS

THIS CREDENZA IS BUILT OF AFRICAN MAHOGANY. THERE are several species commonly available known as mahogany, not all of them true *Swietanias*. African mahogany actually belongs to the genus *Khaya*, related to but separate from the *Swietanias* of various South American countries. It is generally cheaper and more plentiful, and is commonly regarded as inferior to the South American varieties. In fact, although *Swietanias* were originally prized for their greater stability and more interesting figure, a lot of mahogany from Honduras is now very plain, and the original Cuban variety is largely unavailable. The plainness of Honduran mahogany is a result of its straight grain, which can be a useful characteristic. African mahogany, on the other hand, is frequently rowed: alternating bands of grain make it hard to machine and work with anything other than the sharpest of handtools. The visual effect, however, of rowed grain is very dramatic and gives the wood a changing reflective finish — referrred to as chatoyance — of great apparent depth.

Mahogany is an ideal species to carve, being neither excessively hard nor soft. It is not as expensive as other exotics, and the relative instability which manifests itself in greater changes in dimension according to the humidity is easily accommodated by frame-and-panel construction.

CARCASE CONSTRUCTION

THE CARCASE CONSISTS OF A PANELED BACK, SIDES, AND A front frame in which the doors are held. The solid bottom is tongued into the inside of these pieces, and two interior vertical partitions which divide the cabinet into three compartments and provide extra support, are similarly grooved into the stiles of the front and back frames.

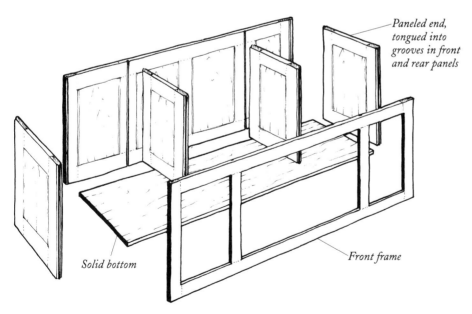

Paneled end, tongued into grooves in front and rear panels

Solid bottom

Front frame

FIG. 131 CARCASE CONSTRUCTION

GLAZED CREDENZA

Make the back first. Note that the top and bottom rails are tenoned into the outside stiles, which are not quite 3 ft. high, since not only will the top add another ¾ in. to the overall height but the plinth also will add another 1 in. or so at the bottom. The three inside stiles are tenoned into the top and bottom rails and so are shorter than the outside stiles.

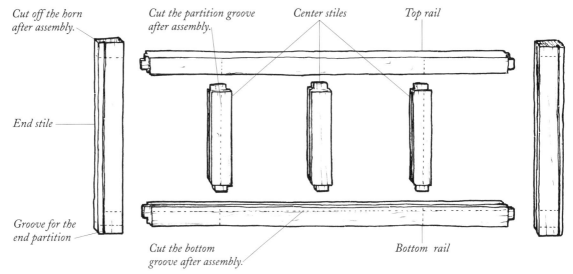

Cut off the horn after assembly.

Cut the partition groove after assembly.

Center stiles

Top rail

End stile

Groove for the end partition

Cut the bottom groove after assembly.

Bottom rail

FIG. 132 REAR FRAME CONSTRUCTION

The exact width of all these members will be a function of the size of the panels. While 3 in. is a good width for the top rail and inside stiles, and 4 in. is a good width for the bottom rail and the outside stiles (since these dimensions will produce a frame with nicely proportioned members that are big enough for all the panel grooving), you must feel free to adjust them to accommodate the panels you may make. These will undoubtedly be made up from two or more widths joined together. If you join the available material so that the grain pattern of adjacent parts looks as well as possible it is all but inevitable that your panels will be other than the specified width. Adjust the framing members accordingly. If you remain insensitive to the individual characteristics of the material you are working with and cut to a predetermined measurement the finished piece will lack a certain wholeness and be little better than something you could have bought from a factory.

With this in mind, decide on the material you will use to make the panels before starting to make the framing. Unless you are certain that the piece will spend its entire life — which could be hundreds of years if you make it right — with its back to the wall, take both sides of the panels into account. The glass doors will allow the insides to be equally visible.

Construct the frame as follows: First saw out the stiles and rails to the correct thickness; a minimum of ¾ in. is acceptable, but 1 in. will make the glazing easier. Cut them to the correct widths and lengths, allowing a little extra length for the outside ſtiles for purposes of mortising. Groove the inside edges of all members to receive the edges of the panels. Note that the inside ſtiles muſt be grooved on both edges. If the rails and ſtiles are ¾ in. thick, cut a centered groove about ¼ in. wide. Whether you do this by hand using a plough plane or a multi-plane, or by machine using a router, shaper or tablesaw, it is easieſt to run the groove the entire length of the member.

Next, cut the tenons on the ends of the rails of the central ſtiles to the same thickness and in the same plane as the grooves. The tenons at the ends of the rails muſt be haunched to fill the outside ends of the grooves in the outside ſtiles. Use the finished tenons to locate and size the mortises they will occupy rather than measuring these separately.

It will be moſt efficient to repeat this process now for both ends before directing your attention to the panels. Apart from the fact that the end frames contain only a single panel each, there is one other important difference between them and the back frame. This concerns the tongues that are formed on the outside edges of the ends' ſtiles. These tongues fit into corresponding grooves cut in the front and back frames, thereby joining all four sides securely and in correct alignment. Do not forget to allow for these tongues when cutting the ſtiles for the ends. Furthermore, the thickness of the front and back frames muſt similarly be taken into account when deciding on the width of the ends' ſtiles. To achieve an apparent end ſtile width of 4 in., for example, the actual ſtile will measure 4 in. less the thickness of the front or back ſtile to which it is joined — plus whatever is needed to form the tongue.

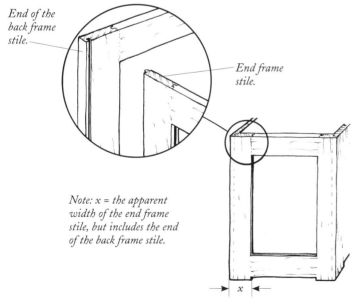

End of the back frame stile.

End frame stile.

Note: x = the apparent width of the end frame stile, but includes the end of the back frame stile.

x

FIG. 133 CARCASE GROOVING

GLAZED CREDENZA

THE PANELS

UNLESS YOU ARE LUCKY ENOUGH TO HAVE UNUSUALLY wide stock you will have to join boards to produce sufficiently wide panels. This may be extra work but on the other hand it does have its advantages. Firstly, you can have fun arranging the constituent parts of each future panel so that the combined figures are more meaningful and effective, and secondly, you will lessen the amount of contraction and expansion that might occur with a wide single board.

Do not overlook this last point. Depending on the species of wood, its condition when used, and its final location, it will change dimension no matter how long it or the piece of furniture it forms part of has been around. One of the main reasons for frame-and-panel construction is to accommodate such change. It is therefore important to leave sufficient room for expansion of the panel in the grooves, as well as provide tongues long enough to continue to fit in the grooves should the panel shrink. A 20 in.-wide panel of African mahogany — even if constructed from material supposedly air-dried, which apart from having better color is also usually more stable than kiln-dried material — can contract and expand by as much as ½ in. Unless you have allowed for such movement, the panels could either fall out of the framing or expand so much they burst it apart.

The panels are the same thickness as the framing. Their tongues are centered, as are the grooves that contain them. They are thus flush with the framing. There is little movement to be expected along the grain, so the top and bottom of each panel may be cut square to ride virtually flush with and against the rails. The sides, however, are beaded as shown in FIG. 134 to disguise any expansion or contraction across the grain.

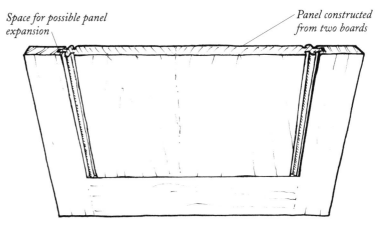

Space for possible panel expansion

Panel constructed from two boards

The panel is beaded on both sides of both edges to disguise any possible expansion or contraction.

The top and bottom edges of the panel are cut flush with the rails.

FIG. 134 PANEL BEADING

THE FRONT FRAME

THE FRAME IN WHICH THE DOORS ARE HUNG IS MADE similarly to the back frame but without any panel grooves. The end ſtiles do, however, need grooves to receive the end ſtiles' tongues. At the same time the dimensions of the rails and ſtiles are somewhat narrower than those of the back, since the door frames have to be taken into account in order to match the proportion of the reſt of the framing. Furthermore, you muſt align the two central ſtiles with the central ſtiles of the back in order that the partitions my fit properly.

PARTITIONS & FLOOR

HAVING MADE AND ASSEMBLED THE FRONT FRAMING, SIDE framing, and back framing, you muſt firſt groove them for the partitions, floor, and buttons before joining them together. The reason for grooving after assembly of these parts is that the grooves necessarily run through both rails and ſtiles.

The partitions, which may be either solid or frame-and-panel, fit into vertical grooves cut in the back of the front frame's ſtiles and the front of the back frames' ſtiles. They might be made as thick as the partition, but the extra work involved in making tongues as shown at *A* in FIG. 135 will avoid the necessity of worrying about how well the joint fits, since the shoulders on either side of the tongue will hide any small inconsiſtencies, and make assembly easier.

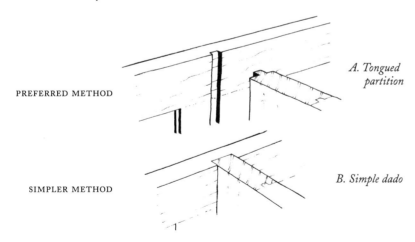

PREFERRED METHOD

A. Tongued partition

SIMPLER METHOD

B. Simple dado

FIG. 135 PARTITION HOUSING

The floor is similarly tongued and fitted into matching grooves cut in the back and sides only. At the front the floor projeċts ¼ in. above the top of the front frame's bottom rail in order to provide a stop for the doors and so there is no tongue-and-groove here. Three or four 1 in. by 1 in. screwblocks are sufficient to secure the front of the floor from below to the front frame, leaving the rest of the floor, which is solid and consequently subject to contraction and expansion, free to float in the grooves at the side and back. For this purpose, make the tongue on the floor flush with its top surface rather than being centered as on the partition in order that any contraction might be invisible, and any gap created thereby, into which small items might fall, might be avoided.

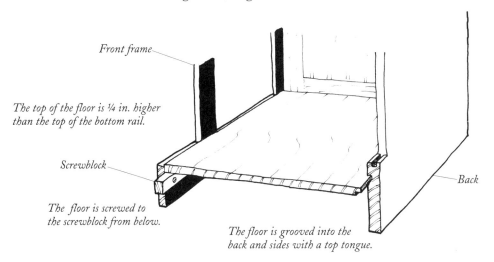

Front frame

The top of the floor is ¼ in. higher than the top of the bottom rail.

Screwblock

The floor is screwed to the screwblock from below.

The floor is grooved into the back and sides with a top tongue.

Back

FIG. 136 FLOOR DETAILS

The last groove to be made is that to receive the buttons that will secure the top of the credenza to the framing. This groove is cut near the top inside face of all four frames according to the buttons or tabletop fasteners you intend to use.

The final assembly of the credenza, while a considerable undertaking, is largely self-regulating so far as alignment and squareness is concerned as a result of the way the constituent parts are grooved and fitted together. The order is: sides and partitions into the back; floor; then front.

THE PLINTH

THE PLINTH IS EXTREMELY SIMPLE, CONSISTING OF FOUR lengths of 5 in.-wide skirting, moulded along its top edge and carefully mitered at all four corners. Its thickness will depend on the profile of the moulding you choose for its top edge — or vice-versa! Fix it by screwing through from the inside of the framing, leaving a ¼ in. reveal between its top and the top of the front frame's bottom rail, as shown opposite.

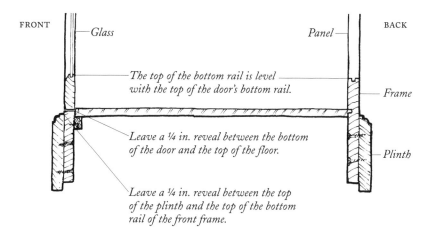

FRONT — Glass

Panel — BACK

— The top of the bottom rail is level
with the top of the door's bottom rail.

— Frame

Leave a ¼ in. reveal between the bottom
of the door and the top of the floor.

— Plinth

Leave a ¼ in. reveal between the top
of the plinth and the top of the bottom
rail of the front frame.

FIG. 137 PLINTH DETAILS

THE TOP

CHOOSE THE VERY BEST BOARDS AVAILABLE FOR THE TOP
since this will be as visible as a tabletop. Allow a sufficient overhang all
round, taking into account that the front and back are bound to move
a little with changing moisture conditions. The edge may be moulded
and even carved. If you use rowed African mahogany, make sure to use
handplanes or, at least, well-sharpened scrapers to finish the surface, since
sanding will achieve a smooth surface but destroy the wonderful changing
reflective quality this wood has by abrading the ends of the fibers instead
of cutting them off cleanly.

Before screwing down the top it will be best to bore the holes for the
adjustable shelf supports. Use a template as a boring guide to ensure that
all holes are aligned, and use a depth stop to avoid inadvertently boring
completely through any member. The shelves should be cleated to keep
them flat, as described in chapter 13. Unlike the mitered cleats used for
the top of the standing cabinet, these cleats may run from front to back on
each shelf, since their front ends will be hidden behind the front framing.
Fix the top to the framing with buttons. These should be especially firmly
fixed in the middle of its ends, so that those at the front and back are able
to slide in their grooves as the top shrinks and expands.

THE GLAZED DOORS

WITH SUFFICIENT FORESIGHT AND PRUDENCE ANY CHANGE
of dimensions will have still ensured that the rails and stiles of each door
are substantial enough to receive the moulding and rabbet for the glass,

hinges, and in the case of the two central doors the meeting rabbets, as well as continuing to match the proportions of the adjacent framing of the ends of the credenza.

The door frames are constructed similarly to the other framing but without the groove necessary for the panels. Instead, you must form a rabbet for the glass on the inside edges. The outer edge is moulded, and in order that this part may meet in a miter at the corners the mortise and tenons must be cut as shown below in FIG. 138. This form of joint, common to glazed framing, has a frank to receive the central part of the moulding rather than a haunch to fit in the panel groove. You can, of course, construct the joint without the frank, but you will lose the advantages that the frank offers in terms of keeping the framing in the same plane. In the case of this credenza this is especially important since there are no mullions, muntins, or extra sash bars to help keep the frame out of winding.

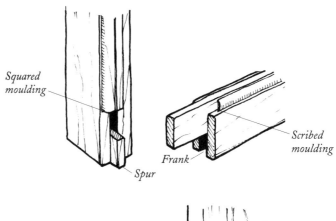

Squared moulding

Frank

Scribed moulding

Spur

Note: The end of the stile moulding is squared off and hidden under the scribed end of the bottom rail's moulding.

FIG. 138 GLAZED DOOR FRAME DETAILS

The thickness of the tenon should equal the central part of the moulding. The rabbet should be wide enough to accommodate the glass and the ¼ in. quarter-round restraining moulding. If you have used the tablesaw to make the various tongues or rabbets, you will have produced enough square-sectioned waste to make these strips. Fix the strips with small roundhead brass pins, since these are easy to remove should the glass ever need replacing. Make them a little over-length so that they must be sprung gently into place. This will help keep them tight and ensure that the glass does not rattle in its frame.

Bead the outside edges of the stiles to continue the design of the paneling and help disguise any unevenness in the gap between door and frame. The bead should ideally be the same diameter as the hinge knuckle. The meeting stiles of the center doors are mutually rabbeted as shown in FIG. 101. Take care that from the front they appear to meet in the center of the bead cut in the right-hand door; this requires that the right-hand stile be made that much wider than the left-hand stile.

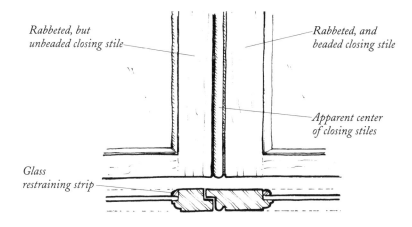

FIG. 139 MEETING STILES DETAIL

Attach the handles with screws inserted from behind the frame, and then hang the doors. Each door should close against the ¼ in. reveal formed by the floor of the credenza and the plinth. You can further guarantee perfect closing by making the front of the shelving flush with the back of the door frame. Use magnetic catches in the area behind the handles, or install bullet catches at the base of the opening stiles, to keep the doors properly closed.

FINISHING

HOW YOU FINISH IS A MATTER OF PERSONAL CHOICE AND depends on the species used. This piece is an ideal candidate for a sprayed lacquer finish, but several coats of danish oil will also work very nicely. The top needs perhaps a little more protection than the rest of the piece and should be treated as a tabletop.

PARTS LIST *for the* **GLAZED CREDENZA**
(Provided as a convenient checklist of parts needed.
See text for remarks concerning dimensions of individual members.
Measurements, where given, in inches)

Top:

    1 piece   84 x 20 x ¾

Back frame:

    overall size   82½ x 34
    2 stiles

    1 top rail
    1 bottom rail
    3 muntins
    4 panels

Ends:

    overall size   18½ x 34
    4 stiles
    2 top rails
    2 bottom rails
    2 panels

Partitions:

    4 stiles
    4 rails
    4 panels

Front frame:

    overall size   82½ x 34
    2 stiles
    1 top rail
    1 bottom rail
    2 muntins

Doors:

8 stiles
4 top rails
4 bottom rails
16 lazing strips   ¼ x ¼ x length as needed
4 handles   4 x 1 x ¾

Floor:

1 piece   83¼ x 19¼
4 screw blocks   3 x 1 x 1

Plinth:

2 pieces   84 x 5 x ¾
2 pieces   20 x 5 x ¾

Interior:

4 shelves   *(to fit between partitions as needed)*

Hardware:

12 buttons *(or tabletop-fasteners and screws)*
4 pair hinges   2 x 2 cabinet butts
4 bullet catches *(or magnetic catches)*
½ gross screws   #8 x 1½ in. flathead
4 panes glass for doors
1 box glazing-strip brads

Pepysian Bookcase

15

PEPYSIAN BOOKCASE

Working in Previous Styles

CHAPTER FOURTEEN DEALT WITH ADAPTING EXISTING DESIGNS, AND SPECIFICALLY DESIGNS OF OTHER FURNITURE TYPES, TO PRODUCE A NEW piece where the purpose and utilitarian function of the piece was the main consideration. This chapter suggests mining the past for a different purpose, namely style. This may be done regardless of function in so far as the piece in question's style is indeed independent of its function.

Different periods of history have produced different styles of furniture. How these styles relate to the tenor and exigencies of the times is often central to an understanding of their genesis and a closer appreciation of their characteristics than might be apparent to an observer ignorant of their place in history, but a certain esthetic is bound to strike a chord in a sensitive observer no matter how far removed in time and place. Some things speak to us across centuries and cultures simply because we respond, without necessarily knowing why, to their shape, their color, their presence, or any of a number of other ineffable qualities. We just like them. This is sufficient reason to attempt to use these aspects in something new we might design.

Designing this way is relatively straightforward if the piece we are considering building is of a type that exists in the chosen style. We have only to discover what constitutes the style and apply the same principles, using original examples as our guide. In the case of much medieval furniture the underlying design parameters were often basic geometric shapes, such as the square and circle, chosen for theosophical reasons such as the perfection of infinity (represented by the circle), and the Holy Trinity (represented by the trefoil, the triangle, and various other three-sided figures). In the case of 18th century furniture the underlying design was often based on interpretations of the various proportions of classical architecture. Other styles may be defined by more obvious characteristics, such as a particular form of decoration. The study of what underlies any given period of furniture is a fascinating pastime although it can lead to ludicrous results if not properly grasped. Trying to imitate a particular style without a proper understanding of what it is that truly constitutes that style can produce silly and ugly anachronisms. But this ought not to deter you from incorporating elements that appeal to you. The point here is not to define good taste but to become aware of other sources of inspiration.

The situation becomes a little more difficult if you wish to design a piece in a style that was used in a period when the piece you wish to build had not yet been invented. Chippendale never made any stereo cabinets because there were as yet no stereo systems. He made plenty of tea trays and pier glasses, however, not to mention more common types of furniture such as tables and chairs. If you can ascertain what it is that makes a Chippendale piece quintessentially Chippendale then there is no reason you cannot build a Chippendale stereo cabinet. This was the rationale behind the design of the Pepysian bookcase.

THE INSPIRATION

THERE IS A SERIES OF BOOKCASES, NOW HOUSED AT Cambridge University, made for the English diarist Samuel Pepys in 1666 that I had long admired for their size and handsome proportions. Unfortunately, they are much too large for today's average home, and most of my books are housed in built-in open shelving. But I recently got my chance to build something along the lines of Pepys's book presses (as the paneled and glazed cupboards made to hold books in the 17th century were called) when I came into simultaneous possession of an 16 ft.-long, 4 in.-thick, and 16 in.-wide mahogany board, and a high-ceilinged shop.

So far as housing books goes, many other designs might have been used with equal success. Indeed, a cursory inspection of bookcases will quickly reveal a class of furniture astonishingly varied in character, especially when compared to groups such as tables and chairs, which, despite an almost infinite variety of styles, all clearly owe primary allegiance to their main functions of providing seating and surface. Bookcases, on the other hand, having come into being long after other types of furniture had been established, are largely derived types rather than *sui generis*. Faced with the necessity of providing for an accumulation of bound books, the first makers of bookcases had a wide variety of existing types of other pieces of furniture to act as their inspiration. As a result the only form of bookcase that might be considered purely and simply a bookcase is perhaps the simple semi-enclosed system of two or three open shelves, free-standing and usually backed. For the rest, their development is easily traced to pieces as diverse as medieval hutches, buffets, sideboards, armoires, and even (in the case of so-called lawyers bookcases) shop-display cabinets.

Contemporary bookcases, more than many other types of furniture, seem to follow this trend: sloping bookcases designed to lean against a wall are obvious adaptations of the ladder; diagonal bookcases have much in common with wine cellar storage; and hanging bookcases are yet another development. But the cross-fertilization of furniture types which has produced such a variety of bookcases is a useful design principle to bear in mind no matter what piece you may be considering. It results most often from combining needs. Requiring somewhere to sit and somewhere to store things you might well end up with the Gothic chair of chapter 16 (or perhaps a more contemporary version). A tall-case clock could be redesigned to house a compact-disc player and a collection of compact discs. The bed which is built over a low system of drawers is another example. The possibilities are endless. The point is not to limit your potential design to established types of the class you want to build.

Nevertheless, glass-fronted bookcases have long been considered the best way to keep books. Books can be seen, cataloged, and simultaneously protected from dust, damp, light, and wear — especially important in the days when most books were leather-bound and expensive. Nowadays, even though many books are cheap paperbacks, it is still a great way to maintain your own library. It can also serve as an elegant way to house and display other treasured accumulations, such as glassware, china, curios, or, in my case, an ever-growing collection of moulding planes.

AN EVOLVING DESIGN

MY ORIGINAL PLAN WAS TO BUILD A SIMPLE CASE WITH adjustable shelving, fit it with glass doors so that the contents could be seen while remaining dust free, mount the case on a stand, and construct a simple cornice, so that the finished piece echoed the general proportions of the 17th century bookcases I so admired. These pieces are frequently characterized by a flat cornice, unlike the often high, scrolled bonnets of much Georgian furniture of the succeeding century. They also tend to have heavier, rather squat, bases that give the appearance of a waistline lower than that with which a 21st century sensibility feels comfortable.

Pepys's book presses were made of oak, as was most furniture of that period. But I was not attempting to build an authentic reproduction, and in any case I had this magnificent piece of mahogany that I thought would provide enough material for the entire cabinet. I also decided to simplify the stand, which in the original consisted of an additional glazed case standing on bun feet, by building a straightforward ball-and-claw, cabriole-legged stand. This form was as yet unknown in Pepys's day, but it was the overall shape and relative proportions of the various parts that I was drawn to imitate.

MATERIALS, DIMENSIONS, & TOOLS

HOW I OBTAINED THE NECESSARY PARTS FOR THIS PIECE, all from the same giant board, are detailed here, but should not deter you from constructing a similar piece using more standardized material. It is also important to realize that I followed no exact proportional system in arriving at finished dimensions. To do so was common practice in the 18th century, when craftsmen were seeking to emulate the classical styles which are at the heart of much Georgian furniture, but I relied primarily on my eye to achieve the kind of balance I felt was demonstrated by Pepys's cases. I estimated rather than calculated the relationships between the parts, as well as the overall dimensions of height, width, and depth. I also allowed the available material to dictate certain fundamental dimensions, since I wanted to keep the work to a minimum. Feel similarly free to adapt the measurements given here to your own purposes. If you appreciate what it is about the original that is so proportionally appealing, by all means change things according to your circumstances and rely on your own eye to preserve the spirit of the original. Otherwise it may be easier to base the overall dimensions and inner proportions on some form of paradigm, as explained in chapter 1.

Apart from the resawing needed to produce the individual boards from my original plank, which was done on a large resawing bandsaw, the entire cabinet was built using only handtools. Since its purpose was to house my various moulding, rabbeting, and other special-purpose planes this seemed appropriate, but most operations could have been performed just as easily with powertools such as tablesaws, shapers, and routers.

CASE CONSTRUCTION

START BY PREPARING THE TOP AND BOTTOM AND SIDES OF the case. I merely sawed off a little over 6 ft. from my board and resawed this to produce the necessary four pieces. After surfacing I ended up with pieces a full ⅞ in. thick. This provides a little more meat for the necessary dovetailing and other joinery that is needed than the ſtandard ¾ in.-thick boards, but using thinner ſtuff is also possible.

Finish all four pieces to the same width, and let the top and bottom into the sides with lapped dovetails as shown in FIG. 140. The bottom back edge of the top, and the top back edge of the bottom are rabbeted to receive the back panel, so be sure to ſtart the dovetails far enough in from these edges not to interfere with the rabbet. For simplicity's sake prepare all carcase and frame parts to the same thickness. This resulted in a ⅞ in.-wide rabbet in my case; if you are working with ¾ in. ſtuff, then the rabbet will be ¾ in. wide.

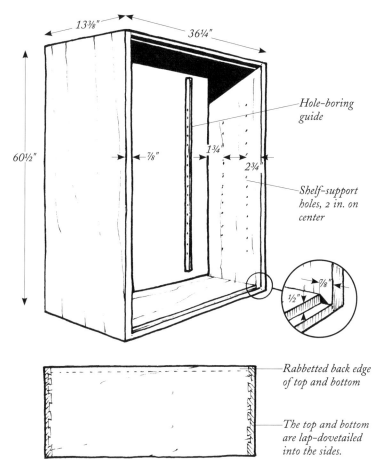

Hole-boring guide

Shelf-support holes, 2 in. on center

Rabbetted back edge of top and bottom

The top and bottom are lap-dovetailed into the sides.

FIG. 140 CASE DIMENSIONS & CONSTRUCTION

Make the back of the case before gluing the sides to the top and bottom since the back, if nicely fitted, will help ensure proper squareness when the carcase is in clamps.

The back, as shown in FIG. 141, is a simple mortise-and-tenon and frame-and-panel construction: two stiles running from top to bottom, joined by three horizontal rails, which in turn are separated by two pairs of muntins. The pattern of the framing is largely arbitrary: in my case it was decided by the width of the boards available for resawing into ¼ in.-thick panels. I felt that at least one center rail was necessary for strength, but there is no reason why two or more might not be used; it simply entails more joinery.

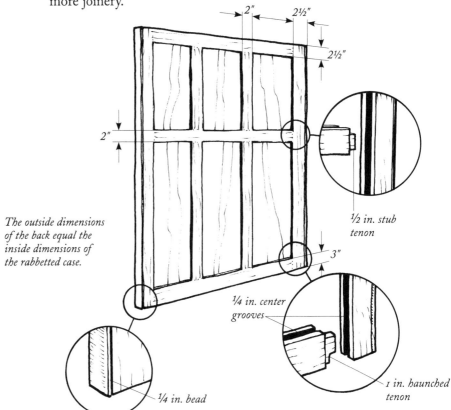

The outside dimensions of the back equal the inside dimensions of the rabbetted case.

½ in. stub tenon

¼ in. center grooves

¼ in. bead

1 in. haunched tenon

FIG. 141 BACK DIMENSIONS & CONSTRUCTION

After preparing all the framing members to length, thickness, and width, cut a ¼ in.-wide and ¼ in.-deep center-groove in the inside edges of the stiles, the top and bottom rails, and in both edges of the muntins and the center rail. Now cut ¼ in.-thick tenons, in the same plane as the groove, at the ends of the rails and muntins. Only the tenons on the top and bottom rails need be very long; 1 in. is sufficient if the stiles are 1½ in. to 2 in. wide, since the tenons on the other members are merely for fixing their location; these may be as short as ½ in.

Lay out the matching mortises directly from the tenons. Note that the tenons at the ends of the top and bottom rails are haunched. It is wise to leave the rails a little longer than their finished size to protect against splitting out the ends of the mortises as they are excavated, and trim them to length only after the frame has been assembled. This is particularly true if you excavate the mortises by hand with chisel and mallet. It is less important if you use a plunge router, drillpress, or horizontal borer. It is similarly wise to leave the stiles a little wider than necessary so that the assembled back can be trimmed to a perfect fit in the carcase before assembly.

Cut the panels to length and width, leaving a little space all round for any possible expansion should the ambient moisture content increase and the panels become wider. At the same time do not make them so narrow that the slightest shrinking of their width will cause them to pop out of the framing. Getting this right is a matter of considering the species you are using, how well-seasoned it is, how impervious the finish will be, and what the conditions are likely to be where the piece will live.

To minimize the appearance of any possible shrinkage, as well as for the sake of neatly recognizing the joint without trying to disguise it, run a ¼ in. bead down the outside back edges of the stiles after the assembled back has been test-fitted in the carcase. When the back has been glued up and trimmed to a perfectly rectangular fit, use it to keep the carcase square while it in turn is glued and clamped, but do not fix it in place.

When the carcase comes out of clamps, remove the back and bore the holes for the shelf supports on the insides of the sides. A strip of one-by-two scrap cut to fit exactly between the top and bottom and bored with a series of ¼ in. holes 2 in. on center makes a perfect boring guide (see FIG. 140). If the strip is marked and always used the same way up, the two columns of holes necessary on both sides will be in perfect alignment. Now the back can be fixed in place with glue or a screw through the top and bottom rabbet.

THE STAND

APART FROM CUTTING OUT AND SHAPING THE CABRIOLE legs, and carving the ball-and-claw feet, the construction of the stand is straightforward, and consists simply of four legs, four aprons, a simple overhanging frame with a sub-moulding instead of a complete top, and a three-sided shoe into which the case fits.

The legs are prepared from four 16¾ in. lengths of 4 in.-square stock. If you do not want to attempt cabriole legs, simply prepare four lengths that are 1⅞ in. square. A short taper might be made starting 4 in. from the bottom. The 1⅞ in. square is the dimension formed at the top of the cabriole leg into which the aprons of the stand are mortised.

To cut out the cabriole shape evenly on all legs, use a template made from something thin but stiff, such as hardboard. Leave a 3 in. length at the top that is 1⅞ in. wide. Draw around the template held against two adjacent sides of the leg, as shown below, so that the knee part of the template touches itself.

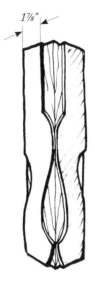

1⅞"

Position the cabriole template first on one side of the 4 in. leg-square, and then on an adjacent face, so that the knees touch.

Draw the outline of the bottom of the foot on the bottom of the square.

FIG. 142 CABRIOLE LEG LAYOUT

The usual procedure is to bandsaw to the template lines, and complete the shaping using a drawknife, spokeshaves, rasps, and files. The feet may be carved to a variety of patterns observed either from existing examples or from published patterns. The shapes of the claws and the balls they hold may vary: genuine antiques can often be identified as to their place of manufacture by characteristic shapes common to particular makers or cities (see FIG. 41 in chapter 3). The most important point to bear in mind for a well-designed foot is to locate the claws evenly around a circle scribed on the bottom of the foot, and then to carve to this line.

Whichever form of leg you choose, excavate the mortises for the tenons of the aprons before you attempt any shaping; the leg is much easier to work on when still square.

I find it preferable to lay out the mortises directly from the tenons at the ends of the aprons. This requires knowing the finished dimension of the square at the top of the leg so that the aprons can be cut to length and then have tenons cut. The aprons are arranged so that their faces are flush with the outsides of the legs. This permits the longest possible tenons, especially if their ends are mitered and almost touch at the bottoms of their respective mortises.

When the joinery is complete, and after any carving has been nicely finished, glue and clamp the legs to the aprons, taking care to preserve the rectilinearity of all four sides. It also helps to perform the assembly on a known flat surface, such as your benchtop, in order to guarantee that the base is not twisted vertically and that all four legs touch the ground at once. If you have made cabriole legs, now is the time to cut out eight 2¾ in.-square knee blocks and glue them to the legs, but not to the underneath of the apron or they may eventually split should the apron shrink. The ogee profile is cut before they are glued in position, but the rest of the shaping is left until the glue has dried.

Make a mortise-and-tenoned, or biscuit-joined, frame whose members are 3¾ in. wide. The front and back members should run from end to end so that no end grain is visible from the front or rear. Whether you use moulding planes or a router to form the ogee profile in the frame's upper outside edge, cut the sides first, using a piece of scrap clamped to the end of the cut. When the profile is formed on the front and back it may be run the entire length with no fear of chipping the ends. Indeed, if any chipping should have occurred when forming the sides, this will now be removed.

The frame is screwed to the top of the aprons with a single screw in the center of each frame member. Since this is not a solid top there is little danger of sufficient shrinking across the width of the front and back frame members to cause any problems. Make sure that the overhang, which should be approximately 1 in. all round, is even on all sides.

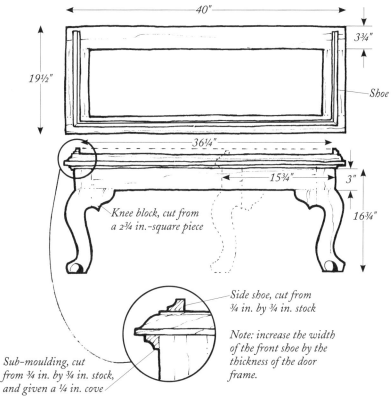

FIG. 143 STAND DETAILS

PEPYSIAN BOOKCASE

Prepare a length of moulding, approximately ¾ in. square with a cove formed on one edge, sufficiently long to be cut into four pieces and mitered together against the aprons, tight under the overhang. Fix this sub-moulding with small finishing nails, and set and fill the holes.

The shoe for the case is made in three parts. The two side pieces should be about ¾ in. wide, so that they may be set in from the upper part of the moulding on the frame's edge by ⅛ in. Their top outside edge should also be moulded in such a way that the combined profile of shoe, frame and sub-moulding presents a coherent whole. Without going into details about the usual 18th century reasons for particular profiles and their components, all of which were strictly modeled on classical architectural models, suffice it to say that alternating convex with concave shapes and keeping all fillets and arrises (flat edges and corners) in proportion generally produces the most pleasing effect. Before deciding on the exact profile, however, read the next paragraph.

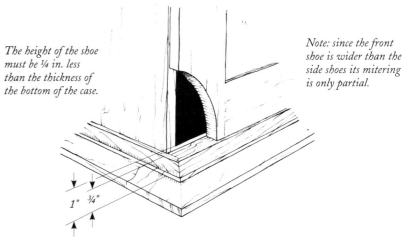

The height of the shoe must be ¼ in. less than the thickness of the bottom of the case.

Note: since the front shoe is wider than the side shoes its mitering is only partial.

1" ¾"

FIG. 144 SHOE DETAILS

The front piece of the shoe is wider than are the side pieces by the thickness of the material you intend to use for the doors to the case. FIG. 144 makes the reason for this clear. It also shows why the height of the shoe must be ¼ in. less than the thickness of the bottom of the case: so that the revealed edge of the case bottom forms a stop for the door. Once you understand the function and limitations of the shoe you will be able to choose an appropriate moulding. Lacking an extensive collection of moulding planes, router bits, or shaper cutters, you can always plane a simple chamfer or bevel along this edge.

The side pieces of the shoe are mitered into the wider front piece. Their rear ends are left square with the back of the case when this is slid into the shoe. All three pieces of the shoe are screwed to the top of the frame of the base, countersinking and plugging where appropriate.

Apart from the applied carving on the front apron, which may be greatly simplified or even omitted, the stand is now complete.

THE TOP

THE BASIC FRAME OF THE TOP IS MADE EXACTLY THE same width and depth as the case, from four lengths 4 in. high. The two side pieces of the frame are blind-dovetailed into the front piece. This joint is sometimes called a secret mitered dovetail. Its virtue here is that while a mitered corner joint is preferable in order to avoid any end grain showing, the dovetailing is an easy way to hold the pieces together without messing around with splines or corner blocks.

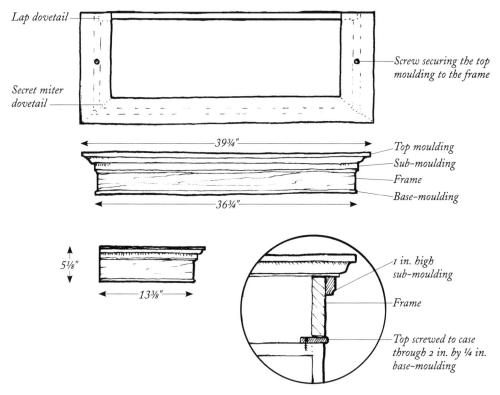

FIG. 145 PLINTH

The joint is made by marking the squared ends of both parts of the joint as if for a miter, and then making a rabbet that stops at the miter line as shown at FIG. 146 in both ends. Once the rabbet has been formed, the dovetails are cut in that section defined by the rabbet, just as for a double-lapped dovetail, and the remaining square portion left at the ends is trimmed to the miter lines. Do not be afraid to tackle this joint, it is easier than you might think. The secret is to be careful in trimming the ends to the miter lines, and this process can be made almost foolproof if you start carefully with a chisel and trim to the line using a shoulder plane and a very simple guide as shown. If the guide, which can be any piece of scrap as long as the joint is wide, is cut to an accurate 45° and clamped to the end of the joint so that the shoulder plane can run on it, it will be hard to form anything other than a perfect miter. As for the dovetails, since they are invisible and will be sufficiently strong no matter how sloppily they are cut, do not waste time striving for the same degree of perfection that might be justified by visible dovetails.

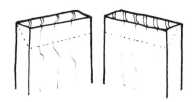

1. Scribe a 45° miter on both pieces.

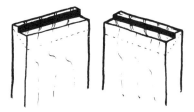

2. Cut a rabbet to touch the miter line.

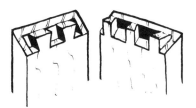

3. Cut lap dovetails and remove waste to the miter line.

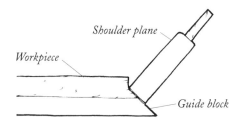

4. Trim the mitered surfaces using a shoulder plane and a guide block.

FIG. 146 SECRET MITERED DOVETAIL

The back member of the frame is straightforwardly lap-dovetailed into the two side pieces, and then all four pieces may be glued together.

A 2 in.-wide strip of ¼ in.-thick wood (which in my case was most conveniently obtained from the offcuts left from the panel material prepared for the case's back) is rounded along its outside edge and glued and screwed to the bottom of the frame sides and front. I formed this round edge with a ¼ in. beading plane. Taking two passes with a small round-over bit also works. Even a block plane and some sandpaper, or a simple scratch stock, will accomplish the same thing. Keep the edge even so that only the rounded portion projects past the face of the frame. Note that this strip is not necessary at the back. Its absence creates a gap under the back part of the frame which is useful in earthquake country: the cabinet may be secured to a wall with a loop of wire passed through this gap. The strips are made wider than the thickness of the frame members in order to provide an inside projection though which the top can be screwed to the top of the case.

To the top edge of the front and sides of the frame screw three mitered pieces wide enough to overhang the outside face of the frame by about 1⅝ in. all round. The bottom front edges of these pieces are moulded with the same profile, upside-down, as the top outside edges of the frame that was screwed to the top of the stand. In the corner formed by the overhang and the frame, fix a sub-moulding 1 in. high by ½ in wide, with a ¼ in. cove formed in its bottom outside edge. This piece is similar to the sub-moulding used on the stand, but its extra height seems better proportioned for the top. The rear ends of the moulded pieces fixed to the top of the frame should be trimmed flush with the back of the frame, and any nails used to secure the sub-moulding should be set and filled.

THE DOORS

THERE ARE VARIOUS WAYS OF MAKING THE DOORS depending on the tools you prefer to use. In their simplest form the doors are simply a pair of mortise-and-tenoned frames with a small rabbet formed on the inside edges to receive a pane of glass which is then secured with a small strip of wood tacked to the frame.

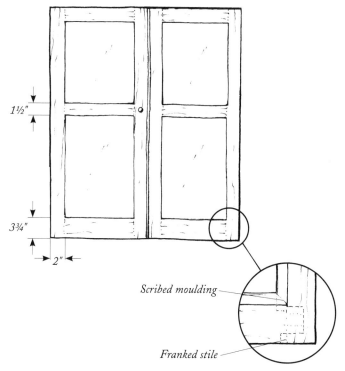

1½"

3¾"

2"

Scribed moulding

Franked stile

FIG. 147 DOOR CONSTRUCTION

Using ⅞ in.-thick material gave me the opportunity to use a sash moulding plane* that formed the ovolo moulding on the outside of the frame and the rabbet for the glass on the inside simultaneously. After the rails were tenoned into the stiles, a part of the ovolo moulding was chiseled away and coped to fit the moulded part of the rail. This is better than mitering the two moulded portions, since if the rail shrinks across its width it never reveals a gap.

The meeting edges of the stiles are half-lapped as in FIG. 148. This allows the first door to be secured to the case when closed with a small barrel or slide bolt at top and bottom, and the second door to be secured to the first door with a simple turn button or mortised lock. Note that the first stile must be wider than the second stile by the width of the lap if both stiles are to appear the same width when closed.

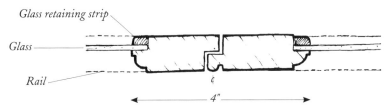

Glass retaining strip

Glass

Rail

← 4" →

FIG. 148 MEETING STILES

A further adjustment becomes necessary to retain the appearance of symmetry if the edge of the second door is beaded. The advantage of the bead is that its quirk echoes the joint between the doors, thereby making this less obvious. For best effect, the widths of the stiles should be adjusted so that the distance from the center of the bead — not the quirk nor the joint — is the same on both sides. A ¼ in. bead here will add congruity to the piece, since this is the same dimension used elsewhere. Additionally, run a ¼ in. bead down the back outside edges of the doors. Not only will this bead help disguise the gap between door and carcase, but it will also align the hinge knuckles with the bead for a very neat effect.

THE SHELVING

HOW MANY SHELVES YOU MAKE IS OPTIONAL. I WANTED AS many as possible to house the maximum number of planes. In order to save valuable mahogany, I edged some used pine with a ½ in. strip of mahogany, and cut a ¼ in. center bead in the face of the strip. Shelving

---

* Sash moulding planes are illustrated and discussed in *The Illustrated Encyclopedia of Woodworking Handtools, Instruments & Devices*, and in chapters 22 and 23 (*Sash Fillisters, and Match Planes*, respectively) of *Traditional Woodworking Handtools*, volumes 1 and 2 respectively of the present series.

in antique cabinets is frequently made out of a cheaper secondary wood. The aged appearance of the used pine not only looked right but also made sense for the possibly abusive use it would receive from the cutting edges of my planes.

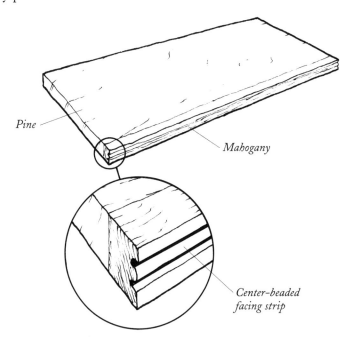

Pine

Mahogany

Center-beaded facing strip

FIG. 149 SHELF DETAILS

The last touch was a departure from tradition: instead of pins or cut-out zig-zag supports for the shelves I used brass shelf-supports. They are neat, easy to use, and match the brass hinges. I am sure Samuel Pepys would have approved had they been available in 1666.

PARTS LIST *for the* **PEPYSIAN BOOKCASE**
(All measurements in inches)

Carcase:

2 sides	60½ x 13⅜ x ⅞
1 top	36¼ x 13⅜ x ⅞
1 bottom	36¼ x 13⅜ x ⅞

Back:

2 stiles	60 x 2½ x ⅞
1 top rail	36 x 2½ x ⅞
1 bottom rail	36 x 3 x ⅞
1 muntin	36 x 2 x ⅞
3 panels	23 x 11½ x ½
3 panels	34 x 11½ x ½

Doors:

4 stiles	59¾ x 2 x ⅞
2 top rails	14⅞ x 2 x ⅞
2 bottom rails	14⅞ x 3½ x ⅞
2 muntins	14⅞ x 1½ x ⅞
16 strips	¼ x ¼ x length as needed for glazing

Shelving:

6 pieces	34 x 11½ x ¾ *(inclusive of facing strips)*

Stand frame:

2 stiles	40 x 5 x ⅞
2 rails	20 x 5 x ⅞
3 shoe pieces	¾ x ¾ x 78 total length
4 pieces	¾ x ¾ x 160 in. total length *(sub-moulding)*

Legs:

4 pieces	16¾ x 4 x 4
8 knee blocks	2¾ x 2¾ x 3

Top:

1 front frame	36¼ x 4 x ⅞
2 side frame	20 x 4 x ⅞
1 back frame	35½ x 4 x ⅞
top moulding	5 x ⅞ x 80 total length
3 pieces	1 x ¾ x 80 total length *(sub-moulding)*
3 pieces	2 x ¼ x 80 total length *(base-moulding)*

Hardware:

4 hinges	2½ in. cabinet butts
2 barrel bolts	2 in.
1 cabinet lack or latch	
1 box glazing strip brads	
24 shelf supports	
½ gross woodscrews	#8 x 1¼ flathead

Gothic Armchair

16

GOTHIC ARMCHAIR

Exploring Different Mindsets

HIGH STYLE ANTIQUE FURNITURE HAS ALWAYS FASCINATED ME AS MUCH FOR ITS EXCELLENCE AS FOR THE WAY IN WHICH IT WAS MADE. TO admire a Louis XV bombé desk, resplendent in all its exotically veneered curvaceousness, encrusted with gilt-bronze mounts, and topped with exquisitely veined rose marble always begs the question of how such fine work was done in shops and with tools that today strike us as primitive.

Nowadays, when every weekend woodworker has a shop equipped with tablesaws, routers, and plate-joiners, competent woodworking seems to require an ever greater attention to precision: setting up jointer knives, finely tuning tablesaw fences, and calibrating runout with micrometers. Even the simplest joinery is commonly approached with an astonishing array of high-tech jigs. To consider the construction of even the simplest piece made in previous centuries without all this power and technology is almost inconceivable. But attempting to replicate something radically different from the kind of thing you are most familiar with can be an extremely useful exercise. It can enrich your design vocabulary with previously unthought of forms and techniques.

The Gothic armchair is a copy of a chair made, so far as anyone knows, sometime in the 15th century. The records are scant. The accession slip in the Metropolitan Museum of Art where the chair occasionally stands in the dimly lit hall of Medieval Furniture notes only that it was given to the museum by J. Pierpont Morgan in 1916, and came from the Hoentschel collection in Paris. It is described as French, but may very well have been made in Flanders, where similar work was produced.

At first I was impressed only by the chair's dark and massive presence. But every time I passed by, on my way to the better lit area where the 18th century American masterpieces are kept, I found myself looking closer and closer. The chair was so old and alien in form, so different from anything having to do with contemporary woodworking, that I could not help thinking about the woodworker who had made it and how it had been done.

The back, made high to impress, keep out the draft, and protect against attacks from the rear, was rough-hewn, showing the axe or hatchet marks plainly, but the front of the paneling was carved in elegant linenfold, and there was a pierced tracery panel at the top of the back flanked by crockets, a frequent medieval carved motif representing curled leaves and buds. At the time it was made chairs were rare and reserved for the most powerful and richest. This had been a very important item, possibly belonging to a bishop or feudal lord: a veritable throne. Despite the fact that the gloomy ambiance lent an undeniable feeling of extreme age and made it easy to imagine its original setting in some dark northern European castle, the fact is that these pieces were most usually originally brightly painted and often covered with rich fabric for comfort and color. Over the centuries the paint has worn off and the wood become smoke blackened so that Gothic furniture tends to be equated with somber oak pieces, almost ebony in appearance.

I looked closer each time, and eventually I made a number of sketches, noting as many details as possible. It became apparent that this was no rude construction; there were aspects of considerable subtlety, and despite a somewhat presbyopic and cavalier attention to the sort of detail that concerns us so greatly today — the perfect fit of every joint and the immaculate finish of every surface — the chair radiated an authority and splendor that could only have been produced by someone very sensitive and sure of his craft. And all this had been done with no tablesaw, no router, no tenoning jig, no electricity . . .

I at last decided to make my own chair, and embarked on a voyage of rediscovery that at times made me feel very close to that anonymous 15th century woodworker as I tried to solve the same problems and think the same way as he must have done, working as close to the vernacular of the time as possible. My dimensions do not duplicate those of the original exactly; I was not able to get close enough to take precise measurements, and in any case I am sure the original units were not in feet and inches.

Furthermore, although I tried to preserve the relative proportions of the parts, I allowed my material to dictate the exact size of the various members, as I am sure did the original maker.

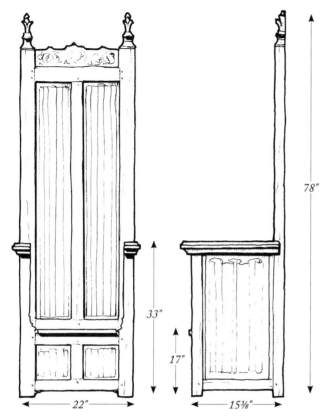

FIG. 150 OVERALL DIMENSIONS

The following directions will bring you very close to duplicating the manufacture of a major piece of furniture from the 15th century, and at the same time may surprise you with both the sophistication and the realization of how much contemporary woodworking still owes to the woodworkers of more than six hundred years ago. Styles may change but the material remains the same, as do many of the ways of working it.

MATERIALS

BOTH OAK AND WALNUT WERE COMMONLY USED IN THIS period, but since both species change color considerably with age, not to mention the fact that much medieval furniture was either painted or covered with painted canvas, there seems little reason not to use any medium-density hardwood that can be carved fairly crisply.

GOTHIC ARMCHAIR

CONSTRUCTION

THE ENTIRE CHAIR, EXCEPT FOR THE HINGED SEAT, IS made using frame-and-panel construction, and virtually all the joinery is mortise-and-tenon. The job may be broken into three parts: making the framed sections; carving the panels, including the pierced section at the top of the back; and assembly, including fitting the seat and making the floor of the box under the seat.

THE FRAMING

THE FRAMEWORK FOR THE BACK IS SIMILAR TO THAT of a paneled door, and consists of two vertical stiles, three rails (bottom, seat, and top), and two muntins. The front is similarly constructed with two stiles forming the front legs and arm supports, connected by two rails that, together with a short vertical muntin, enclose the front panels. The front is joined to the back by the arms, the seat rails — which do not interrupt the side panels but which run along their inside surface — and the bottom rails.

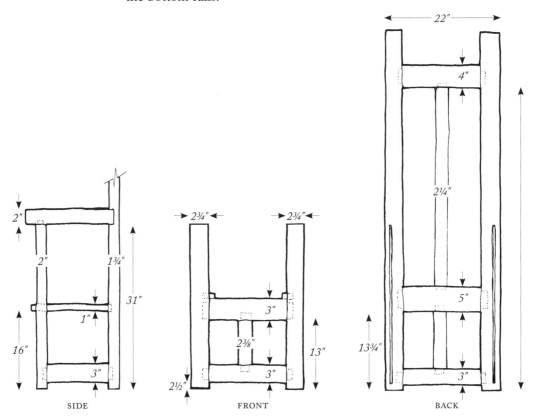

FIG. 151 FRAMING DIMENSIONS

It seems a little perverse to reduce lumber that is already more prepared than what was readily available in the 15th century to a more primitive ſtate by duplicating the rough-hewn surfaces of the original's back and nether surfaces, so begin by preparing all the above mentioned parts to the given dimensions to be as ſtraight and as square as possible.

Note that several members need to be initially prepared larger than the finished dimensions in order to accommodate subsequent shaping. These are: the tops of the rear ſtiles, which will be carved into crocketed finials; the arms, which will be coved top and bottom on their outside and front surfaces; and the front ſtiles, which will be reduced above the seat level after a carved transition. Be sure also to leave extra length for the various tenons needed on the muntins, rails, arms, upper ends of the front ſtiles, and both ends of the seat support.

A special word about the arms: the outsides do not run all the way to a point flush with the back of the rear ſtiles. This is because their tenons muſt ſtop short of the groove formed in the inside of the ſtiles in order to allow the back panels to seat properly, and it is easier to cut the end of the tenon and the end of the outside portion of the arm to the same length. It is, however, important to make this tenon quite as long as possible in order to provide ample area for the pin that will secure the tenon.

Cut the mortises necessary to receive these tenons after forming the grooves needed to receive the various panels. This will ensure that the mortises and grooves line up as is normal and moſt convenient in frame-and-panel work. Note, however, that the grooves in the front ſtiles which will receive the front panels ſtop at the height of the front top rail, and be sure to lay out the ſtopped grooves in the front of the rear ſtiles, which will receive the side panels, to align properly with the grooves in the side bottom rails. Laying out the arms requires moſt attention since at the ſtart

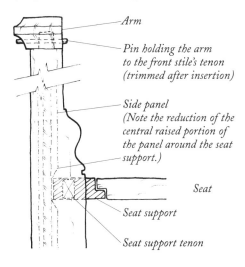

Arm

*Pin holding the arm
to the front stile's tenon
(trimmed after insertion)*

*Side panel
(Note the reduction of the
central raised portion of
the panel around the seat
support.)*

Seat

Seat support

Seat support tenon

FIG. 152 FRONT LEG DETAILS

none of their prepared faces will be flush with any other face of either the front or rear stile. For similar reasons it is best to lay out the mortises for the seat supports after the rest of the framing has been temporarily dry-assembled.

Finally, remember to form a rabbet along the inside top edge of the seat supports to receive the matching rabbeted edge of the seat, as well as along the bottom corner of the bottom rails to receive the floor of the seat box.

SHAPING & MOULDING THE FRAMING

ALL THE FRONT INSIDE EDGES OF THOSE FRAMING members that enclose panels are chamfered. The chamfers meet in mason's miters, which are square-cornered at the bottom and curved at the top, except at the top of the side panels, where the overhanging arm precludes the forming of a chamfer, and where the chamfers on the uprights run up to the underneath of the arm at the front, and, because of the way the back of the arm is joined to the rear stile, are stopped a little below it at the back.

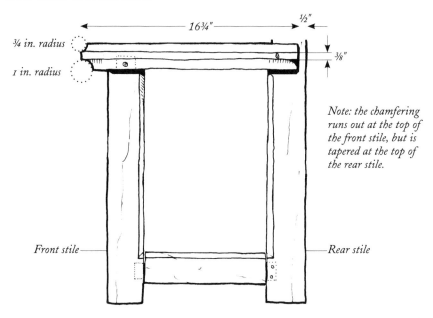

¾ in. radius

1 in. radius

16¾"

½"

⅜"

Note: the chamfering runs out at the top of the front stile, but is tapered at the top of the rear stile.

Front stile

Rear stile

FIG. 153 SIDE PANEL CHAMFERING DETAILS

When making the mason's miters, note most particularly that the horizontal chamfers on the rails can be run to the end of the member, but that the chamfers on the vertical members should be stopped at the level of the abutting rail, and the corner then finished after the frame is assembled to ensure a smooth transition.

Similarly, the narrow groove that outlines the chamfers at the sides and tops of the forward facing panels must also be formed after the framing is assembled to ensure a smooth continuity. You may be tempted to form these chamfers, miters, and grooves mechanically, but it is readily apparent from their irregularity that the originals were cut freehand. It is not the perfection of the details but the overall robustness of an integrated design that gives the chair its power and presence.

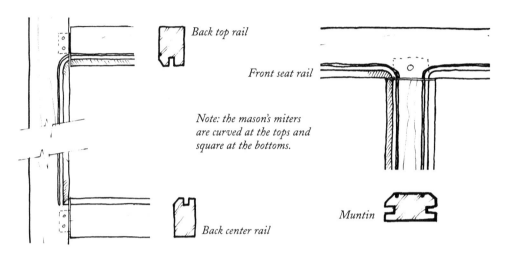

Back top rail

Front seat rail

Note: the mason's miters are curved at the tops and square at the bottoms.

Back center rail

Muntin

FIG. 154 MASON'S MITERS

When chamfering the rear stiles note two important details: at the very top, above the top rail and just below the carved finials, the upper end of the chamfer is stopped square, and a drop is formed in the corner.

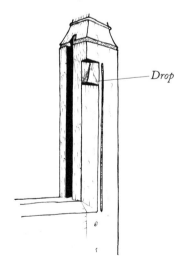

Drop

FIG. 155 CHAMFER DROP

GOTHIC ARMCHAIR

Next, reduce the thickness of the upper part of the front stiles so that their inside surfaces are flush with the inside faces of the arms. The variously curved transition section just above the seat may be cut with a bandsaw or, as was probably done on the original, by making several depth cuts with a backsaw and chiseling the waste out, fairing the profile with rasps and files.

The upper and lower coves formed on the outside and front edges of the arms are not equal! They may be started as bevels and then hollowed with gouges or, more easily, by using a round plane. Whatever method you employ, form the coves on the front, across the grain, first. Any chipping or splitting that might occur at the sides will then be removed as the side coves are formed.

Lastly, carve the crocketed finials shown in FIG. 156. Be bold; do not worry about perfection. Saw close to the profile with a narrow-bladed saw, and remove the waste with carving tools. Cut the defining lines between the leaves last. Be sure only to keep the heights of the various leaves and the tops of the finials and the lower protrusions equal on both stiles.

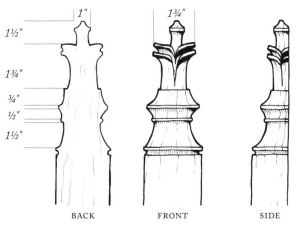

BACK   FRONT   SIDE

FIG. 156 FINIALS

THE PANELS

NINE PANELS ARE NEEDED: THE WIDE, PIERCED CARVED panel at the top of the chair; two side panels; two front panels; and four back panels, of which only the two longer upper ones are carved, the lower pair being simply fielded on both sides. The original panels were all single pieces, and I was fortunate to have sufficiently wide lumber to duplicate this, but there is no reason why you may not make up individual panels from several narrower widths.

Start by cutting the panels to size so that they will fit in their grooves with enough room for any possible expansion. This is more important across the width than in the length; but the grooves should be deep enough so that should the panels shrink they will still be wide enough for their edges to remain hidden in the grooves.

Now feather the backs gently to define a rectangular field. This was done very coarsely on the original; the concern seems to have been only for fit, and not for appearance. Note that the backs of the side panels form the inside of the seat area and must be formed with an additional depression across their width at the point where the seat supports will butt up against them, as shown above in FIG. 152.

Lay out the areas to be carved into linenfold and cut rabbets on these surfaces extending to the edges of the linenfold area and to a depth that will produce an edge thin enough to fit in the grooves in the framing.

The linenfold pattern is the same for all panels, and may be easily produced using a regular plough plane and various round planes to form the hollows, and then rounding the convex sections with hollow planes or even a narrow block plane, or less easily with various router bits, and finally carving the ends with appropriate gouges.

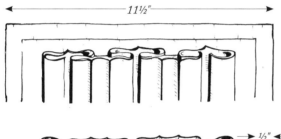

Note: the linenfold pattern is similar for all panels, the dimensions of the folds expanding or contracting as necessary.

FIG. 157   LINENFOLD PATTERN

PREPARING THE LINENFOLD PANELING

THERE ARE INNUMERABLE VARIATIONS OF LINENFOLD paneling; those used in the Gothic chair duplicate the original pattern, but there is no reason why other, simpler patterns may not be used. Since the process is essentially the same no matter how many folds are involved in any given panel, the process is described here using a basic single fold, the which is sometimes referred to as parchment fold or *parchemin*.

With the experience gained in forming a single fold, designing more complicated examples is simply a matter of repeating the following steps, also illustrated in FIG. 158 below:

1. Prepare a panel big enough for the grooved framework.
2. Rabbet the edges thin enough to fit in the framework's grooves, and wide enough to leave the center of the panel raised.
3. Shape this raised center portion of the panel to form the folds.

GOTHIC ARMCHAIR

4. Carve the top and bottom ends of the shaped panel to define the fold or folds of the 'linen'.

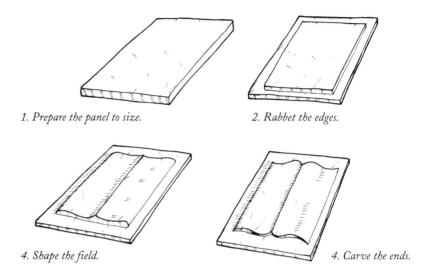

1. Prepare the panel to size.

2. Rabbet the edges.

4. Shape the field.

4. Carve the ends.

FIG. 158 CARVING PROCESS

SHAPING THE FOLDS

STEPS ONE AND TWO SHOULD PRESENT NO PROBLEMS, provided you remember to size the panel to allow for the usual expansion and contraction of panels within grooves, and providing you make the width of the rabbet sufficient to place the raised portion of the panel at least ½ in. or more in from the inside edges of the framing. If the panel needs to be made up of several boards in order to achieve the needed width, make sure to align the constituent boards so that grain is running in the same direction. This will make planing the folds easier.

The usual instructions given are first to plough grooves the length of the panel corresponding to the future hollows. This is hard to do with handtools such as plough planes since the hollows are often too far from the edge of the panel to allow the tool's fence to be used. A tablesaw is not much help either, since the groove made with a regular blade is too narrow and the groove made by a dado headset is too wide. Using a router can be similarly impracticable given the amount of set-up needed. Much easier than any of these methods is to pencil in a few rough guidelines and begin at the deepest points of the future hollows with any round plane less than ¾ in. wide.

Once the round plane has formed these relatively small grooves, the procedure is to widen the grooves until their inside edges meet in a sharp arris at the center of the panel. This may be done using a round plane between ¾ in. and 1¼ in. wide in such a way that the groove is widened but not deepened. This is achieved by tilting the plane sideways; the groove will widen on the side opposite to the plane's tilt. Using only your fingers as a fence to guide the round plane, or even moving the plane completely freehand, you will be surprised how nicely you will be able to work gradually closer to the center line and eventually produce a remarkably straight arris. Remember this is carving, not precision joinery.

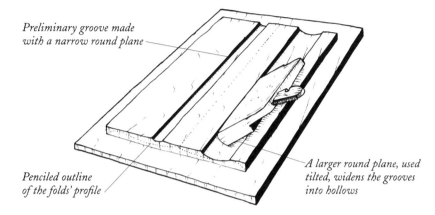

Preliminary groove made
with a narrow round plane

A larger round plane, used
tilted, widens the grooves
into hollows

Penciled outline
of the folds' profile

FIG. 159 FORMING THE HOLLOWS

To shape the edges of the depressions where they rise to the surface and turn into the convex portion of the fold, a block plane will suffice. Where the rounded over portion of the profile doubles back on itself a certain amount of undercutting is necessary. This can be greatly emphasized if you possess specialist planes such as side rabbets or snipesbills, but an ordinary hollow plane around ¾ in. wide will produce enough of a curve for a satisfactory profile. Note only that you cannot form a rounded over profile with a hollow plane narrower than the desired profile since the edges of its cutting iron will cut into the curve.

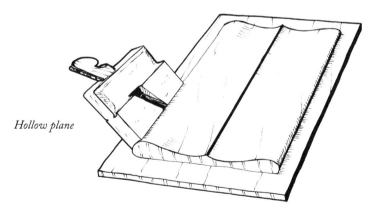

Hollow plane

FIG. 160 ROUNDING OVER

GOTHIC ARMCHAIR

Once the basic profile has been formed, a little ingenuity with side rabbet planes, including the common metal versions made by Stanley or a gentle gouge, will produce sufficient undercutting at the edges of the folded over portions of the profile.

CARVING THE ENDS

ONE OR TWO SIMPLE CARVING GOUGES ARE ALL THAT IS needed here. The secret for success is first to pencil the required finished outline both on the top and the end of the panel.

Two patterns are illustrated, the first (FIG. 161) is that for a simple single fold panel and requires only vertical cuts, which may be made using appropriately shaped gouges. Most linenfold panels have a fairly shallow profile and so the vertical cuts required even at the highest points of the fold will not be very deep, but the usual technique used by carvers to form outlines, using a V-shaped parting tool to describe the outline, and then deepening the cut with a gouge, can make life a little easier.

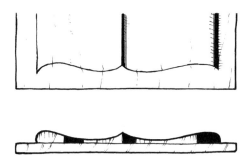

FIG. 161 SINGLE FOLD PATTERN & PROFILE

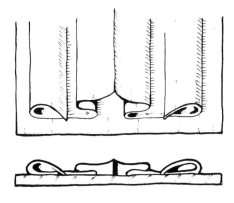
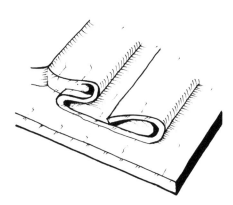

FIG. 162 FOURFOLD PATTERN & PROFILE

The second pattern is very similar to that used on the Gothic chair. When starting work on the still square ends confusion can be avoided if you work first from the top of the panel, cutting in the required outline, but keeping an eye on the end so that none of the downward cuts go deeper than the level of the various folds. In fact, if you first reduce the height of the wood to these various levels the subsequent shaping of their outlines as seen from the top of the panel will be easily understood.

To enhance the effect once the basic outline has been formed, a little judicious undercutting at those points where the 'linen' folds over itself is very effective; just pay attention so that you do not remove any material that should form part of any inferior folds.

ADDITIONAL PATTERNS

LINENFOLD PANELING IS BY NO MEANS UNKNOWN IN MANY older buildings and churches in larger American cities, and many museums have examples of furniture of the oak period, such as the Gothic chair itself in the New York Metropolitan Museum of Art. It is extremely common in older buildings in Europe, and there are many good books illustrating different examples. The varieties are endless; there is a room in Hampton Court Palace in England completely paneled with linenfold no two panels of which are alike!

PREPARING THE PIERCED PANEL

CARVING THE PIERCED PANEL IS NOT DIFFICULT IF THE pattern is first carefully drawn on the panel. Because the panel needs to be thick enough to accommodate the beveling and lower-level cusping described below, it will be necessary to form a rabbet on the back edge of the sides in order to allow it to fit in the grooves in the inside of the stiles. The bottom of the panel sits on top of the top edge of the top rail with no groove or corresponding tongue.

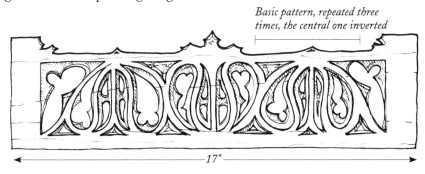

Basic pattern, repeated three times, the central one inverted

—17"—

FIG. 163 PIERCED PANEL

GOTHIC ARMCHAIR

Bore holes large enough to receive the blade of a coping saw, a fretsaw, or even a narrow keyhole saw in the corners of the pierced parts, and saw these sections out, cleaning up the corners and fairing the insides with chisels. The front edges are all beveled, leaving a fairly even band at the front, from which the triangular cusps that protrude into the pierced areas, sometimes meeting each other, emerge at a somewhat lower level. A small recessed triangle is cut in the interior of all the cusps, and the two unpierced triangles at the top are decorated with low-relief oak leaves, the background to which is stippled with punch marks that may be made with the point of a fairly large nail or a metal nail set. All openings at the back of the panel are lightly chamfered

ASSEMBLY

ASSEMBLE THE VARIOUS PANELS WITHOUT GLUE INTO their respective framing, gluing and pinning the tenons as follows: First glue and assemble the back, and then glue and assemble the two sides, sliding the side panels into the incomplete, three-part frames formed by the front leg, bottom side rail, and arm. Now assemble the two front panels into the framing formed by the seat and bottom rails and their connecting central muntin. When this part is assembled affix the brackets shown in FIG. 164, and join the completed front to the two previously assembled sides.

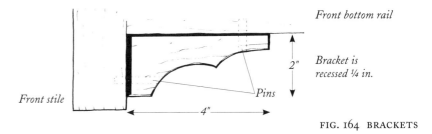

Front bottom rail

2"

Bracket is recessed ¼ in.

Front stile

Pins

4"

FIG. 164 BRACKETS

Before assembling the now complete front-and-side unit to the back, insert the front ends of the seat supports into their mortises in the back of the front legs. The horizontal depression formed across the center of each side panel will help to keep the seat supports somewhat level, but an extra pair of hands to help guide their back ends into the back legs, as well as seat the back edge of the side panels in their respective grooves, will make this part of the assembly a lot easier.

Draw all tenons close with clamps if necessary, and bore for the pins. If clamping and boring is too unwieldy an operation you may prefer to draw-bore the mortise-and-tenon joinery by first boring for the pins only through the mortises, inserting the tenons and marking them with an awl inserted through the holes bored in the mortises, and then boring the tenons slightly closer towards the shoulders. This will cause the pins when inserted to draw the joints tight.

The pins should be made from square stock whose four corners are chamfered to create an octagonal pin. Make one end slightly smaller so that each pin may be started in its hole, and then drive them home with a mallet. Any protruding ends may be planed flush. No glue is necessary. Indeed, any glue used on the mortise-and-tenon joinery in the original may well have long since failed with little effect on the chair's integrity since the pinning, in combination with the shouldered tenons, is more than sufficient to hold the framing firmly together. The panels and the seat-box floor will in turn maintain squareness.

THE SEAT

THE ORIGINAL SEAT IS MADE FROM ONE BOARD, RABBETED underneath at the sides only, to fit into the rabbeted seat support, and attached to the seat rail in the back by two large pairs of iron staples. The crudeness of this hardware has been tempered by the patina of centuries, and is probably best replaced by a pair of unobtrusive butt hinges mortised into the back edge of the seat and then attached to the seat rail. By leaving the flooring of the box, which consists simply of rough boards nailed into the rabbets formed in the bottom edges of the framing under the chair, to last, attaching the seat is made a little easier.

The original chair's seat is secured by a large lock mortised into the front's top rail, but this appears to have been a later addition and may be included or omitted as you desire.

FINISHING

THERE ARE YET TRACES OF COLOR IN THE CREVICES OF the original, indicating a polychromatic finish typical of much medieval furniture, as well as series of small nail holes around the arms indicating the use of attached fabric for color or cushioning. But a simple oil finish, or even a coat of wax, is all that is needed to afford minimum protection to the chair. A few centuries of being dragged from smoky castle to smoky castle will effect its own patina. The original bears a multitude of scars and dents suggesting a rich history, but neither these nor the rough simplicity of the overall construction detract one bit from a magnificent presence.

GOTHIC ARMCHAIR

PARTS LIST *for the* GOTHIC ARMCHAIR
(All measurements in inches)

Back frame:

2 stiles	78 x 2¾ x 1¾
1 top rail	19½ x 4 x 1¾
1 seat rail	19½ x 5 x 1¾
1 top muntin	45½ x 2¼ x 1¾
1 lower muntin	11¾ x 2¼ x 1¾
2 top panels	45¼ x 7½ x ¾
2 lower panels	9½ x 7½ x ¾
1 pierced panel	17 x 5

Front frame:

2 stiles	32½ x 2¾ x 2
2 rails	19½ x 3 x 1¾
1 muntin	11 x 2⅜ x 1¾
2 panels	11½ x 7½ x ¾
2 brackets	4 x 2 x 2

Sides:

2 arms	16¾ x 2 x 2
2 panels	26 x 12
2 seat supports	15½ x 1 x 2½
1 seat	16 x 14 x ¾
40 pins	2 x ½ in. diameter

Hardware:

2 butt hinges	2 x 2

SELECT
BIBLIOGRAPHY

FURNITURE DESIGN & CONSTRUCTION IS THE FOURTH IN THE PRESENT SERIES OF BOOKS ON WOODWORKING, EACH VOLUME OF WHICH IS INTENDED TO BE READ as a stand-alone work, but all of which taken together constitute a sequentially developed grounding in the craft. As such they are listed here, together with various other titles that have long been among my favorites, arranged according to the 'Three Pillars of Design'.

VOL. I: *The Illustrated Encyclopedia of Woodworking Handtools, Instruments, & Devices.* 1974. 3rd ed. Bearsville, New York: Blackburn Books, 2000
     — *A comprehensive alphabetical pictorial index to the tools of the various woodworking trades common in Western civilization from the 18th century to the present.*

VOL. II: *Traditional Woodworking Handtools: A Manual for the Woodworker.* Bearsville, New York: Blackburn Books, 1998
     — *Organized by major tool classes, this is the basic user manual for both the amateur and the professional woodworker.*

VOL. III: *Traditional Woodworking Techniques: Fundamentals of Furniture-making.* Bearsville, New York: Blackburn Books, 2004
  — *A practical introduction to the principles of furnituremaking and a reference to many of the more interesting aspects of the craft.*

FUNCTION

Macquoid, Percy, and Edwards, Ralph. *The Dictionary of English Furniture.* Country Life Limited, 1927
  — *The primary reference to English furniture from the Middle Ages to the Late Georgian period.*

Ramsey, Charles G., and Sleeper, Harold R., *Architectural Graphic Standards* : New York: John Wiley & Sons, Inc., 1932
  — *The standard reference for all things architectural, including furniture; the earlier editions are equally useful (and more attractive) for the aspiring furniture designer.*

Palladio, Andrea. *The Four Books of Architecture.* New York: Dover Publications, Inc., 1965
  — *First published in Venice in 1570 as a practical guide, this work is our link to the Roman architect Vitruvius and through him to formal classical design and the belief that beauty is rooted in ideal form and harmony.*

CONSTRUCTION

Boison, J. *Industrie du Meuble: Principes de Construction, Éléments Généraux.* Paris: Dunod, Éditeur, 1922
  — *A trade school text based on traditional techniques that deals with fundamental wood science, furnituremaking wood conversion, and a host of construction and joinery techniques, illustrated by high-style French furniture.*

Frank, George. *88 Rue de Charonne: Adventures in Wood Finishing.* Newtown, Connecticut: The Taunton Press, 1981
  — *One of the best books on the least understood areas of furnituremaking; history, anecdotes, and techniques.*

Hayward, Charles H. *Woodwork Joints.* ca. 1960. Reprint. New York: Drake Publishers, Inc., 1970
  —*The basic primer for traditional joinery techniques, with many illustrations from the basic joint families.*

Hoadley, R. Bruce. *Understanding Wood: A Craftsman's Guide to Wood Technology.* Newtown, Connecticut: The Taunton Press, Inc., 2000
— *The book that explains what wood wants to do, how and why; essential for all who would build anything to last.*

Hodgson, Frederick T. *Modern Carpentry: A Practical Manual.* 1902. 2nd ed. Chicago: Frederick J. Drake & Co., 1902
— *Although originally written for end of the 19th century joiners and carpenters, this book has an excellent section on casemaking. as well as containing much useful information for drafting and setting-out.*

Mehler, Kelly. *The Table Saw Book.* Newtown, Connecticut: The Taunton Press, Inc., 2003
— *The essential text for what has become the icon of contemporary woodworking.*

Moxon, Joseph. *Mechanick Exercises: or the Doctrine of Handy-Works.* London: 1678
— *Generally regarded as the first book on British woodworking tools and techniques. A useful reprint of the 1703 edition was published in 1975 by The Astragal Press, Morristown, New Jersey.*

Pain, F. *The Practical Wood Turner.* Reprint. New York: Sterling Publishing Company, Inc., 1979
— *A straightforward introduction to turning, at the side of a genuine craftsman.*

Villiard, Paul. *A Manual of Veneering.* Princeton, New Jersey: D. Van Nostrand Company, Inc., 1968
— *An excellent introduction to an important furnituremaking technique, complete with instructions on pressmaking.*

FORM

Chippendale, Thomas. *The Gentleman & Cabinet-maker's Director.* London: 1762
— *Most easily obtained in a Dover Books edition, this is one of the definitive 18th century furniture books.*

Hayward, Charles H. *Antique Furniture Design.* New York: Charles Scribner's Sons, 1979
— *A close look at the structure and construction techniques of various examples of furniture from the 17th and 18th centuries.*

Le Corbusier (Charles Edouard Jeanneret). *The Modulor: A Harmonious Measure to the Human Scale Universally Applicable to Architecture* and *Mechanics*. Birkhäuser, Basel: 2000

> *— A great investigation into the practical use of the Golden Mean, by one of the 20th century's most important innovators, who once said: ". . . the chair is architecture, the sofa bourgeois."*

Saarinen, Eliel. *Search for Form: A Fundamental Approach to Art*. New York: Reinhold Publishing Corp., 1948

> *— An analysis of what constitutes form and beauty, that should be always in the mind of the designer.*

SELECT BIBLIOGRAPHY

INDEX

Numbers in boldface (e.g., **312**) indicate pages with illustrations.
References to ranges greater than two pages (e.g., 106–109) may
also include illustrations.

FINIS